✔ KU-536-562

The Process of Network Security

Designing and Managing a Safe Network

Thomas A. Wadlow

ADDISON-WESLEY

An Imprint of Addison Wesley Longman, Inc.

Reading, Massachusetts · Harlow, England · Menlo Park, California
Berkeley, California · Don Mills, Ontario · Sydney
Bonn · Amsterdam · Tokyo · Mexico City

Library of Congress Cataloging-in-Publication Data

Wadlow, Thomas A.
The process of network security : designing and managing a safe network / Thomas A. Wadlow
p. cm.
Includes index.
ISBN 0-201-43317-6
1. Computer networks—Security measures.   I. Title.

TK5105.59.W34 2000
005.8—dc21

99-058362

Senior Acquisitions Editor: Karen Gettman
Production Coordinator: Jacquelyn Doucette
Compositor: Octal Publishing, Inc.

ISBN: 0-201-43317-6

Text printed on recycled and acid-free paper
1 2 3 4 5 6 7 8 9 10—MA—04 03 02 01 00
First printing, February 2000

This book is dedicated to my mother,
who raised a family full of interesting
and curious characters.

Contents

Preface

A friend of mine said to me the other day that he wanted his old Internet back again. Things worked as well as they needed to. Everyone was nice. You could send mail to people you'd never met, and you'd typically get a nice reply. People gained access to different machines all around the world, which was given more or less freely, so you could log into those machines and see what they'd accomplished this month or just chat with friends. If something needed to be done, a bunch of smart people got together and did it, without too much fuss or bother. It was a nice place, for the most part.

He really wasn't serious, this friend of mine. He makes his living using the Internet we have today and by speaking about the Internet we'll have tomorrow. He gets most of his news from CNN's Web site and the computer industry-specific sites such as Slashdot and Freshmeat. I can't remember the last time he traveled without a laptop; you can send him e-mail anywhere he travels, and (if you get past his filtering software) he'll answer it from Tokyo or Singapore or Paris. The Internet is probably the most complicated thing created by the human race, and yet it is (relatively speaking, of course) easy to use and just about everywhere you'd want it to be.

But I understand his point. The Internet isn't the friendly place it used to be. What was once a small town, where neighbors were friendly and you could leave your door unlocked, is now the largest (virtual) community in the world, and it's growing bigger every day. There are bad parts of town, and there are muggers and thieves and con men, just as in every other city on Earth. You can't get beaten up, but you can be robbed of your time and in some cases of your money.

For all that, the Internet is probably the safest community of its size ever in existence. But that isn't something to take much comfort in. The reason I say this is that I and other members of my profession are called on to look at the security of sites on the Internet from time to time. I know the Internet is mostly safe, because the doors to most places are still unlocked and yet major catastrophes have not happened. Reasoning from that, it appears that most of the people on the Internet are not Bad Guys. Not yet, anyway.

Of course, this can change at any time. And it has begun to. The 1990s saw an ever-growing number of people systematically trolling for computer weaknesses. These people are not trying to attack a specific site; rather, they are just fishing to see what they can catch. The late 1990s saw the beginning of Internet attacks for political reasons. As this book was written, the news media referred to the conflict in Kosovo as the "First Internet War" because of several hostile incidents that occurred and also because much of the unofficial communication between sides was taking place over the Internet.

The Internet is becoming a dangerous place. But it is important to see this in perspective. Any large community has its bad neighborhoods, robberies, muggings and trouble spots, but that doesn't mean it is impossible to live and work there safely. The trick is to keep your eyes open, take reasonable precautions, and not act foolishly. The same rules apply to the Internet.

But computer security means far more these days than the ability of one person to protect himself or herself from the dangers that can arise on the Internet. It's one thing to protect yourself. It's a very different thing indeed to protect a hundred computers, or a thousand, or ten thousand.

This book is intended for the people facing that formidable challenge and the people who will assist in such an endeavour. It is not a tutorial on how to become a hacker. Nor is it a technical manual on how to run a large computer network. Many other sources cover those subjects, for better or worse. My goal here is to give a person charged with the responsibility of running the network security for a large organization a tool for understanding the language and practices of network and computer security, and to provide some hints along the way to save some time and some scraped knuckles. As with any large project, there are many ways to approach these issues. I don't claim that this book is an exhaustive survey of all possible ways. It is, however, a collection of good methodology and tips and tricks, with some warning signs at the rough spots, that have worked for me.

So who am I? Well, I am an electrical engineer by training, but I was swept up into computer science in my high school and college years. My first experience with the Internet was in the late 1970s, when I discovered that I could connect from Carnegie-Mellon University, where I went to school, to a machine in London, England, over something called the ARPANET, which was just appearing on the scene at that time. Like many others at CMU, I worked in the university Computer Center. Unlike many of my colleagues there, I've kept much the same job ever since, running larger and larger collections of computers and their networks at Lawrence Livermore Laboratory, Schlumberger's Palo Alto Research Center, Xerox's Palo Alto Research Center, ParcPlace Systems, and Sun Microsystems Laboratories. Along the way, I've learned a few things about keeping large collections of machines happy and healthy and about keeping the Bad Guys out and the Good Guys working. Now I find myself as the Chief Technology Officer and Vice President of Security for Pilot Network Services, Inc., a company I helped to found and whose function is to handle Internet security for our customers, a diverse collection of some of the most dynamic and interesting (as well as the largest) companies on Earth. The principles we use to run our business safely can be found in this book. That may strike you as odd, creating a book that says how we do our business, because it enables people to compete against us, using our own principles. Well, read on. If you still think it's easy, give it a shot. We welcome the competition.

Acknowledgments

A great many people helped me with the production of this book, directly or indirectly, but I'd like to thank several specifically:

Dr. Martine Droulers and Dr. Celine Broggio, wonderful friends who fed me delicious food and gave me the use of their French seaside attic to finish the book. *Fromage!* Eileen Keremitsis, who put up with my grumbling, made sure that I wasn't working *too* hard, and was ready with an invitation to dinner whenever I needed one. Dennis Allison, who tempted me back into the book-writing business after a long absence, and Karen Gettman and Mary Hart of Addison-Wesley, who made sure that I stayed the course. Steve Riley, Joseph Balsama, Steve Rader, John Stewart, and Clifford Neuman, who read the entire manuscript and whose numerous and insightful comments I found very helpful. And of course, the people at Pilot Network Services, who are the hardest working and nicest bunch of security folks I've ever met.

Tom Wadlow
San Francisco, California, USA
Le Crotoy, Picardie, France, 2000

Chapter

1

Understanding Security

IN THIS CHAPTER:

- What Are We Protecting?
- Thinking Like a Defender
- The Reader of This Book
- The Organization We Are Protecting
- The Process of Security
- How Do You Know That the Process Is Working?
- Trend Analysis

This book is not about "Security." That's a concept that may seem odd to the person who just bought the book or who is leafing through it, considering a purchase. But if you think about the word itself, you can begin to understand why. An exercise book or a diet book or a therapy book are not about "Health" but rather about a process that one can follow to move toward "Health." "Health" is one of those ideal states you can never completely achieve. Instead of being an achievable condition, "Health" is a comparative one. You may be adequately healthy or wonderfully healthy or healthier than I am, but you can never achieve a state of perfect "Health." A state of perfect "Security" is never achievable, either. But the process of improving your network and Internet security, which is what this book *is* about, is one well worth knowing and understanding.

To understand a concept, sometimes it's helpful to go back to first principles. What exactly does it mean for something to be secure? To learn the answer to that, a good place to start is to define what it is that you are securing.

What Are We Protecting?

There are many different kinds of security, and all are focused on the thing they are protecting. Nuclear weapons demand one type of security, rock concerts another. A security breach of one can end the world, another will merely sound like the end of the world.

For the purposes of this book, we will be protecting neither extreme. The challenge of this book is to discuss security for an organization, an enterprise of some kind, usually a business. Some of the topics we will discuss can be of use to an organization of any size. Others will require the resources of a large company and may not be appropriate for smaller or poorer entities.

I've defended the networks of many organizations, large and small. Over the years, I've picked up a few things that seemed to me to be important. Wherever possible, I'll try to make you aware of these points with the following typographic convention:

> *Security should be commensurate with the value of what you are protecting. Part of that value is actual value; another part is the work it will take you to rebuild; another, more subtle part is the work it will take you to trust your network again.*

Many books are about the security of a single type of machine or about highly technical issues of configuration of a specific piece of software. This book is more a philosophical discussion than a technical tutorial. Most of the issues related to securing a large, complex network are not technical. They are related to how the defenders think about their network.

Thinking Like a Defender

Security is not a technology. Technology solves problems of physics and engineering. They are repeatable processes, and enough careful measurement and thoughtful design and thorough testing can squeeze enough bugs out of a box to make it completely reliable.

In security engineering, some of the components are people, and they can be nasty, devious, clever people who lie and cheat and steal. They can also be honest, trustworthy, helpful people who are bright and work hard but sometimes get tired and don't understand all the implications of what they are seeing. When you try to automate a process, you are essentially working to remove people from the system to avoid these variable qualities. You want the steel from a factory to be just as good on the days when the workers are in a bad mood as it is when they are in a good mood. Automation lets you do that.

But in a situation where the difference between a major intrusion and a minor one is an article that appeared in yesterday's *Wall Street Journal* or the knowledge that a product is shipping next Tuesday or that the system administrator will be on vacation for the next two weeks, you'll never be able to automate a security system to account for all of the variables. There have to be people in the loop as defenders, because there are always going to be people in the loop as attackers.

The Reader of This Book

The person for whom this book is written is a computer/network security adminis-trator at a reasonably large organization, which we will discuss in a moment. This administrator is responsible for keeping the organizations's production network safe from attack. The organization is large enough that several people work with this security administrator in a team. The members of the team have moderate-level technical skills with the machines they supervise, even though they may or may not be responsible for the day-to-day system administration of those machines. They are all competent programmers to the degree that they can read and understand programs, can install source code packages from the Internet, and are familiar with most of the workings of the operating systems they use.

Parts of this book are targeted to the person heading the team, who shares the same technical skills and may, in fact, have somewhat more experience in this area. This person is the interface between the security team and the management of the organization for which he or she works.

The security team described here is the only group responsible for the day-to-day security of the network, which implies a moderate-size organization.

The Organization We Are Protecting

If you are a five-person real estate office, with individual Internet dialup connec-tions for all your Windows 98 desktop PCs, this is not the book for you. This book is targeted at the protection of a medium- to large-size organization, using several dozen to several thousand machines all speaking TCP/IP and connected to the Internet via one or more dedicated high-speed links. This organization relies on its network for day-to-day, minute-to-minute conduct of business. It is a Big Deal if the network is unavailable for an hour. Many of the machines are desktop computers of various types, but some of the machines in this network are business-critical, and their continued security is of major importance to the management of the organization.

The operations of this network and of the business-critical machines are the responsibility of other groups in this organization, not that of the security team. If a disk drive fails or a file has to be restored from a backup tape, someone else does it. The security team is responsible for the operation and management of all equipment relating to the security of the network.

The Process of Security

We have said that security is not a technology. You cannot buy a device that will make your network secure, nor can you buy or write a piece of software that will make your computer secure. The fallacy of those statements is in implying that security is a state you can achieve. You can't. Security is a direction you can travel in, but you'll never actually arrive at the destination. What you can do, and what this book is about doing, is managing your acceptable level of risk.

Another important aspect of security is that it isn't static. In many ways, working the Internet security industry is like trying to climb up an endless down escalator. You can race up a few steps, then stop to catch your breath, and when you're rested, you find that the escalator has moved you back down toward or beyond your original starting place. In order to stay even, you must continually expend effort. In order to get ahead and become more secure, you must expend even *more* effort. And like an escalator, it's not just the amount of effort you expend; the effort must be in the correct direction.

If you remember only one concept from this book, remember this one:

> *Security is a process. You can apply the process again and again to your network and the organization that maintains it, and, by doing so, you will improve the security of the systems. If you stop applying the process or have not yet started, your security is becoming worse as new threats and techniques emerge.*

What is the security process? Well, in many ways it is similar to the ancient Greek triad that is taught to engineers the world over (Figure 1-1):

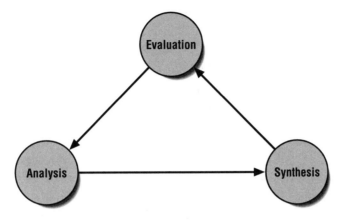

Figure 1-1: Greek triad

Analyze the problem you face based on everything you know.

Synthesize a solution to it, based on your analysis.

Evaluate the solution and learn where it did not live up to your expectations.

And then start the loop all over again and again and again. This is, of course, how you design anything. The process of security, which we will explore throughout this book, expands on this endless loop and adds a few twists of its own.

Learn everything you can about the threats that face you. The Internet is full of information about many things, and that includes information about how to break into systems on the Internet. Finding information can range from very easy to nearly impossible, however, and you need all of it. And the information changes every single day.

Design as well as you can based on what you've learned before you implement anything. Very often, in the hectic world of technology, the synthesis comes long before the analysis. As organizations grow, it is sometimes easier to slap a couple of boxes in place and get things working, then worry about the little details (such as whether somebody can break in through your new Internet connection) later. But more often than not, a weekend's worth of research and an afternoon's reflective thought can save an awful lot of time and money later.

Think pathologically about the design and beef it up to be on the safe side. "Thinking pathologically" is something we discuss in great detail later. The ability to do this, to "think evil thoughts," is what separates the security designer from all other types of designers.

Implement it the way you designed it. There is a famous story about a very large building in New York City that was built in the early 1970s. The architect modeled the building very carefully, because he was concerned about extra stresses from wind channeled through Manhattan's famous "concrete canyons." He tested the model for winds coming from the north, south, east, and west, learned a few things, and designed special welded joints that would distribute the load properly onto the foundation. A year or so after the building construction was finished and the building was fully occupied, an architecture student called the architect and asked for a meeting. After some persuasion, the architect agreed. The student, as an exercise, had duplicated the model of the building, but, employing some new technology, the student had tested it for stresses against the corners of the building instead of the wall faces. Under some conditions with an angular wind load instead of a perpendicular one, the model collapsed, and the student wanted some reassurance that this had been accounted for in the actual design. The architect admitted that he had not modeled for diagonal wind stresses, but he said that the welded joints he'd specified ought to be able to handle the load. He offered to take the student up into the building to see the joints. They entered the inspection corridor, halfway up the giant building, and the architect turned ashen when he realized that the joints that had been built and were supporting the skyscraper were bolted, not welded, and were inadequate for the stresses that would be imposed by a major windstorm. At some point during construction, a plan had been misinterpreted, and the welding had never been done. A great deal of time, money, and anxiety were expended over the next year, relocating some of the tenants of the building, carefully replacing each joint while still supporting the skyscraper, and working with the city government to plan for an emergency evacuation of thirty square blocks of midtown Manhattan if a storm approached from the right direction.

Continuously recheck it to make sure that it hasn't changed. It takes time to change physical structures, but the configuration of a computer or a router can be changed in an instant, and such changes can have a profound impact on the security and maintainability of a machine. Quite often, major changes are made in what is intended to be a temporary fashion, but temporary changes have a way of becoming permanent if there is no feedback mechanism to call attention to them.

Practice running it to make sure that you understand it and can operate it correctly. All the security technology in the world won't make a bit of difference if, when the alarm goes off, everyone looks at each other with a blank stare because nobody knows what to do. A properly monitored and operated security system based on weak technology is, in most cases, much more secure than a poorly operated system based on great technology. The skill with which you operate your network security systems makes more difference to your overall security than any other single factor.

Think pathologically about the implementation, and beef it up to be on the safe side. There are many aspects of a production network that are not considered in a typical design. Consider, for example, a rack full of logging machines and network sniffers, used for security. The way in which they are integrated into the network might be elegant and effective, but if all the devices are powered by a single circuit and the circuit breaker should trip, what would the effect be on the overall security of the network? Especially if the machines that notice that sniffers and loggers are down are also on the same circuit?

Make it simple for people to do what you want them to do. It is very easy to design a system that is "secure" if you require massive amounts of authentication and paperwork to be filed in order to do simple things. The system will be secure because no one will use it. The art of designing security into a system is to do so so that normal users of the system are fairly unaware of the security measures you've taken, as long as they do what they are allowed to do.

A true artist in the design of secure systems would apply this principle not only to authorized users of the system but also to unauthorized ones. A system that entices unauthorized users to do things that quickly cause themselves to be detected and neutralized is a system that will be much easier to secure.

Make it hard for people to do what you don't want them to do. This principle also applies to both authorized and unauthorized users. You want to design a system in which dangerous changes are difficult to make, are noticed immediately when they are made, and require authorization and justification.

Make it easy for you to detect problems. A huge amount of information is available in any network that is pertinent to the security of that network, but much of it is not logged, and what is logged is often ambiguous. Careful work with each component and with the logging system can improve this situation, but even more effective is proper design. If you design a device that accepts connections for e-mail, file transfer, remote login, and many other services from arbitrary locations, you'll need a great deal of context to disambiguate a legitimate access from an attack attempt. If you design for separate devices, each accepting one protocol, and each connection is allowed only from specific sources, then a file transfer request from an unauthorized source to a box that does only e-mail can be treated as an attack, with no further analysis required. The cost of extra hardware for major services quickly disappears as it is amortized across an entire organization, but the cost of extra work for monitoring and missing a potential attack signature because of bad design continues for the life of the network.

Make it difficult to hide what you don't want hidden. The idea that something is "hidden" implies a watcher who does not see. In most networks, there is very little watching going on, which is one reason networks are easy to attack. Your chances of catching an attack as it is in progress are relatively small, compared to your chances of noticing an attack by analyzing the information you log about your network. The more events you log and the more thoroughly you analyze them, the more likely you are to see the footprints of your attackers. Much more than half of the battle is knowing that an attack is in progress, and so your ability to see what is happening within your network should take up much more than half of your efforts.

Test everything you can test. How do you know that your logging system is working? How do you know that your log analysis tools are operating properly? How do you know that your packet filtering is still filtering packets? How do you know that your packet sniffers are still alive? If you don't know how to test them, then you really don't know. If you do know how but haven't tested them recently, then you still don't know. You should find ways to test everything you can possibly test, starting with the most important things and working through them all. Passive tests (such as whether or not a particular packet filter has logged any activity recently or whether a sniffer has seen a packet recently) allow you to monitor your network without increasing the traffic load. Complicated tests make it more difficult for changes to go unnoticed. A test that noticed that a particular machine was still logging traffic but not responding to pings would suggest that something very odd and possibly hostile was happening.

Practice everything you can practice. The people in your organization are as much if not more a part of your defenses than anything you can mount in a rack in your machine room and connect to the network. In order to defend the network, they must know their roles and be skilled in them. They must know what their responsibilities are regarding the security of your network. A well-organized and regularly scheduled set of practice sessions, typically including your security staff but sometimes including other people in the organization, trains your people in a way that no other activity can and makes it clear that security is an important part of your operations. And on the day when the attack is not a drill, your people will be ready to handle it and it will be handled correctly.

Improve anything you can improve. Make it simpler, make it faster, make it more robust. Make it more comprehensive, make it smarter, make it easier to understand. Make it better documented, more up to date, more fun to train on. Make it more testable, more fault-tolerant, more fail-safe. Make it log better. You can always find places to apply your skill and ingenuity, and the more time you spend doing so, the better you'll understand the environment in which the system you are improving resides; the better your understanding, the better your defense.

Repeat this process endlessly, at all levels of detail. You can apply this process to any part of your network, from full network design to individual component to process and procedure and instructional drill. The process is what keeps you safe and alert, and the more zealously you apply it, the harder it will be for one of the Bad Guys to slip past you and cause trouble.

How Do You Know That the Process Is Working?

In many ways, this is the most frustrating part of a career in network security. The answer is that you may never know for certain. Consider how you would quantify the answer to the following question: "How many times, in the course of a month, is my car *not* stolen because of the alarm system I had installed in it?" Clearly, a single theft that is avoided and thus an insurance claim that you didn't have to file and the time and trouble of a police report that you did not have to undertake would pay for the cost of the alarm. And your alarm may in fact have paid for itself in the first week after its installation. But even though a thief did walk by your car, see the alarm, and choose not to steal the car, you cannot *prove* that such a theft was avoided.

Something similar will happen with the security you provide for your organization. Attackers will lightly scan your network, see that the obvious holes are not open, and move on to select another target. In many cases, this activity will not be distinguishable from that of legitimate or accidental activity. An attack has been averted because of your diligence, but there is no way you can prove it well enough to take credit for it.

There is a danger here. Much of the business of security has been tainted with the policy of selling through FUD (fear, uncertainty, and doubt). It's an easy sell because the threat is difficult to measure, and a master of the FUD technique has an unlimited well to tap because people can always be made a little more afraid, uncertain, or doubtful. But a management team that needs to reduce their spending a bit will always be tempted to look at the security organization, especially if they haven't seen any major success stories from them recently. It is a paradox. Your success is impossible to quantify, but without quantification, the process will appear to be a failure or unnecessary and therefore be cut back.

The answer, as with many paradoxes, lies in restating the problem. Rather than trying to quantify the value of what you are *not* doing, namely defending against attacks that are never attempted because of your defenses, quantify the value of what you *are* doing, namely applying the process of security. How many drills were conducted? How many action items resulted from each one? How many anomalies were detected by log analysis? How quickly were they resolved? How many modifications were requested to the network that required security review? How rapidly were those requests answered? How many were permitted and how many denied? These are quantifiable elements of your work that can be reported on and analyzed for trends. It seems like a lot of hard work, but consider this: An attack that knocked out 10 percent of your monitoring capacity would be a major catastrophe that you would work very hard to prevent. Why then would a budget cut of 10 percent be handled any differently than such an attack, if it could be avoided by better quantification and reporting?

Trend Analysis

The last half of the 1990s was a time of amazing growth for the Internet, as well as for networks within organizations. Capabilities that were amusing diversions in 1995 were business-critical systems in 1999, and this trend shows no signs of slowing down in the next decade. The Internet has spread to encompass most of the planet. With that growth comes an increase in crime, fraud, and network abuse. Many computer security professionals feel that the use of the Internet for terrorism and acts of war is inevitable in the coming decade, and that places your network and your computer systems on the front line of each and every war, major and minor, anywhere in the world.

Your organization may never be a focus of international terrorism. Indeed, the odds are that it will not be. But based on my experience and the experience of others in my profession, the chances are excellent that someone will jiggle the Internet "doorknob" of your organization some time within the next week of your reading this sentence. Whether that doorknob yields easily or not and what they are allowed to find beyond it depends on what you do, how well you do it, and how regularly you continue to do it. The purpose of this book is to give you a structure that will allow you to do your work better.

Chapter
2
Writing a Security Policy

IN THIS CHAPTER:

- Pitfalls
- Staging a Coup
- Contents of the Policy

There's an old joke that goes something like this:

> *A security guard working the evening shift at a factory sees a little man leaving the factory, pushing an empty wheelbarrow. The guard, suddenly suspicious, stops him, and the man asks why. "I just want to be sure you're not stealing anything," the guard says gruffly. "Check all you want," says the man, and the guard does but can find nothing suspicious and allows the man to leave. The next night, the same thing happens. This goes on for a few weeks, and then the little man stops appearing at the gate.*
>
> *Twenty years go by, and the guard, now retired, is sitting at a bar when the little man walks in. Recognizing him, the retired guard goes over, explains who he is and offers to buy the man a drink if he'll answer a question. The man agrees, and the guard says, "I was sure you were up to something, but I could never figure out what you were stealing." The little man took his drink in his hand, and as he raised it to his lips, he said: "I was stealing wheelbarrows."*

The point of this is, of course, that security measures don't mean much if your guards don't know what they are guarding.

Ask a corporate executive what the purposes of the security teams are and you'll probably get a response that boils down to "They are there to keep us secure." If pressed, most people could go a bit further in describing the physical security side of the job: keeping unauthorized visitors out, making sure doors that are supposed to be locked remain locked, assisting in an emergency. It's much less likely that the same people would understand what the computer security team is there for. At best you'd probably get "To keep hackers out of our network." It is the job of the network security team to take that vague description and amplify it to the point where it can be used to set priorities and be figured into budgets.

If you ask computer security professionals what the single most important thing you can do to protect your network is, they will unhesitatingly say that it is to write a good security policy. If you ask them to show you their policy, there's a good chance they'll sheepishly grin and ask you to come back next month, when it's finished.

A security policy serves several purposes:

- It describes what is being protected and why.
- It sets priorities about what must be protected first and at what cost.
- It allows an explicit agreement to be made with various parts of the organization regarding the value of security.
- It provides the security department with a valid reason to say "no" when that is needed.
- It provides the security department with the authority to back up the "no."
- It prevents the security department from acting frivolously.

The creation of specific security policies is covered in far more detail in other books than it would be possible to cover here. Books such as *Information Security Policies Made Easy* by Charles Cresson Wood (www.baselinesoft.com) are dedicated to helping you write immensely complex policies or extremely simple ones.

Pitfalls

If a good security policy is the single most important thing you can create to make your network secure, why do most organizations find it so difficult to create a workable policy? There are several major reasons.

Priority. A policy is important, but somebody needs that Web server put on line this afternoon. If you require that people stop putting out what they perceive to be fires to take time to agree on your security policy, then you'll find it difficult to succeed.

Internal Politics. In any organization, large or small, a number of internal factors affect any decision or practice.

Ownership. Oddly enough, in some organizations, the fight is between several groups who want to own the policy, and in others, the fight is between several groups who most explicitly do *not* want ownership of the policy.

Hard to Write. A good policy is an inordinately difficult document to get exactly right, especially if it is to be comprehensive. You can't think of all cases and all details in advance.

Here are some trade-offs that seem to offer insight into these problems and how to get around them.

- A good policy today is better than a great policy next year.

- A weak policy that is well-distributed is better than a strong policy no one has read.

- A simple policy that is easily understood is better than a confusing and complicated policy that no one ever bothers to read.

- A policy whose details are slightly wrong is much better than a policy with no details at all.

- A living policy that is constantly updated is better than one that grows more obsolete over time.

- It is often better to apologize than to ask permission.

Staging a Coup

There is a way that you can get a decent policy in place for your organization. It's not perfect and not without its risks, but if you can manage it, you'll save yourself a lot of time and trouble. The process looks like this.

1. *Write a security policy for your organization.* Say nothing specific. State generalities. This policy should cover no more than five pages. It should take no more than two days to write. Consider writing it over the weekend, so you won't be disturbed. Don't ask for help. Do it yourself. Don't try to make it perfect, just try to get some key issues written down. It doesn't have to be complete, and it doesn't have to be crystal clear.

2. *Find three people who are willing to become the "security policy committee."* Their job is to make rulings on the policy and amendments to the policy, not to change it. The people on the committee should be interested in having a security policy, should be from different parts of the organization, if possible, and should be willing to meet briefly perhaps once or twice per quarter.

Make it clear that enforcing the policy and taking heat for any problems with it is your responsibility, not theirs. Their job is to be judges, not enforcers.

3. *Create an internal Web site with the policy on it and a page describing how to contact the security policy committee.* As amendments are written and approved, add them to the Web site *as quickly as possible*.

4. *Treat the policy and the amendments as if they were absolute rules of law.* Do nothing to violate the policy, and allow no violations to occur. At some point, your management may come to notice this. Allow and encourage them to become involved as much as possible, except that they should not simply eliminate your policy and leave you with nothing. Steer them toward creating a new and better policy. You will not get them involved unless they want to be, and this is an excellent method for involving them. If they remain involved, you get a policy with management buy-in. If they get caught up in other things, your policy remains in place.

5. *If someone has a problem with the policy, have the person propose an amendment.* An amendment can be no more than a single page. It should be as generic as possible. To become an amendment, two of the three (or more) policy committee members need to agree.

6. *Schedule a regular, off-site meeting to consolidate policy and amendments.* This meeting should take place about once a year and involve you and the security policy committee. The purpose of this meeting is to take the policy and any amendments and combine them into a new five-page policy statement. You can involve the committee in the writing, if you'd like, but the best way is probably just to take a weekend and write another draft of the policy, taking all the amendments into account.

7. *Repeat the process again.* Put the policy on your Web site, treat it like law, involve management if they wish to become involved, add amendments to the policy as need be, and review the whole thing in a year. Keep doing so for as long as possible.

There's a lot of work embodied in these simple steps, but this process works as well as anything and better than most for getting *something* useful in place as quickly as possible. Granted, if you can get early management buy-in, assemble a committee of the right people, and get them all to meet and agree on a process and a policy, you'll get better results. But getting all those things to happen is even harder and more time-consuming than the process shown and less likely to actually produce a workable policy.

The reason that this process is called a "coup" is that you are not involving your management in the creation of the policy as much as you otherwise might. This might seem dangerous, and it may be, so act carefully. You could go the safe route and build consensus, but historically such approaches result in a great many meetings and a very small number of security policies. Look at the odds. Your management is probably as busy as you are and as uninterested in attending lots of fruitless meetings as you are. If you simply create a reasonable policy, adopt a flexible attitude toward changing it to meet the needs of the organization, and create a process by which it can be changed that is immune to your "whims," then the chances are excellent that what you've created will be what the organization officially adopts. Or the organization will react to your policy by creating a completely different one. Unless your relationship with your employer is so bad that they discount every suggestion you make (and if that is the case, allowing you remain in charge of security is pretty foolish), the new policy as well will be strongly flavored by your ideas. The only real trick is not allowing the situation to be one in which your policy is rejected but not replaced. The more obviously reasonable your policy is, the less likely this is to happen.

Contents of the Policy

The rest of this chapter describes issues that you should consider for inclusion in your policy.

What Are We Protecting?

Describe in reasonable detail the types of security levels that you expect to have in your organization. For instance, you might characterize the machines on your network as follows:

Red   Contains extremely confidential information or provides mission-critical service.

Yellow   Contains sensitive information or provides important service.

Green	Able to access red or yellow machines but does not directly store sensitive information or perform crucial function.
White	Unable to access red, yellow, or green systems but not externally accessible. No sensitive information or function.
Black	Externally accessible. Unable to access red, yellow, green, or white systems.

By doing this, you've now provided a vocabulary to describe every machine on your network and the level of security each machine should be accorded. You could use the same nomenclature to describe your networks, as well, requiring, for example, that red machines be connected to red networks, and so on.

Methods of Protection

Describe, at a high level, your priorities for the protection of this network. For example, your organizational priorities might be as follows:

1. Health and human safety

2. Compliance with applicable local, state, and federal laws

3. Preservation of the interests of the organization

4. Preservation of the interests of partners of the organization

5. Free and open dissemination of nonsensitive information

A listing in that order would say, in effect, that employees should protect company information but not at the cost of breaking the law or endangering their own safety or the safety of others.

Describe any general policies for access to each category of system; for example,

Category	Network	Access	Qualification Cycle
Red	Red networks only	Red-cleared employees only	Monthly
Yellow	Yellow and red networks	Employees only	Quarterly
Green	Yellow, red, and green networks	Employees and cleared contractors	Yearly
White	White networks only	Employees and contractors	Yearly
Black	Black networks only	Employees, contractors, and public (through cleared access means)	Monthly

The qualification cycle describes how often a machine of that type should be audited to prove that it is still configured correctly for its security status.

Responsibilities

Describe the responsibilities (and in some cases, the privileges) that are accorded each class of system user.

General

- Knowledge of this policy
- All actions in accordance with this policy
- Report any known violations of this policy to security
- Report any suspected problems with this policy to security

Sysadmin/Operations

- All user information to be treated as confidential
- No unauthorized access to confidential information
- Indemnified for any action consistent with systems administrator code of conduct

Security Administrator

- Highest level of ethical conduct
- Indemnified for any action consistent with security officer code of conduct

Contractor

- Access to specifically authorized machines in specifically authorized fashion
- Request advance authorization in writing for any actions which might be interpreted as a security issue

Guest

- No access to any computing facilities except with written advance notice to security

Appropriate Use

Describe the ways in which employees should or should not use the network.

General

- Minimal personal use during normal business hours
- No use of the network for outside business activity
- Access to Internet resources consistent with HR policies

Sysadmin

- Responsible access to sensitive or personal information on the network
- All special access justifiable for business operations

Security

- Responsible access to sensitive or personal information on the network
- All special access justifiable for business or security operations
- Use of security tools for legitimate business purposes only

Contractor

- No personal access at any time
- Minimal use of the network and only for specific reasons relating to specific contracts

Guest

- No use of the network at any time

Consequences

Describe the way in which the magnitude of a policy violation is determined and the categories of consequences. Some examples follow.

Security Review Board

The Security Review Board consists of three director-level or above employees of the company. A Security Review Board is convened by the Chief Security Officer. Decisions of the Security Review Board can be appealed to executive management of the company. Evidence can be presented by the security department and the employee in question.

Penalties

Below are listed the categories of actions the Security Review Board can take.

Critical

- Recommendation for dismissal
- Recommendation for pursuit of legal action

Serious

- Recommendation for dismissal
- Recommendation for garnishment of wages

Limited

- Recommendation for garnishment of wages

- Formal reprimand in writing

- Unpaid suspension

Chapter

3

Who Is Attacking You?

IN THIS CHAPTER:

- The Nature of the Beast
- Security as an Evolutionary Strategy

In the military, it is called threat analysis. The study of the threats to you and your network is a crucial part of developing a defense that will actually accomplish the goal of defending your network.

Implicit within the idea of threat analysis is the difference between computer security and all other forms of computer technology. For most computer applications, the issue at hand is a problem you must solve. Measure properly, think hard enough, test thoroughly, and you can devise an approach that will solve the problem adequately or, in many cases, perfectly.

Computer security is different. In this field, you don't just solve problems; you defend against threats. If you study hard enough, you can understand a computer problem completely because it is a matter of physics and electronics and software. But a threat comes from a human attacker, not a machine. People are much more difficult to quantify and predict. And therefore they are much more dangerous. The importance of the human element cannot be overstated. Security is not a technology problem, it is a social issue. If you treat it as a problem that can be solved by technological means, you're leaving yourself open for attack.

The people trying to attack you will range from benign to nasty, from simple to devious, from stupid to clever. Your job is to design a defensive strategy that will keep all of them out, including the nasty, devious, clever ones who know too much about your systems. And that is impossible. No defense can withstand every possible attack. No company could afford such a defense, even if it existed. No business can be conducted through such a defense. You could take every computer your company has, weld them in a giant steel ball, place that ball at the bottom of the ocean, and the machines would still be vulnerable to some kinds of attack. But the attacker wouldn't find it easy. And that is the key.

You can't make it impossible to successfully penetrate your systems. But you can make it awfully difficult. You can also adjust the level of difficulty to match your budget and your business needs.

A fundamental principle of all security systems is this:

> **_An attack will be successful if the attacker has sufficient_**
>
> - skill
> - motivation
> - opportunity

Your goal, as a designer of security systems, is to second guess those three qualities to minimize the number of attackers who could conceivably succeed. Combine this with your budget, and you are defining an acceptable level of risk, the key parameter for every defensive system.

You must set up a situation in which an attacker must have a very high skill level and a very high level of motivation and be able to make use of a vanishingly small opportunity in order to succeed. To do that, you must understand something about your attackers.

The Nature of the Beast

Attackers come in three basic varieties:

- Browsers, campers, and vandals
- Spies and saboteurs
- Disgruntled (ex-)employees and (ex-)contractors

Their skill levels can vary wildly, as can their motivation levels. You cannot control those factors, but you can control the opportunity each group has to damage your network.

Browsers, Campers, and Vandals

Likelihood of attack:	High
No. of potential attackers:	Large
Motivation:	Low to medium
Skill:	Low to high

These people are the most common attackers on the Internet, and they are the ones you will almost certainly be probed by. They probably aren't targeting your business specifically, but if you have resources that can be exploited, someone from this group will probably attempt to do so if it appears that they can get away with it.

You can think of this class of attackers as wasps. Wasps have a knack for finding little holes through which they can enter your attic. If they can't get inside, they are unlikely to go to extraordinary means to gain entrance, but if they can get in they'll look around to see what they can use. A wasp that finds a way in and finds a hospitable environment is likely to bring back more wasps. Soon, you have a nest of wasps living in your attic. And once you discover this, you'll have a difficult and expensive time getting rid of the wasps safely. Simply attacking them is foolish and dangerous. Ignoring them means that you can never use your attic again, and anyone who tries is in danger. And sooner or later the wasps will try to visit the rest of the house.

To get rid of them, you'll need a good plan, carried out by people who know what they are doing. And if you don't find and fix the hole that allowed them to enter in the first place, you'll get rid of one nest and return in a few weeks to find another.

The types of attack posed by this group are as follows:

- Browsers want to find a way in, often just for the challenge of doing so. Once in, they want to look around to see what they've accomplished.

- Campers have found a way in and see resources they can make use of. Your 1.5-Mbps T-1 line is a lot more attractive as a means for launching further explorations than their ancient 14,400-bps modem. Your computers compile programs faster, have more disk space, and are more accessible to them and their friends.

- Vandals are often campers who've been discovered. If you find your systems in use by outsiders and destroy what the outsiders have left on your systems without closing the holes they used to get in, you can easily find yourself subject to retaliation.

The skill level of this type of attacker can vary widely. Most common today are the "script kiddies." These attackers don't really understand what they are attacking, but they have tools written by people who do understand. Those tools, combined with a failure by the defender to close common holes, add up to a penetration. If you find it comforting that your network was penetrated by a kid who didn't really know what he was doing, perhaps you should find a different line of work.

This type of attacker is the one that makes the news the most often. You know: "Fourteen-year-old boy breaks into Pentagon computer." Unsurprisingly, this type of attacker is almost always close to the profile of a fourteen-year-old male. Boys of that age can be clever, devious, and looking for a way to look cool in the eyes of their friends or looking for a way to make friends. They are at the age when outwitting authority figures is enormously attractive and when peer pressure is at its peak. Computer intrusion is fun. It's easy enough to do once you know how, but learning how takes enough time, concentration, and intelligence that not just anybody can do it. And doing it successfully makes you feel powerful, which is something that will attract fourteen-year-old boys, especially alienated, unpopular ones, like moths to a flame.

This is not to say that all attackers will be boys or that a fifteen-year-old is no threat. Far from it. But if you can make your systems safe from highly motivated teenage boys, you're doing a pretty good job of keeping them secured.

Keep in mind that what motivates a teenage boy or any attacker may not be what motivates you. When designing a defense for your networks, don't just think about defending the parts that are valuable from your perspective; defend the parts that are valuable from the perspective of your attackers as well.

Browsers, campers, and vandals are quite common on the Internet today. In fact, they represent the bulk of the attacks launched on the Internet and probably the bulk of the attacks that succeed. The community of people who do this is evolving at a furious rate. Concerns about international encryption legalities and return on investment don't faze them at all, because, for the most part, there is no money in this type of activity. It is done because it's fun and seems like a cool thing to do.

Defensive Strategy

- Do not provide unauthenticated public resources that can be taken over by campers.

- Scan your public resources periodically to ensure that they have not been compromised.

- Eliminate features of your Internet presence that would be particularly attractive to these types of attackers.

- Stay very current on attack methodologies. Collect exploit scripts where possible and make sure that your systems are not vulnerable.

The last point is a tricky one. Resources for collecting exploit scripts are like good, inexpensive restaurants. Their character changes dramatically once everybody knows about them—often for the worse. In many ways, the process for developing resources for exploits is a microcosm of what this book is about. If I included a list of useful sites, I would be doing the readers of this book no great service, because the sites popular as this book is written are unlikely to be of much use weeks or months after I create the list. Having a list is not nearly as important or useful as developing the skills to make your own list. Becoming familiar with the landscape of security resources on the Internet is an essential part of your job. Start just by looking up "computer security" on any reputable search engine and follow the links you find. Keep notes. Remember that the Web site you are browsing may be scanning you as well, so browse from a locked-down machine on a network that will not suffer from the added attention. Doing that will get you to exploit sites quickly enough, but what you will learn in the process will help you to understand what you find when you arrive.

Spies and Saboteurs

Likelihood of attack:	Depends on your business
No. of potential attackers:	Usually low
Motivation:	Medium to high
Skill:	Medium to high

This type of attacker is the one the movies lead you to expect: the skilled computer expert who types a few well-chosen commands into a laptop and suddenly has access to the command and control systems of his target. It looks great on film, but it rarely (if ever) happens that way in real life.

Which is not to say that spies and saboteurs don't exist. They do, but the game is risky, the stakes are high, and the rewards are low and come only after endless days of painstaking work. In the days of the Cold War, the spies would have been government agents, the goals political. A perfect example can be found in Cliff Stoll's book *The*

Cuckoo's Egg, the true story of an attack on computers at the Lawrence Berkeley Laboratories by East Germans.

These days, with the Cold War ended, the spies are more likely to be freelancers and the goals industrial. While this scenario lacks the romance of stealing nuclear secrets, it also lacks the danger . . . to the spies. They have a much better chance of succeeding and a much lower chance of getting caught. And even if they do get caught, the ability of a U.S. company to locate let alone extradite an Internet-based spy from Bulgaria or Taiwan is practically nonexistent.

A typical characteristic of this type of attack, if one could be said to exist, is that the attackers are specifically targeting you. They know what you do and to a large extent how you do it. They've made a study of your company and your network and perhaps even your employees. They may have gone through your trash looking for clues.

These attackers are highly motivated, primarily because they expect to get paid. This is both a strength and a weakness, however. People who perform criminal acts for money tend to develop a finely honed instinct for what their risk is worth. They will do some things, will want more money for others, and will not take some actions no matter how high the price because of the risk of getting caught. But desperation can change those limits, so you cannot always count on them.

A good analogy here would be that of car thieves. They range from the street punk trying to snatch a purse off the back seat of a car up to a "professional" looking for a specific model Mercedes to sell to a chop shop on order. They have a specific target in mind, and they perform reconnaissance work to verify the target's value and minimize their risk. They have a bag of tricks that help them get in and get out as quickly as possible. If anything goes wrong before they've committed, they can walk away and try another car later. If anything goes wrong after they've committed, they do whatever they can to get out safely.

The car thief analogy can extend a bit further in the case of saboteurs. These people are specifically targeting you also, but they don't want to acquire something from you. They want to deny you the ability to perform some function. In other words, they don't want to steal your car; they just want to prevent you from driving it. This gives them much more freedom of operation and much less chance of detection. A car thief has to approach your car in order to steal it. A saboteur can make your car undriveable with a ball bearing and a slingshot from a hundred feet away.

In many ways a saboteur is like a vandal, but they have some key differences: The saboteur is targeting you specifically. The vandal commits random acts of service denial or damage. The vandal is operating purely for emotional gratification. The saboteur has some larger goal that is served by the sabotage. Saboteurs are much less common than vandals, but they do pose a threat worth considering.

Spies are not very common on the Internet today. As more and more commerce shifts to the Internet, and as more and more of value is available via the Internet, this type of activity will become more common, because the motivation for it, primarily money, will increase.

Defensive Strategy

- Appear, from the outside, to be a risky target to attack.
- Eliminate well-known means for denial-of-service attacks.
- Limit what is publicly known about your defenses.
- Guard your core business systems especially well.

Disgruntled (Ex-)Employees and (Ex-)Contractors

Likelihood of attack:	Medium to high
No. of potential attackers:	Depends on your business
Motivation:	High
Skill:	Medium to high

These attackers are the most dangerous of all. If a successful attacker needs skill, motivation, and opportunity to succeed, this group can have those qualities in spades. You trained them to have the skills, they are disgruntled, meaning that you've given them the motivation to succeed in attacking your company, and because they may still be known and trusted, or worse yet, may still be employees of your company, they may well have the opportunity.

Those three things taken together constitute a serious threat to your network. In fact, most serious attacks on a computer system or network in which significant money is lost tend to have people on the inside who match this profile. Sometimes the insiders are difficult to spot, but they are likely to be there.

There are plenty of reasons to be careful about an inside attacker. Consider the following attack scenario:

> Dave slid his car into the familiar parking space outside Red's Place, a bar just a few blocks from work. He'd been coming here for years, as it was a popular hang-

out for his crowd at Megacorp. They'd had some good times here: birthdays, bachelor parties, and celebrations of milestones at the office. But recently, Dave wasn't coming to celebrate. He'd gotten into the habit of stopping by for a few drinks after work and grumbling to anybody who'd listen about his new supervisor, Bill, the little jerk who used to be his assistant and was now making Dave's life miserable.

As he settled onto his usual stool at the bar, Dave was greeted by a couple of the other regulars. His pal Charlie spotted him from across the room and came over to say hello. Charlie was fairly new at the bar, but he'd been hanging out for a couple of weeks and was a friendly sort who'd stand for a round or two now and then. He was a good listener, too, and that was what Dave needed.

Charlie signaled the bartender for a round of the usual drinks and chatted with Dave until the glasses arrived. Dave drained his first drink in one swallow and signaled for another. "Geez, Dave, what's wrong?" said Charlie.

"The little creep was on me again today," said Dave through clenched teeth. His second drink arrived, and he took a good sip. "Ten years at Megacorp and now I can't do anything right, according to that jerk!"

"Yeah, he sounds like an idiot all right," said Charlie. "Reminds me of a manager I knew over at Quasidyne. Thank God somebody finally took care of him!"

"Whaddya mean?" said Dave, the booze already beginning to hit him. Charlie went on to explain that the Quasidyne manager had been in charge of a big demo for upper management. It seems that a few of the boys had installed a virus on the manager's system that popped up during the demonstration with a few choice phrases that did not win him the favor of his superiors.

"The guy's now in charge of printer maintenance for MIS," Charlie said, laughing. "He won't be any trouble at all now . . . and the best part is that he could never figure out who did it. It was completely untraceable!" Dave looked thoughtful. "Yeah, I'd sure like to do something like that to Bill. That'd teach him a lesson."

At that point, Charlie grunted sympathetically and changed the subject. But a few days later, he appeared at the bar with a floppy disk. "Just put it in Bill's machine, wait till it beeps, and take it out." Dave did just that the next day, while Bill was in a meeting. Afterward, he threw the floppy into the river, as Charlie had told him to do. But days went by and nothing happened. "I guess it didn't work. Sorry, man," said Charley. After a while, Charley stopped coming around to the bar, and Dave forgot about him.

But Charley didn't forget about Dave. He thought about him every time he used the Back Orifice server that Dave had installed on Bill's machine. He could examine files, sniff the network, collect passwords, and relay attacks to other machines, all *from the comfort of his home and protected by a bogus ISP account. The information he was getting from Megacorp was making him a star at Quasidyne. . . .*

A dangerous form of insider threat comes when a trusted employee quits or, worse yet, is fired. Any network security system must be designed to account for this scenario. Oddly enough, however, the threat comes not so much from the skill of the departing employee as from your underestimation of the threat posed by that employee. If the chief security architect for a firm is fired, everyone, including the architect, knows that if anything bad happens, the architect will be first on the suspect list. Because of this, and because the architect has a professional reputation to maintain (or salvage, in the case of his being fired), the architect has great reason to reduce his motivation to attack his previous employer.

If the second assistant to the chief security architect is fired, however, there is a potential for much more harm. The expectations are fewer for this person, and the security precautions taken may be fewer as well. That is where the real danger is, because this person, while he may not be as well known as the chief, was probably responsible for real systems and probably knows enough to pose a very serious threat. He doesn't have the reputation to protect, and if it is clear that he is not considered a suspect, he has the skill and motivation to pose great danger.

Defensive Strategy

- Appear, from the outside, to be a risky target to attack.
- Keep your employees and contractors happy.
- Develop a plan for firing employees that covers security issues, such as

    Eliminating computer system access immediately.

    Warning the terminee that he or she will be high on the suspect list if an attack occurs.

    Creating a situation in which the terminee simply cannot abuse the system.

- Develop a plan for firing employees who are aware of key details of your security infrastructure.

Security as an Evolutionary Strategy

Flowers have bright colors that attract bees. This is not to say that flowers make a conscious choice about it, but flowers that attract bees survive and bees that can easily find flowers survive. A system develops in which the most easily seen flowers and the bees with the best eyesight for those flowers reproduce; others do not.

Our networks shape our attackers, and our attackers shape our networks. Each new attack strategy sweeps through the Internet; then there are victims, and soon there are defenses.

If you want the attackers to survive, then wait for them to attack, and make slight improvements to your network each time you detect a problem. That gives the attackers a chance to grow and learn and adapt. If, instead, you want to climb a rung higher on the evolutionary chain, think of this strategy for survival:

> Make your networks formidable and unattractive to attack. Make attackers practice their attacks elsewhere, before they come to you. Develop and monitor information sources that tell you what new attacks are being tried, and defend against them as quickly as you can. Think up new ways of attack, and defend against them before your attackers think of them.

Following this principle moves you higher on the "food chain" and makes it exceedingly difficult for an attacker to cause you any harm. But it requires ongoing work. And it poses several difficulties, which we discuss in other chapters:

- If your defenses are too effective, will your management perceive this as a sign that, because there are no attacks to defend against, you are spending too much money on security?

- If you are depending on other organizations to post defenses that you will then use, what are your responsibilities with regard to posting what you have learned?

Chapter

4

Security Design Process

IN THIS CHAPTER:

- Thinking About Security
- Principles of Security
- The Shape of Your Defenses
- The Shape of Your Security Organization

Security is an interesting business and a different one from many other forms of human endeavor. If your goal is building an airplane, you can tell when you're done because the airplane flies. If you build a building, the day the tenants move in is the day your work is completed. There may still be work to be done in either case, but there comes a point when the work is effectively complete. Security is different. You can secure a building, reaching the point where you think most of the work has been done, and suddenly a thought occurs to you, perhaps from a passing conversation, that points out a huge gap in your defenses. You thought you were nearly finished, but suddenly you're back at the beginning of the process and must rethink all your plans and strategies. If you consider security as a goal, you'll encounter this phenomenon again and again.

The real key to understanding how to secure a building or a network or a computer system is to see security as a process, not a goal. It's a lot like gardening. Just because you weeded your garden a month ago, there is no guarantee that new weeds haven't begun to sprout. A well-tended garden is a pleasure to work with. A garden that has been ignored for a year is a mess that takes a lot of work to clean up. The moment you begin to ignore it, weeds begin to creep in and bugs start eating your plants.

Understanding that security is a dynamic process that requires constant attention gives you a philosophical basis for taking action. It also gives you reasons to lose sleep, worrying about what you might have overlooked.

In this chapter, we discuss some fundamental principles of the security process. Security is an art, not a science. Like viewing a painting or hearing a symphony, a shift in perspective can make a huge difference in how well a task has been accomplished. So while there are no absolutely correct answers to the questions that face you, there are many, many wrong ones. The principles listed here are a good starting point for designing networks that are reasonably secure. Undoubtedly, you will develop more of your own as you go along.

Thinking About Security

Security, as we've said, is a process, not a state or a goal. But what exactly is that process, and how can it be applied? A good way to understand the process is to think about the conditions that spawned it.

In the last chapter, we discussed the types of attackers that can threaten your network. Without attackers, the way in which we would design computer networks would probably be very different, and more attention would be focused on details of performance and ease of use, rather than security. Now, imagine a network like that, and picture what would happen to it when the first malicious attack was launched upon it. Because the network was designed with no safeguards whatsoever, an attacker would be able to completely control any aspect of the network. The situation would be similar to that of people born without an immune system suddenly being exposed to disease for the first time. The disease would ravage them, and they'd die quickly.

An immune system is a very good analogy for what we are trying to create here. We want to design our network to resist attacks, and we want that resistance to be adaptive so that new attacks are countered quickly.

Immune systems have served people well for the history of the human race. But they have not served perfectly. Plagues have ravaged humanity over the centuries, and even diseases that are survivable, ones with which our immune systems can cope, sometimes incapacitate us for days or weeks. But humanity has an advantage, developed over the last century or so, that gives our immune system a capacity unprecedented in the history of biology: vaccines.

A vaccine is a means through which your immune system can learn how to counteract a disease without your ever having been exposed to the disease or having had to contract it. A vaccine allows your immune system to benefit from the experience of other people many miles or years away from you. It's an amazing thing, when you stop and think about it. A vaccine gives our immune systems the capacity to learn from the experiences of others in exactly the same way that our senses, language, and writing give our brains the ability to learn from the experiences of others.

And that is exactly what we want to build into our computer networks: the ability for a network to resist many different kinds of attacks by design; the ability to adapt the design of the network and the protection mechanisms within it to new threats; and the ability to learn of those threats before they actually threaten our network.

Having such an ability is no guarantee of network "health," just as a person possessing a good immune system whose vaccinations are up to date may still get a cold from time to time. But what it means is that most common threats can be dealt with without troubling the network, and there is also a means to deal with the occasional threat that has not been anticipated.

The process of preparing for known threats, anticipating new threats, and having a system for dealing with threats is what we are calling the process of security. A more elaborate definition follows.

Security

- Learn everything you can about the threats that face you.
- Design your system as well as you can based on what you've learned before you implement anything.
- Think pathologically about the design and beef it up to be on the safe side.
- Implement it the way you designed it.
- Continuously recheck it to make sure that it hasn't changed.
- Practice running it to make sure that you understand it and can operate it correctly.
- Think pathologically about the implementation and beef it up to be on the safe side.
- Make it simple for people to do what you want them to do.
- Make it hard for people to do what you don't want them to do.
- Make it easy for you to detect problems.
- Make it hard for people to hide their attempts at penetration.
- Watch for signs of penetration attempts.
- Think pathologically about the signs you see.
- React quickly and decisively toward the penetration attempts you detect.
- Test everything you can test.
- Practice everything you can practice.
- Improve anything you can improve.
- Repeat this process endlessly, at all levels of detail.

It may seem like a complicated process, but, like any way of thought, it simply takes some getting used to. The more you apply it, the better you'll get at it, and the better you get, the easier it will be to apply it.

The trick with this process is that you *have* to apply it, if just to stay even. Like the garden, if you ignore it, weeds will soon begin to grow.

Principles of Security

The process of security directs you to what must be done, but a designer needs more than that. This book is not a "cookbook" of secure network design, in which you can simply look up a prefabricated solution and apply the recipe. The threats and design constraints change much too rapidly for that, and the Internet is accelerating the process. Such a book would be obsolete in months. The purpose of this book is to make you aware of the issues so that you can understand what is involved and create your own design that meets your needs and yet does not overlook important aspects.

What follows here are a number of fundamental principles regarding security.

> *If you don't know what you are defending and why, you can't defend it.*

Few security experts would disagree that the single most important thing you can do to secure your networks is to write a security policy describing what you are protecting, why you should protect it, and how you think it should be protected. Some security experts have actually written such policies. Many would sheepishly admit that they have not. Some goals in writing a security policy:

Keep it understandable. A security policy that nobody reads is useful as kindling for a fire but not much else. A security policy that everybody reads but nobody understands is not much better. For a policy to do any good at all, it must be in the hands of the people who are expected to live by it, and they must read and remember it.

Keep it relevant. Your security policy will, of necessity, be a large document. But putting 300 pages on an employee's desk and saying, "Read this and live by it" is not likely to be successful. Ultimately, the quality of your work will be judged by how memorable it is to the people who need to know it, not by how many pages it covers. The finance person doesn't need to know all the details of your off-site tape storage policy, but he or she does need to know what to do when the phone rings and somebody asks for their account and password.

There is a temptation to write long elaborate policies simply because the bulk impresses upper management. Fortunately, there's a good way to get the best of both worlds. Create a number of policies, each intended for a very specific audience within your organization. Individually, each policy can be short, straightforward, and understandable, but taken together they will be massive enough to impress anybody.

Know what is *not* relevant. Some parts of your policy should cover topics you do *not* want everybody to know about. There are two basic ways to accomplish this, and you ought to have both. First, you need a section that describes to everybody the type of information you consider to be sensitive, not to be discussed with outsiders. This section might include topics such as details of security mechanisms (such as the authentication system), phone numbers for internal organizations or dialin access, design of the network, and any other issue relevant to your organization. This list should contain no details about these topics, only enough discussion so that employees can identify them.

The second section is the classified one. It is kept in strictest confidence and can be viewed only by people with the highest level of trust. This section is the "conscience" of your security organization. It lists all the different issues that are extremely sensitive, in whatever level of detail necessary to make your security people aware of the issues involved. The purpose of this section is to allow the people who have to make judgment calls about sensitivity issues to have a basis for judgment. Why is this necessary? Well, consider the way security people tend to behave. Things that they are not supposed to talk about they don't talk about. That is as it should be. But consider also that organizations change over time. If the first generation of your security team *never* talks about the Asmodeus Project because they know how secret it is supposed to be, the third generation will be completely unaware of it, and a mention of it may go unnoticed. You need an explicit, up-to-date list of issues that are sensitive so that your team will have an organizational memory of what they are not supposed to discuss.

Give it teeth. A security policy works only if people take it seriously. That boils down to two basic things:

- They must know in advance from reading the policy that they can be disciplined if they take or fail to take certain actions.
- People who violate the policy must actually be disciplined in accordance with it.

Both principles are equally important. Fail to follow through on either one, and your policies are worthless. The employees also need to take responsibility for staying current with the policy.

Difficulties arise in assigning and enforcing penalties. Work this issue through early on, because a day may come when, for perfectly good and justifiable reasons, you have to ask your vice president of sales to fire his top performer while your company is straining to meet its quarterly numbers, or you have to ask your vice president of engineering to fire his chief designer. If that day comes, you have to have the bugs worked out of this system or else you'll be laughed at.

You need a way to do this that establishes the guilt of the offender to an adequate degree, makes it clear to those applying the sentence that the punishment is justified and equitable, and has the continued, proven support of the top management of your organization. This is a tough thing to accomplish, and no two organizations do it the same way. A good way is to establish a security review board, which sits in judgment. Following are some guidelines:

- A big case is easier to win if you've already worked out the bugs on many, many smaller cases.
- The security team should act as prosecutor, not as judge.
- The judges should be from all areas of the company, and upper management should be well represented. They should have a reasonable amount of practice in the process before being asked to handle a big case.
- Besides punishment, the judges should get to decide a reasonable number of rewards for doing things correctly, as well.
- The security team should be painfully honest and conspicuously unbiased about the cases they present.
- Abide by the decision of the judges.
- The process needs to be somewhat formal, and a public record must be kept.

Keep it current. Every security auditor has had the experience of being handed a beautifully written policy document, only to discover that most of it applies to a department or computer system or project that is long gone. A security policy must be an ongoing process, just like the network security it represents. If you fail to keep the document alive, it very quickly becomes worthless.

Distribute it to the people who must live up to it. Having a great security policy means something only if people other than the security team actually read it. But of course, if you pass around a thousand-page document, few will read it at all, let alone carefully. A very good way of distributing a policy is to create an internal Web site for it, make sure that the site is linked to other internal Web sites, and then keep the policy Web site current. If you are smart, you'll also arrange the policy Web site so that pertinent sections can be printed out easily. Then you can have printed copies of specific sections, such as the general policies that all employees are supposed to abide by, distributed at times and places for which they are appropriate, such as orientation meetings for new employees.

The worst time to develop a new policy is in a crisis. A crisis is typically a situation with too much adrenaline and not enough perspective. Both factors make it very likely that whatever choices you make will be wrong. Thinking through problems before they occur and deciding on a strategy to handle them may not always work, but it has a much better chance of success than shooting from the hip.

Nevertheless, you will develop policies in a crisis. Plan for it. Have a mechanism for sanity checking a policy you come up with on the fly, distributing it to the people who need to know it, and then reviewing it after the crisis has ended. If it still looks good, include it in "the book." If it doesn't, write a better one, and put that in. And by all means, once you've done the postmortem review and decided on the correct policy for a particular situation, communicate it to all the relevant people in your organization.

Security is never an absolute quantity.

Anything can be broken into, if the attackers have sufficient skill, motivation, and opportunity. Your goal, therefore, is to second-guess these three qualities so that you can reduce the number of attackers who can successfully attack you.

SKILL

You can defend against the skill level of attackers in two ways:

- *General skill level.* This is the skill and knowledge required of an attacker of any network. If you've applied all vendor patches, reduced the number of ways of entry to your systems to the bare minimum, applied all known lockdown techniques, and brought your systems to the state of the art in security measures, then the general skill level of an attacker would have to be very high. If you've left known holes open or are vulnerable to simple techniques, an attacker would need only a low general skill level.

- *Custom skill level.* This is skill in and knowledge of your specific network. If, in order to bypass your intrusion detection system, an attacker has to have knowledge of the system that cannot be deduced from the system itself, such as an invisible sniffer listening on the network, or knowledge of a cryptographic key that requires a huge effort to crack, then your network requires a high custom skill level.

A good system would require both a high general level and a high custom skill level. A system requiring a high general level but a low custom level would be difficult for outsiders to crack, but easy for insiders. A system requiring a low general level would be easy for anybody to crack, insider or outsider. What you want is a system that is difficult for both groups to abuse.

MOTIVATION

In a network that demands a high motivation level of an attacker, the attacker must be extraordinarily persistent in order to succeed in a penetration. You can defend your network against attackers' motivation by addressing these factors:

- *Satisfaction.* A network is satisfying to break into if it yields after an interesting struggle. A network penetration is unsatisfying if the struggle is uninteresting and the amount of gain is very little. A well-designed security system will always be satisfying to penetrate, but by changing the rules and allowing the attacker very little gain from any single penetration, and making the probability of detection (and thus immediate response) very high, you can change the satisfaction into frustration. The goal of any defensive system in motivation management should be to deny satisfaction to the attacker and maximize the attacker's level of frustration.

- *Tenacity.* You want to require of the attacker a *great* deal of patience to get anywhere. And you want to minimize the amount of work that the attacker can get done per unit of time, so they not only have to wait but also have to waste a great deal of their own time to get anywhere. Better still is to require the attacker to work very hard between attacks, if that is possible. An example of this would be a security system that requires an attacker, after each failed attempt, to move to another location on the network.

- *Ego.* An attacker can be especially motivated if his or her ego is involved. If a defense is designed to personally insult the attacker or to try and make him or her feel stupid, many attackers will redouble their efforts to penetrate. A defense that is as boring and impersonal as possible is less likely to engage an attacker.

OPPORTUNITY

The opportunities presented to the attacker should be as few as possible. An opportunity is a means of access into your network that can be operated and perhaps abused by the attacker. For example, if a system runs the FTP file transfer service, then an opportunity is available to abuse the service. If, however, the service is configured so that only certain networks have access to it and so that all known security holes have been patched, then the opportunity is reduced. If the network itself is configured to minimize access to the FTP server, then opportunity is further reduced. If the FTP service requires strong authentication for login, then opportunity is reduced even more, and if the service is not present on the system at all, then opportunity is dramatically reduced.

Following are some general ways to minimize opportunity:

- *Parsimony.* Your systems should offer the minimum number of opportunities to the attacker as possible. If you don't want a machine to offer a service, it should not have that service configured, and better still, it should not allow that service to start, even accidentally.

- *Justifiability.* Any outside access opportunity (and therefore possibly accessible to an attacker) must be present for a very good reason or not present at all.

- *Completeness.* Any service available on your network should be fully up to date with all known bugfixes, patches, and security modifications.

- *Awareness.* The network should monitor itself and be aware of any attempt to violate policy; it should also be able to notify the proper people about such a problem.

- *Robustness.* Any limitation of services applied to a part of your network should be replicated throughout the entire network. Thus, if a machine does not offer FTP service, FTP service should be blocked on that machine, and the network itself should not allow FTP connections to that machine.

An ever-present factor in any network design is the resources you have at your disposal to implement and manage the network. By balancing your budget against your modulation of the three attacker qualities, you can develop a sense of your acceptable level of risk (ALR). The ALR is the key design parameter of any security system.

People make mistakes.

You will make mistakes. Design your network so that a single mistake will not compromise its security. It is an impossible goal but one worthy of pursuit. The closer you can come to this state, the harder it will be for an attacker to compromise you. This is what is known in military terms as "defense in depth." You want to design your network in such a way that the compromise of a single device does not result in penetration.

A good way to do this is to adopt a policy known as *restrictive design*. The Internet as a whole has a *permissive design,* which says:

> *Everything that is not specifically forbidden is allowed.*

A restrictive design is exactly the opposite of this. It says:

> *Everything that is not specifically allowed is forbidden.*

From a security standpoint, this architecture has a number of advantages. If combined with adequate logging, any attempt to make use of the network in a way not intended by its designers will be immediately noticed. Exclusive of logging, any unapproved attempt at using the network will probably fail as well. The difficulty with such a network philosophy is operational. It limits the flexibility of the network and requires security approval and potentially large reconfigurations every time a new service is added. But if you can work around the operational difficulty, a restrictive network policy tends to make your mistakes immediately obvious and can significantly lessen their consequences.

Attackers will make mistakes. Don't count on them, but be prepared to exploit them to your advantage.

One of the reasons a network should require a high custom skill level is to *force* the attacker to make mistakes by lack of knowledge about your systems. An attacker who does not make such mistakes under these circumstances may be an insider or a recently terminated employee.

Vendors will make mistakes. Don't assume that everything works as advertised. A network component, whether router or computer or other device, is a very complicated system. It is extremely difficult to specify *exactly* what a complicated device will do under all circumstances, and the chances are good that neither you nor your vendor completely understands the consequences of doing unusual things to these devices.

If you measure it yourself, you will know. Don't badger your vendor to do the measurements for you. Badger them for the ability to do the measurements yourself.

> **Knowing that you are under attack is more than half the battle.**

The defenses of any network fall into two categories:

- Defenses that work when you aren't looking
- Defenses that require your attention in order to work

Let's call the first type *passive defenses* and the second type *active defenses*. Clearly, therefore, the easiest way for an attack to succeed is for the attacker to defeat your passive defenses while not triggering your active defenses. It follows that a very bad situation for you to be in would be for you to be under attack and not know it. Consequently, a good set of priorities for your defenses would be as follows:

1. Defeat as many types of attack as possible with your passive defenses.
2. Detect and report any attacks that occur.
3. Deploy active defenses and cut off the attacker as quickly as possible.

Once you know that you're under attack, there are many things you can do to handle the situation or at the very least to frustrate the attacker. To know that you're under attack, you've got to have the following capabilities:

- Ability to detect an attack in progress
- Ability to notify the security staff of an attack

Because the ability to know that you're under attack is so important, you should devote a significant portion of your ongoing efforts to improving and testing your ability to monitor events on your network. If something happens on your network but you don't notice it, it can't help you at all and it can easily hurt you. If you notice it but don't interpret it correctly, the same consequence applies, but you may be able to learn from your mistake.

The Internet is a rich source of information and attack signatures if you develop the skills to find them. Any well-known attack signature that applies to your network and that you cannot detect and trigger an alarm about is one that an attacker can use against you. Developing tools to find them, which can be adapted to new signatures as they occur, should be an essential part of your network monitoring plans.

A more difficult type of monitoring tool to perfect is the kind that helps you spot unusual situations on your network that you did not anticipate. This type of tool will always be more prone to false alarms, because it is looking for less easily quantifiable conditions. One good approach to designing this type of tool is to use a statistical approach and develop a profile of various characteristics of your network. For example, if a key server is normally idle on Sunday mornings and a tool notices that on a particular Sunday the machine is working quite hard, it would be worth investigating. If you notice that a machine that normally does not run a particular service has now started running it (or vice versa), that is something worth investigating, as well.

As you develop these tools, think of ways that you can test them. If an attacker can prevent your alarms from sounding, he's got the advantage.

> ### Defend against the attacker as well as the attack.

There are two main components to any defensive system. Passive defenses guard against the attacks you know about. In theory, if they are adequate and remain adequate, they are all you really need. Every attack will simply bounce off them and never bother you. But you might make mistakes. You might misconfigure a passive defense. You might not learn of an attack in time to set up its defense. Or someone might try out a new attack on your network before *anybody* has learned of it. For that matter, what about denial-of-service attacks, which can be attenuated but often cannot be blocked?

What you want is a layered defense that combines passive defenses, which operate against the attack, with active defenses which operate against the attacker. Once someone has taken hostile action against you, what rule requires that you allow them to try again? Remember the three characteristics of a successful attack: sufficient skill, motivation, and opportunity. The basic design goal of your passive defense is to require an arbitrary attacker to have a high level of skill and motivation and to present the attacker with a low level of opportunity. Once someone has attacked your network, the attacker is no longer "arbitrary." You can quickly present an attacker with *no* opportunity by refusing to accept any network traffic at all from him.

A blocked attacker must either find a way around a total block or move to another network location to attack again. When you put a block in place, it should be against not just the source address of the attack but against an intelligently selected range around such a host. This makes it difficult for an attacker to make a simple change and attack again, and it requires him to move to another network or another dialin server or another service provider. There is nothing to stop him from doing so, but the more diligently you pursue this policy, the more annoying it will be for the attacker and the more motivation he will require to continue the attack.

The keys to blocking well are as follows:

- Sufficient monitoring to allow you to distinguish hostile acts

- Sufficient judgment to allow you to decide to implement the blocks

- Sufficient control over your network to allow you to implement the blocks

- A review process to determine when and how to remove the blocks (quickly if it was a mistake, after a long period of inactivity if not)

> *Train as you fight; fight as you train.*

Having active defenses is all well and good, but if you never test them and never practice using them, you won't find them to be very helpful (or even functional) when you need them. A good network defense has been rehearsed. Rehearsals give you a way to test your procedures and eliminate bad ones and improve good ones. Drills give you a way to become familiar with established procedures and to see how they work in action. A proper drill should be as much like a real attack as you can manage, at least in one particular aspect. By varying the aspects and the intensity of the drill, you can focus on various kinds of problems and your responses to them. A drill can be as simple as a bunch of people together in a conference room talking, or it can be a full-blown exercise with real attacks staged by a team pretending to be attackers. The more you do, the better you'll get, and the less likely a real incident will be to surprise you.

> *Good components will not save you, but bad components will surely hurt you.*

The steel that goes into a bridge is not picked off the scrap heap, nor is it chosen because it is popular or politically correct. Someone sits down and analyzes the requirements and carefully selects what the bridge is to be made of and how it is to be constructed. This is called *engineering*. Your network should be engineered correctly, as well.

Of course, you'll have constraints. All projects have constraints. The trick is to find a solution that will work within the constraints or to reshape the constraints to allow for a better solution at a minimal cost. One way to do this is to carefully select which parts of your network require careful selection and which do not. Clearly, you will need to be far more selective about your core routers than you will about which computer goes on the receptionist's desk.

Whenever possible, you want to use best-of-breed components. There will be more discussion of this later, but the idea of best of breed is to pick what is most critical about the function you are trying to accomplish, find out who distributes a program or package that best accomplishes that task, and then work backward from there to select components to support the best-of-breed system. It is common for people to select components based on what they already have or already know. For some parts of your network, that may work acceptably, but for your security system it can often put you at a disadvantage, sometimes a quite severe one.

One difficulty with this approach is that the computer market changes so swiftly, and the security market is even swifter still. Yesterday's best of breed may not be today's. But you can't continuously update to the current best-of-breed systems without huge disruptions and expenses. A good way to handle this dilemma is this approach:

- Divide your components into categories, according to their importance with regard to your security.

- Apply best-of-breed selection rigorously to the most important components, and decrease the rigor as much as you feel comfortable with for lesser components.

- Select a review period for each category, based on its importance to security and the rate at which the market for the components improves its technology.

- Review each component at the end of its review period, and decide whether or not to update or replace it. Note that this is not the same thing as applying vendor patches. Those should be applied as quickly as possible after a stable patch is released.

Often, it is cheaper to partner with your vendors on improving existing components than it is to rebuild from scratch every year. Vendors are usually starving for sensible customer input, and if you can arrange to trade your insight for information about new products or the ability to test and comment on experimental products, both you and your vendor will benefit, and you will have much more stability in your network without doing so at the expense of your security.

Despite that, rebuilding key parts of your network from scratch every once in a while is not necessarily bad. The network you can design after two or three years of running a secured network may be quite different from the one you designed at the beginning. You'll have a better understanding of every process involved, and you'll be able to optimize the design for the way you actually work. A fresh start helps to flush many of those annoying vestiges of previous designs or previous projects that often creep into a continuously running system as well. But a complete redesign is not a panacea. Part of what you'll be doing is trading old, well-understood problems for new, perplexing ones. It is probably better to redesign a subsystem at a time on a regular basis and then work to flush the vestiges away as quickly as you can.

A good time for a redesign is when moving to a new facility. Many people feel that the "cheap" way to move is to pick a day, turn everything off, haul it to the new building, and turn it back on again. Sometimes this is unavoidable. But as a veteran of many moves, I can say that the overall cost of building new systems fresh, with better wiring plans and a more intelligent layout and configurations you have time to test, is much cheaper in the long run. Complete duplication is not necessary, but adequate testing time for your core systems is.

Rust never sleeps.

Any defensive system you build will begin decaying as soon as you stop paying attention to it for several reasons:

- The older it is, the more people will know about it. The more people know about it, the more ways to attack it will emerge.

- The less you pay attention to it, the easier it will be for it to be changed, either accidentally or maliciously. Neither type of change is likely to improve the security of the system.

- The less time your people spend working with a system, the easier it will be for them to make mistakes in operating it.

Your network design needs to incorporate procedures for regular maintenance, periodic testing, and occasional full auditing of every major part of your defenses.

> ### *Security is everybody's business.*

That is a warning, not a slogan. Everyone in your organization will have an opinion about security. Typically, these opinions tend to be in one or more of the following areas:

- We need to do more about security. In particular, we need to do it more the way I think it ought to be done.
- Our security is a joke. Last week, I had a problem, and the security department didn't help me at all.
- Our security people are doing the wrong things. The other day I wanted to do something, and all they did was criticize me and stop me from doing it.
- Why are we spending so much money on security when we should be spending it on something I care about?

People are normally aware of security only when they are inconvenienced by it. It's often tempting for the security department that works hard to expect that people will notice what a good job they are doing. This rarely (if ever) happens. Consider ways in which you can improve on areas such as the following:

- *General security awareness.* What are the fundamental principles of maintaining a secure site, and how is our organization addressing them?
- *Specific security statistics.* How many security problems have we had this month? How rapidly were they addressed? How does this compare with other, similar organizations?
- *Basic security questions.* What is our security policy? Where do I find it? How do I understand it?

Your goal here is to increase the perception of value of what you do within your entire organization, as well as to provide people with tools for thinking about the issues you face every day so that they can act as an early warning system for you. Sometimes that can result in more false alarms than you might care for, but you'd rather deal with that situation than with complacency or active disinterest.

The best kind of security problems are the ones that don't happen. The way you accomplish this is by training and by continually reinforcing the basic security message. You don't need to create an armed camp in order to accomplish this, and doing so would be counterproductive. If your employees know, at a general level, why security is important to your organization and what it takes to be secure, then opinions such as those listed a few paragraphs back will not be given voice because the people will have a basic idea of the answers to the questions. It will be an uphill struggle, though, and will require continual attention on your part. Two things you can do to help are constant and effective communication and recognition and reward for correct actions. Classically trained security personnel can find this precept difficult to embrace, because most security training focuses on exactly the opposite concepts. But if you look at the bigger picture and focus on problem prevention, you can save yourself a lot of work in the long run.

> ### *If security conflicts with doing business, security will probably lose.*

This is the other side of the previous issue. You cannot make your network into a fortress unless doing so is the only way you can do business. Security measures are often the enemy of flexibility. If your business depends on flexibility and your network security is inflexible, then a clash between the two is inevitable, and you will lose.

It follows, therefore, that you should have a thorough understanding of how your organization does what it does before you try to constrain your network. This is to say not that you can't influence your business operations with arguments of security but rather that you should attempt to do so carefully and with advance planning. "We've always done it this way" is a remarkably powerful argument, especially combined with "We don't have the time/money/people to do it differently." This issue is much less of a problem in very new organizations, but if you find yourself, as many security professionals do, in the position of trying to improve the security of a well-established enterprise, then you'll face this problem again and again.

When dealing with legacy security issues, the hidden danger is that you can find yourself responsible for keeping them safe but powerless to change them. It's much better to recognize the danger up front and bring it into focus. Oddly enough, this recognition is often better done *before* you have a good understanding of the problem. Schedule a meeting with your management and tell them you are concerned about a particular set of issues, naming them explicitly. You don't feel that you can take responsibility for their security until you've investigated further. Be careful to imply not that you feel that everything else *not* on the list is OK but that these problems are particularly troublesome.

At that point, with management aware that you think there may be problems and that you intend to look into them, you'll want to ask your management the following questions:

- If I find out that this issue really does pose a serious security problem, how much effort do you want me to devote to fixing it?

- Who in the management team should I work with if there are any problems with fixing this?

- If I get serious resistance from the groups that this problem affects, how much support will I have to change things so that the security issues are not so severe?

If you can get these questions answered satisfactorily, then you should write a memo to all the people attending this meeting and your boss, summarizing the meeting and the answers to the questions. Then move forward with your investigations, and use the memo to justify doing carefully what you believe needs to be done. This means not necessarily doing it all your way, but rather involving all parties in hunting for a mutually agreeable compromise, which errs on the side of security rather than danger.

If you cannot get satisfactory answers to these questions, then you are in the difficult position of having responsibility but not authority. Your only function in that case is to take the blame when things go wrong.

Trust wisely.

You will have to trust some people. Don't trust blindly. People working for your company should live up to some kind of standard. People working for your security group should live up to a higher standard of trust because of the damage they could cause by abusing trust. Background checks are inexpensive ways of getting a sense of how trustworthy a person may be. They are not foolproof, but they offer some touchstone of safety.

It is easy to go overboard on checks, however, and there are laws to prevent you from doing so, in many cases. Set your criteria fairly. Don't use them to eliminate alternate perspectives. Review the criteria with your legal people and your human resources department. And apply them fairly to all applicants.

Sometimes you'll trust the wrong people. Design so that mistakes in trust cannot seriously hurt you. Security is all about people. People are rarely all good or all bad. They are complicated. Situations change, loyalties shift, and last year's star employee can become this year's management challenge.

You must prepare for people's unpredictability. What would you do if your most trusted employee went to work for your competition? Do you have the infrastructure in place to eliminate that person's access to your network? Can you review what that person did in the month before they quit? Have they signed the proper nondisclosure agreements? The wrong time to answer these questions is when you are holding the resignation letter in your hand.

Consider this from the employee's point of view, as well. He or she may have no malicious intent at all, but if you haven't done your job, the burden of suspicion will be on the person quitting. They are at the top of the list of suspects for any problem for the next six months or more—as will you be if you change jobs. So you owe it to yourself and the people who trust you to create a process that is fair and precludes as much as possible a former employee, even one trusted with vital information, from damaging your network.

Trust is not a transitive quantity. I may trust you and you may trust Bill, but that does not mean that I have to trust Bill. Policies and procedures should have ways to measure trust other than the word of another employee. Background checks can be taken to extremes and abused, but, especially for people trusted with the security of your network, some level of checking is quite appropriate.

Security is a matter of perspective.

An attacker who cannot get the whole perspective of your network is at a disadvantage. This principle can sometimes be confused with "security through obscurity." The thought there, which has been used to justify many bad security practices, is that if a system is difficult to understand, it will be difficult to break into. There are several problems with this approach, not the least of which is that it may not be true at all. A system that is difficult to understand may be trivial to break into, if viewed from the right perspective. But because it is difficult for you to understand, you may think that no such perspective exists.

Properly managed, however, obscurity can be your friend. In a system that is well-designed, well-implemented, and well-understood by the defenders, that is properly monitored, whose design and implementation have been reviewed by competent, qualified third parties, making key details of the system difficult for attackers to find and use can only help you. But the key is that the system should be designed so that attackers who know a lot about it can still not penetrate. Obscurity, like cayenne pepper, is fine if used in the right places and in the right quantities. A dinner entirely of cayenne would be inedible.

A defender who cannot get the whole perspective of the network is at a disadvantage. Your own people must be able to understand what they are supposed to defend. They must be able to monitor and control the systems they are charged with. If they are not trained or are kept from information that helps them understand what they are protecting, then it will be impossible for them to form the mental model of your network that is essential to being able to defend it. Picture yourself in the Middle Ages, defending a castle. If you know where only half of the gates are, the protection you'll give that castle is worthless.

Sometimes a fresh perspective is essential. We are, in many ways, the sum of our experiences. Other people have had useful experiences as well. And the more you focus on the network you are defending, the less you can sometimes see of what is right in front of you. Sometimes it is helpful to carefully select a qualified outsider or two and have them look over what you've done.

You want them to answer the questions you should be continually asking yourself:

- Is the system I built really the system I designed?
- Are my defenses adequate for the state of the art in attacks?
- Are my defenses adequate for the things I'm defending?
- What have I overlooked?

Making this a regular part of what you do can be painful, as nobody likes their work to be criticized. And selecting someone who can criticize your work in a way that has value and meaning is difficult also. But if you build an outside sanity check into your security process, you'll learn a great deal about what you are trying to do and be able to improve the security of your systems and networks far more than you could do alone.

One difficulty often faced by smaller organizations is that they employ only one security person. This is a dangerous situation, because a single person, working alone without feedback from colleagues and meaningful criticism and reinforcement from peers, can easily overlook significant problems. The "too close to the trees to see the forest" problem is a very real one. As any engineer knows, feedback loops are what keep complicated systems manageable, so you have to design them into your personnel strategy as well as your technical defenses.

The Shape of Your Defenses

We've talked a lot about your network defenses, but what will they look like? Every network will be different, but a good representation of a generalized defensive system might look something like the diagram in Figure 4-1. The figure shows the layering of the various defenses as they would be applied to any network. Let's discuss the different pieces.

Organizational Network

This is the network you are protecting, the reason for security in the first place. Your security will work best if the network is designed with security in mind. A strong defensive layer around a weakly secured network is a poor idea, because a single, really good penetration can leave your network in ruins, as can a disgruntled insider. That type of poor network design is called "a hard-candy shell with a soft, chewy center" by security designers. Your organizational network, no matter its size, should be designed for functionality, robustness, and security in more or less equal measures.

Passive Outer Defenses

The defenses that surround your network and guard each and every connection of your organizational network to the outside world are the ones that react to attacks that you know about. They are the walls of your castle, your moat. They are called passive defenses because they are designed to work whether you are paying

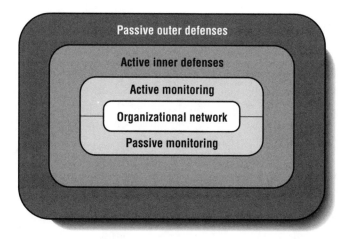

Figure 4-1: Layering of network defenses

attention to them or not. As an example, imagine an attack through the "finger" service (a way to ask a remote computer who is currently logged into it). Your passive outer defenses would include the following measures:

- All routers configured to block the finger request inbound
- All routers configured to block the finger response outbound
- All computers configured to not run the finger response software on boot-up
- Finger response software deleted from all computers

Such a set of actions would be a very good defense against the finger service attack, and they would work, day or night, until someone changed something (or in this case, many things) that made "finger" work again. Variations within your passive outer defenses would be modifications that allow some services to work under certain conditions, such as the source of the request or the time of day.

Active Inner Defenses

Passive defenses will keep you safe from many things as long as they remain in place, regardless of your attention to them. Following the castle analogy, they are your drawbridge and gates. Active defenses require your participation. Active defenses are designed to allow you to take action against attackers. Another way to think of this is that passive outer defenses apply the "rules" of the game the attacker is playing with you when they attempt to penetrate. Active defenses are the part of your defensive system that allow you to change the rules to suit yourself.

Passive Monitoring

The defenses described permit you to defend against the finger attack but not to be aware that such an attack has taken place. The passive monitoring system is the collection of modifications to network components that cause them to log that an event has occurred and the systems that receive that logging message and interpret it. Passive monitoring is a part of the network's response to particular stimuli in which the occurrence of the stimulation is recorded.

Active Monitoring

If passive monitoring is based on what your network components and your sensors bother to tell you at any given time, active monitoring is essentially a series of hard questions that you force your defenses to answer for you. Looking at the finger defense earlier, it will block that particular attack, and the passive monitoring system will tell you if that particular attack happens to have been blocked today, but it may be months before someone tries that attack again. Active monitoring allows you to ask your defenses if this protection is still working—perhaps by simulating a finger request and watching if the appropriate messages are logged; perhaps by reading and analyzing the router configurations to determine if the finger block is still in place; perhaps by scanning your internal computer systems to determine if a finger server is running on any of your machines.

The Shape of Your Security Organization

At several points, we've discussed the idea that active defenses require your attention in order to work correctly. At some point, you should have been wondering whether the profession of security engineering would ever allow you to sleep, eat, or take a vacation. If your personal attention were required at all times, you couldn't. Of course, that cannot be the case in any good design. What you need is a security organization to run your defenses (Figure 4-2).

The intention of the figure is to illustrate how the various parts of your organization bring themselves to bear on an attack. The first three parts are the ones that directly respond to an attack, and the training portions at the bottom act to support the rest of the organization.

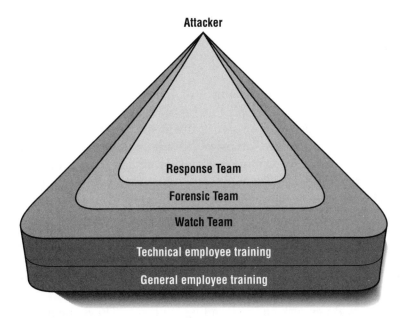

Figure 4-2: Security organization

Let's discuss the various parts of your security organization. The goal of this discussion is not to suggest that this is the only possible way of arranging such a team, but every component we discuss should be represented in some way in any design you do. In a very small organization, all these functions might be embodied in a single, very, very tired person. A huge enterprise might have dozens of people in each team, certain people with overlapping responsibilities. How you organize it will depend heavily on your network, your requirements, and your resources. Just be sure to cover all the bases.

Response Team

The Response Team is directly responsible for meeting any serious attack. They operate the active defenses of your organization and work to assess and coordinate repair of any damage caused by an attack. They are responsible for ensuring that any holes in your defenses that have been used by an attacker to penetrate are discovered and repaired and that any modifications made by the penetrator are also discovered and completely restored to their correct configurations. Some of this work they do themselves; some they do in conjunction with the Forensics Team.

Apart from attack response, the Response Team is charged with the the active study of available attack methods and the system verification portion of the active monitoring, as well as the management of the monitoring and logging systems. If a new attack method is reported, the Response Team must design a way for the defenses, both passive and active, to defeat this method and to report on the attempted attack.

Forensics Team

The Forensics Team provides in-depth research and assistance to the response team. They are tasked with developing an intimate knowledge of the network they are protecting. When a penetration occurs, the Response Team is in charge of reacting *rapidly and decisively;* the Forensics Team is in charge of investigating *thoroughly and carefully* and confirming, refuting, or adding to any rough estimations arrived at by the Response Team. To put it another way, the Response Team decides what to do *now;* the Forensics Team decides whether that was enough and prepares a detailed plan for any additional work that must be done.

Watch Team

The Watch Team is the twenty-four-hour-a-day eyes and ears of the security organization. This team is responsible for monitoring the warning system that guards your organizational network and responding to alarms. They schedule any routine work that must be done and test various systems on a regular basis to make sure that everything is operating as it has been designed to do.

In an attack situation, the Watch Team is responsible for declaring an emergency and holding the fort until the Response Team and the Forensics Team can take over the situation. In many standard cases, the Watch Team may be able to handle routine matters without declaring an emergency. While the Response Team and the Forensics Team handle an attack, the Watch Team continues to monitor the network looking for other problems.

Employee Training

Security is a matter of perspective, and perspective is often a matter of awareness and education. Training groups are tasked with creating awareness and presenting opportunities for education to the rest of the organization. The technical branch works with the people who need to be aware of security policies, practices, and procedures as a part of the design of their systems, both internal and external. The general branch trains all employees in their responsibilities as network citizens with regard to security and security awareness.

Chapter

5

Building a Security Team

IN THIS CHAPTER:

- Employee Characteristics
- Job Functions in a Security Team
- Training and Cross-Training
- Interviewing Security Candidates
- Background Checks
- Hiring
- Firing

You have to assume that the people attacking your network may be devious and clever, because assuming otherwise is an invitation to disaster. The people defending it should be a good match for them. One of the hardest parts of computer and network security is building a team of people to set and carry out your security policies.

Employee Characteristics

Who should I be looking for? First and foremost, you're looking for good people. That is true in any job, but it is especially necessary in the computer security field. These are the people you'll be trusting with the defense of your company's business function, so they'll need to be worthy of trust and capable of defending your network adequately.

Should I be hiring hackers? I use the term *hacker* very little in this book because the word means different things to different people. A hacker can be a Good Guy or a Bad Guy. To describe the Bad Guys, I use the term *attacker,* which has no ambiguity. An attacker is always a Bad Guy. Hackers have many motivations, but attackers want to cause damage or steal resources.

In the context of hiring, use of the term "hacker" is inevitable. Everybody has heard the story of the kid who broke into the system of a major corporation and then ended up working for them to make their computers more secure. It's a great story, but the reality is less encouraging.

Let's look at the idea in another context. Imagine a kid with an interest in burglary tools and techniques. Such a kid could study these aspects of the criminal arts for years and get quite good at their practice. He might have a good future as a police detective or a corporate security consultant or a mystery novelist. But if he were to use the skills to break into a bank, he'd be a criminal, no matter how noble his motives. Using the skills to knowingly commit a crime is a sign of poor judgment on his part. Using the skills to break into a place without realizing that the act is a crime is poor judgment of the highest order. Poor judgment is not the kind of quality you want to rely on to protect your business.

Demonstrated skill as an attacker does not guarantee that the person will also be a good defender. What makes an attacker good is some amount of cleverness and a great deal of persistence and patience. Attackers need to keep probing and probing until they find a weakness they know how to exploit. They need to keep learning more weaknesses and how to exploit them to make the game quick enough to be fun (or profitable, in some rare cases). If you know enough holes and how to spot them quickly, you can move through many systems quite easily and it becomes most enjoyable. A big part of the fun for many attackers is showing their friends how clever they are.

What makes a defender good is enough cleverness to outthink an attacker and the thoroughness to give the attacker few or no footholds in the systems. Defenders are strong on consistency and measurement. They are concerned with details but not blinded by them. The fun for a defender is being right, blocking attackers, and keeping secrets. What you are looking for is good defenders, not good attackers.

Should I be hiring from conventional security forces? Another group that would seem to be ripe for recruitment is people trained to secure facilities and situations. These would include police, military security, and three-letter government agencies. In the computer security world, these folks are the ones who worry about "guns, guards, and gates" (GGG). The idea is that computer security is a subspecialty of GGG-type security and that it is easier to train GGG people in computers than it is to train computer people in GGG work.

Sometimes that may be true. There are many GGG people who have made the transition to computer security successfully. But the transition is not an easy one. Computer security is a highly specialized field, and a great deal of training and experience are needed to do it well. Experience doesn't come quickly or easily. It is hard work, and it takes a long time to learn. In many cases, the lesson GGG people have to learn is that their training in physical security is not relevant to network security. In a GGG world, attackers have to be physically present at some time in some way. They have to try to bluff the guard with a fake ID or smuggle the bomb into the compound. With network security, the target can be in San Diego and the attacker can be in Bulgaria, attacking through several phony ISP accounts. With physical security, an attack is a rare event. With network security, you may be attacked six times a day, from different sources all over the planet. It is a very different world. Nevertheless, if you find people with experience in both the GGG world and the network world, they are worth considering.

Who should I be hiring, then? The best choices for network security people are people who are skilled computer programmers who have experience in "thinking evil thoughts" but enough restraint and judgment not to act on them. You want people who are good defenders.

You also want to select a variety of people. Different perspectives are important. This means that some people should come from the guns, guards, and gates world. Others should have differing philosophies on how to secure networks. And you probably want to shave that line between attackers and defenders as close as you can to get people who can think like attackers but still remain trustworthy and defend well.

Job Functions in a Security Team

A security team must handle a lot of different functions. Not all of them may require a separate person, but each function must be covered somewhere in the organization. Some jobs (such as watchstander) may require several people. The list below is not exhaustive, of course, because you can always think of more things for people to do, but if you've covered most of these functions in your organization, you're doing pretty well.

Authentication. Handles all aspects of user, administrator, and security authentication. Responsible for the system by which the network can verify the identities of users. Handles all design aspects of the system, including selection of authentication mechanism(s), configuration of key authentication servers, physical security of pertinent aspects of the authentication system, and design of the operating procedures to be used by the security operations personnel.

Communications. Manages all formal communications in and out of the security group, such as general alert messages, incident reports, and advisory messages. Responsible for creating clear, concise, and informative messages that reveal only the information they are supposed to reveal and for preventing misunderstandings due to miscommunication or insufficient communication.

Damage Control. Handles second-level damage assessment. Coordinates repairs and workarounds to prevent secondary penetrations. Has good ability to work against real-time threats.

Development Engineer. Responsible for integrating various products and software packages into a coherent system that handles a needed function. Writes new code or modifies existing code to implement new services or improve existing ones.

Development Engineering Manager. Ensures that development projects are scheduled and tracked. Coordinates development work with security architect.

Documentation. Writes various aspects of security documentation, such as policies and procedures, documentation for various systems within the security infrastructure, and/or operational manuals for watchstanders.

Documentation Manager. Manages all security documentation. Responsible for ensuring that documentation is written to consistent standards and is accessed by authorized personnel only. Keeps documentation current and relevant.

Dogfighter. Handles combat with attackers in real time. Does first-level damage assessment. Prime function is to stop attacks and stabilize the system. This position is a skilled subset of incident response.

Forensic Analyst. Determines attack methodology and works with other specialists to develop temporary and permanent deterrence and detection mechanisms. Investigates security incidents, looking for penetration methods and damage to systems, including subtleties.

Forensics Team Manager. Coordinates all actions of the Forensics Team.

Host Security. Responsible for the design and implementation of security systems and software resident on general-purpose computers. Coordinates with general systems administration groups elsewhere in the organization.

Incident Response—Level 1. Does triage on security incidents, handling basic ones and calling in more senior people for complicated ones. Keeps things moving through the system. Focuses on quantity of events processed first.

Incident Response—Level 2. Handles more complicated incidents that are expected to take longer to resolve. Focuses on quality of events processed.

Internal Auditor. Validates that all internal systems have been implemented according to specifications. Enhances specifications as needed to account for new attacks. Coordinates upgrade/repair work with host and network specialists.

Law Enforcement. Manages all communications with law enforcement agencies. Maintains a relationship with law enforcement and creates a perception of credibility with them for your organization.

Logging. Manages the system by which events are logged. Responsible for maintaining valid logging from all systems and fixing problems when they occur.

Network Security. Responsible for the design and implementation of the network security architecture as well as the security configurations of each network component (routers, hubs, switches). Coordinates with the general network management group elsewhere in the organization.

Physical Security. Responsible for badges, access control mechanisms, logging of physical access control point transactions, keys. Coordinates with plant security, if that department exists.

Policies and Procedures. Manages and tracks the security policy document. Responsible for version updates and distribution. Coordinates with HR department to make sure that all employees have read the latest versions.

Press Liaison. Responsible for all contact between the security organization and the press. Responsible for making sure that any press coverage of your company is handled according to your security policy (e.g., no sensitive computer information visible in published photographs). Point of contact for any press coverage of a specific security incident relating to the organization.

Researcher. Keeps up to date on latest attacker exploits and holes. Educates the security team on fixes, workarounds. Coordinates with internal auditor to determine vulnerability of internal systems to latest known issues.

Response Team Manager. Coordinates all responses to a serious incident. Manages the incident response personnel.

Security Operations. Handles day-to-day operational issues regarding security, such as addition or deletion of records within authentication systems, maintenance of key security servers and services, security aspects of tasks being carried out by IS operations.

Security Operations Manager. Tracks incidents and responses. Ensures timely reporting of incidents. Tracks statistics on incident handling. Coordinates with IS operations.

Security Architect. Central coordinator for all aspects of security. Develops new policies. Resolves questions regarding the applicability of existing policies to novel situations. Designs new subsystems to comply with both the letter and spirit of the security policy.

Systems Administrator. Responsible for management of systems and services within the security group. A sysadmin separate from the IS group is typically required for security because of the increased sensitivity of security systems and the need to keep closer track of exactly how and when security systems are modified.

Watchstander. Monitors the various sensors and analysis tools to determine if an attack is in progress and to initiate a standard response for standard situations or call in incident response specialists if the situation should warrant it.

Training and Cross-Training

The previous section listed a lot of different functions and specialties. No practical security team can have a different person assigned to each category listed; in a small business, all functions may be handled by one person. And yet, all the functions must be covered, and the coverage must allow for vacations, unexpected sick leave, accidents, resignations, and sometimes even terminations.

The number of people in a security team varies depending on the size of the network that must be protected, the value of what is being protected, and the specific demands of the particular organization. The Laugh and the Wow tests (see Chapter 9) can be of some help here in gauging the size of the team you ought to have, but they will not be of too much help in actually building a team of that size. It is rare that a network security team is too big. It is much more likely to be too small. Small teams suffer from several typical problems:

- Missing skill sets

- Absence of redundancy

- Inability to cope with crises

- Stress-related attrition

The market for skilled security people is growing, and while the pool of talent is also growing, supply is nowhere near demand. Consequently, your best bet is to find good, smart people and train them. An aggressive training program, the practice of cross-training multiple people for different specialties, and enough people to compensate for absences due to training can produce a formidable security force. But creating such a team is a challenge for any organization.

Training for security teams comes in a variety of forms:

- Coursework

- Conferences

- Trade publications

- Internet research

- Drills and war games

What you want to develop in your people are two key faculties: *experience* and *taste*. Experience is obvious, it is essential to becoming competent in almost any endeavor. The business of security is about handling and preventing problems, and in that line of work, experience counts for a lot. It is important, however, to keep experience in perspective and use it as a tool for progress, not a means to avoid progress.

The faculty of taste is much less obvious. Taste is something akin to the elusive ability to put together clothing into an ensemble or to select quality artwork or to match wine with food. Taste comes, in part, with experience, but many people who have good experience have poor taste. Others seem to soak up taste through their pores and display a good sense of it even though they have little or no experience.

Taste in the world of computer and network security is the ability to recognize, select, and implement solutions that meet your security needs, both explicitly and at levels you may not have considered, that scale well over time, and that are adaptable and maintainable. Someone with good taste can do this, though they may not be able to explain exactly why they made the choices they did. Taste is the ability to do the "right" thing.

Given such a vague definition, it is nearly impossible to train people in taste. Most people don't get it, and those who do often have a hard time explaining "it."

What you can do, however, is expose your team to the process of making decisions and the consequences of the decisions. Taste in anything is an ability to discriminate between the quality of several different alternatives. Anyone who has been exposed to *Zen and the Art of Motorcycle Maintenance,* by Robert Pirsig, has a built-in reluctance to define the word "quality," but people can be exposed to the opportunity to choose and the opportunity to evaluate the results of choices. That type of training cultivates fertile ground for taste to grow in, but it does not guarantee that taste will develop.

But given the unpredictability and rapid change in the field of computer and network security, a security group whose members know more or less what the "right" thing is and how to do it will be a lot more useful and productive than a group that doesn't get it. So it's worth some time to develop a sense of security "taste" in both yourself and your group.

Interviewing Security Candidates

There are many books and courses on how to conduct successful interviews, and that information need not be duplicated here. There are some areas that are unique to the security business that we should discuss, however:

> **Trustworthiness.** The people on the security team are guardians of a great deal of sensitive and dangerous information about your organization and the people who work there. You can design complicated and elaborate safeguards to prevent security people from knowing more than they should, but the chances are good that you will not do so. The world changes rapidly, and you'll be lucky to keep up by doing things in a straightforward fashion, so you'll probably trust your security team more than is strictly necessary. Whether you do or not, you want your team to be as trustworthy as possible.

> **Thinking Evil Thoughts.** The ability to think like an attacker is the essential quality of a good security professional. Many organizations look for people who think "outside the box," which refers to the ability to look beyond the problem specification and come up with a solution to the real, unstated problem or to find a way to bypass the problem altogether. A security person who can think evil thoughts is one who not only can think outside the box but knows how to break into the box, copy the contents, modify them subtly, and leave no traces of having done so—and knowing all this, *never* puts it to use.

Background Checks

In addition to skills, temperament, and intangible qualities, your security people should be able to pass a thorough background check.

Background checks serve two major purposes. First, they tell you facts about prospective employees that you ought to know before you hire them. Second, they tell the candidates that you are serious about the security of your organization. You're trusting your employees with your livelihood, so you should check them out before you hire them.

Consider, however, that background checks can interfere with the hiring process. And remember that there are laws about this kind of thing. You must get your HR department involved in the design of your background check process so that you are on firm legal ground.

A good background check should verify that applicants are who they say they are and that they are reasonably trustworthy. A number of private agencies can assist in verification. A decent background check can be run in the United States on a U.S. native-born citizen for a few hundred dollars. You'll want to define sensitivity levels for various jobs so that appropriate background checks can be run as a part of the hiring process. A reasonable set of levels might be the following:

- *No check required.* Temporary workers, such as catering staff or carpenters, who are allowed only in open areas and generally have some level of escort, would not require a background check.

- *Basic check required.* Longer-term temporary staff with unescorted access or people working in support jobs such as loading dock or lobby reception positions would need a minimal check. This type of check would verify basic application information and would look for problems such as a law enforcement record and a history of personnel issues.

- *Full check required.* Most security employees, especially those with access to internal documentation and facilities, would need a pretty careful check. This check would add to the basic check answers to questions such as "Has this person worked for our competitors?" "Has he or she been trusted with sensitive information in other positions?"

- *Deep check required.* Employees given a great deal of trust within your system should be thoroughly checked. The check would encompass all other checks and also ask questions such as "Would this person's financial situation leave them open to bribery?" "Can we confirm application information through sources not listed on the application?" "Is or has this person been under a great deal of personal stress now or in the past?"

Hiring

Having located an ideal candidate for your security team, you now need to hire the person. There are many issues, such as salary and compensation, that go along with hiring anybody and are far too complex to be covered here. One issue that deserves mention is that of expectations. It is your job, as an employer and as the architect of your security policy, to lay out in advance what you expect of your security personnel—items such as the following:

- Nondisclosure agreement

- Intellectual property agreement

- "Acceptable behavior" agreement

- Comprehension of security policies as they apply to the specific position

All agreements should be written and available for the prospective employee's inspection well before they must be signed. People who will be a good asset for your organization will tend to take such things very seriously and so want time to read them. Having them available to be read—and making them well-written and understandable—will make the first exposure these prospects have to your security organization be an informative one.

Signing these documents should be a condition of employment, and you must be prepared to tell a good candidate that he or she cannot come on board if the candidate does not want to sign. Make your agreements fair and make them protect both the signer and the organization, and most people will sign them.

Firing

Despite the careful interviews and the background checks, sooner or later you're going to need to fire a key security person. That is a task fraught with danger, so you need to take the time and make your policy long before you need the policy; the heat of the moment is the worst time to create a policy.

Disgruntled key security employees present, in theory, an extraordinarily dangerous situation. They have and have had for an unknown amount of time the skill, motivation, and opportunity to create serious trouble. By firing them, you can significantly increase their motivation to cause you pain and anguish.

You have, however, one major advantage if the person you are firing wishes to continue to work in the security world. A security professional who is being fired knows or ought to know that he or she is at the absolute top of the list of suspects should anything go wrong in the near future. An excellent strategy is to create a document that states exactly that and require the employee to sign the document as an acknowledgment that he has read and understands it, (he or she should not be required to *agree* with it, and that should be clearly stated as well) on the day of hire. He or she should also be asked to read and sign it again on the day of leaving employment by your organization. The legal standing of such a document is somewhat unclear, but that isn't really relevant. The purpose of this type of document is to remind the employee about what is at stake here, which is the employee's reputation in the field of computer security. A professional would never attack a previous employer under any circumstances. You need to remind this person of that fact, and the fact that you are watching, before the person leaves.

Paperwork is important, but the technical aspects of firing a key security person should not be ignored either. Every once in awhile, you should ask yourself the following question: "How quickly could I guarantee that X has no more access to the network?" naming a key security player in your organization. Imagine, if it helps you to think it through, that you've just heard on the news that X is a key suspect in an international atomic terrorist organization, and now you've got to disable his ability to get into your network. How quickly can you turn off his ability to log into the computers? How certain are you that you've turned it *all* off? How thoroughly can you review X's last few hours or days of access? Could he have other means of access that you aren't seeing?

Good answers to these questions will depend on the systems you've built and how well you run them. But you need good answers in order to write a reasonable policy. Add this question to your list: "How would I fire Y and disable her access without giving her an opportunity to damage my systems in the process?" If you walk into her office, fire her, and give her two weeks to clean out her desk without taking away her computer access, you could be wide open. If you walk her out the door directly from being fired, there are legal and ethical issues to consider. You need to find a means that will be both fair to the employee and present you with an acceptable level of risk.

Another aspect of firing is how you accomplish the actual act itself. This is a good candidate for "scenario-based design," in which you pick a number of job titles and then work out a checklist for exactly what you would do to fire a person of each title. Don't get bogged down in actual names; just work through the scenario based on positions. For example, developing a checklist for each of these jobs would quickly point out the issues you need to deal with in your environment:

- chief security architect
- security watchstander
- chief engineer
- senior design engineer

- engineer
- salesperson
- receptionist
- vice president
- accountant
- programmer
- senior programmer

Your checklist needs to handle the following issues:

- How and when the employee is notified
- Estimation ("friendly" versus "unfriendly") of the kind of termination
- What process you would go through to cut off any network access the terminee has
- What process you would go through to determine what the terminee has been doing on the network for the last several days
- How you would coordinate network security issues with physical security issues (there are many, especially for an "unfriendly" termination, but they are outside the scope of this book)
- How you would deal with requests for access to personal data stored on your network
- Determining that the terminee has valid copies of all key documents (nondisclosure agreements, acknowledgment of security policies, etc.)

You might take an hour or two with several security people in a room and brainstorm a basic checklist for, say, an engineer, and then meet with your HR and physical security people and brainstorm based on that list to come up with a basic checklist. Then you can examine that checklist for each of the other jobs and to see what variations you might need.

Chapter
6

Fortifying Network Components

IN THIS CHAPTER:

- What Is a Network Component?
- Component Types
- Selecting Components
- Component Categories
- Fortifying Components
- System Fortification

Much of what people think about computer security is inspired, for better or worse, by Hollywood. Even though many people won't admit it out loud, the images conjured up by films such as *WarGames, Sneakers,* and *Hackers* and several James Bond films can dominate the way people treat security problems. This is especially true for people whose only exposure to computer security has been through the movies.

A classic element of films like these is the master computer or computer network. The software is written from scratch, as a custom project, often by a single (usually evil) genius, who understands and controls all aspects of it. The system resists all attempts at access, displaying the infuriating "Access Denied" message over EvilCorp's logo. Then Our Hero learns that the evil genius is driven by the untimely death of his son, and the son's name is the access code that will allow full control of the machine. Our Hero foils the evil plan and saves the world.

It makes for a fun movie, but it isn't necessarily so in real life. Computer security in the world we live in is limited by several crucial facts:

- First, and most important, security people are the good guys, not the bad guys. (Evil geniuses intent on world destruction are invited to read somebody else's book.)

- Second, security systems are not likely to control the means for the destruction of civilization or the suppressed cure for cancer or the secrets of alien creatures; rather, they are the means by which we protect our companies' business.

- And finally (and most relevant to this chapter), security systems are not written from the ground up by geniuses (evil or otherwise) but are built from hardware and software bought off the shelf and customized to fit business needs.

How to take off-the-shelf components and software and turn them into a piece of a secured network is the subject of this chapter.

What Is a Network Component?

A network component is an active device on your network that provides some function for which security is a relevant concern and whose internal state can be made to affect the security of the network in some way. The classic examples are servers, workstations, routers, and terminal concentrators. Elements of a network that do not provide any means of security control, such as cables and simple hubs, are not included. Some types of hubs, such as smart hubs or switching hubs, could be included or excluded depending on whether security measures were implemented on them.

Network components can be further subdivided as *simple components,* such as routers and terminal concentrators, and *complex components,* such as servers and workstations. A simple component is a component designed to handle one basic task, such as network routing, and whose configuration is handled in a more or less uniform manner. A complex component is one whose function can be varied and shared among several different tasks and whose configuration is handled in different places and different ways and may vary according to the function being implemented. With a Cisco router, for example, you have two basic choices for configuration: what version of the operating system kernel you run and what you put in the configuration file. For the most part, that makes it a simple component (though the configuration of a Cisco router is by no means simple). You can make it be a router in a lot of different ways, but you'll never make it a file server or a Web server. It is not a general-purpose component. A Sun workstation has many more possible functions in addition to being an OS: It can be a file server, a DNS server, a streaming audio server, a database server, a Web server, or a router, it can run custom software, or it can be all of the above. Who will be allowed to log in? What privileges will they have? It is therefore a complex component because it is a far more general-purpose device.

Purists at this point will be saying to themselves, "Wait! Even cables can have a security function! The presence or absence of a cable can permit or deny access to some system. Why, then, aren't they included in this definition?" The answer is that you have to draw the line somewhere to be realistic. For the purposes of this chapter, we include only components that are active in some way, meaning that two identical devices connected in identical ways can be made to behave differently based on some internal state that can be changed by the designer—or by an attacker. A cable does not have this property. However, the issue of physical security, in which the connection points of a cable can be shifted to nefarious ends, is an important one, and will be dealt with elsewhere in this book.

It is also important to note that, while a router is, *in general,* a simple component, it is also a computer, and a sufficiently dedicated attacker might be able to find a way to make it become capable of tasks other than routing. The scale of complication for network components is not binary; it is a gradient. One of the skills a good security designer must learn is how to control network components based on what they are while not being blind to what they could become and not becoming paralyzed by the infinite possibilities. That skill is worth more than all the cookbook fortification recipes ever written.

Component Types

There are two major ways in which we can break down the types of components we can use in constructing a secured network:

- What can it do?
- Where can it do it?

The first criterion describes what functions the component can assume. Note that this can be far more than simply what you intend to do with it. It describes what a component *could* do under any circumstances—the component's degree of "general purposeness." A workstation has a high degree of "general purposeness"; it can be used as a desktop machine or a file server or a router or a dialin server, and it can be easily converted from one purpose to another and serve multiple purposes simultaneously. A router has less "general purposeness." It has much less storage and is much less amenable to being reprogrammed. It tends to serve a smaller number of more or less fixed purposes. A hub has even less ability to be modified and is more specialized still. A cable has no processing power and is extremely specialized.

The second criterion is location—not location in the physical sense, but location in the network sense. Another way to think about this is the degree of access that a machine has to network resources. If a machine is directly connected to the Internet, it has access to all the resources of the Internet and the Internet has access to any resources the machine provides. If a machine is separated from the Internet by a router, then the router may be used to deny some types of access to and from the Internet. If a machine has multiple network interfaces, then it has access to the resources available on all those networks. If it has just one, then it is limited to the network resources available through that one interface. A network interface is anything that can be used for remote access, so that includes a modem as well as more conventional devices.

These criteria help you to determine risk and to select and configure components capable of limiting risk. A component with a high degree of "general purposeness" and a high degree of "connectedness" is one that should be selected, fortified, and monitored with great care (Figure 6-1). This is true regardless of your intentions for the use of the component. A component with much less utility access can tolerate less rigid controls. Remember the words of your mother: "Better safe than sorry."

> *Rule of Thumb: You should always apply somewhat more care than a component seems to require, within reason, just in case you've miscalculated.*

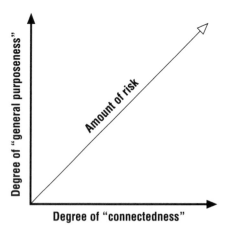

Figure 6-1: Estimating risk

In other chapters, we discuss the process by which you can select the level of security that is adequate for a given level of risk. For the purposes of this chapter, we refer to the level of security required simply as being "appropriate" for that component. It's important to bear in mind that a component near the perimeter of your network with a high degree of network access and a component deep in the center of your network with a low degree of network access may be implemented using the same hardware and software, but they still remain different components, handling different functions, posing different levels of risk, and thus requiring different levels of "appropriate" security.

Selecting Components

Knowing which components to select is half the work in fortifying them. If you choose well, then the ongoing process of keeping the components secure will be much easier and therefore much more likely to be accomplished. If you choose poorly, it will be very difficult to reach the security level you want, let alone to stay there. Remember that today's new toys are tomorrow's legacy equipment. You want to select components that can be made secure and kept secure.

Criteria for Selecting a Component

- Can be configured to withstand known attacks.
- Has successfully withstood known attacks.
- Is likely to withstand newer attacks.
- Historical flaws are well known.
- Newly discovered flaws come to your attention reliably and quickly.
- Manufacturers have a history of responsiveness in determining and correcting flaws.

Some of the following rules are obvious, but all are important, if the equipment you choose is to be useful and securable and remain so.

Select components that can be configured to withstand known attacks. Most equipment comes from the manufacturer in a configuration that will allow customers to use it successfully as quickly as possible. Manufacturers have learned through painful experience that if a customer cannot get a device to work, they will shift to another device that they can make work, even though the other device may not work as well in the long run. If a manufacturer ships a network component configured to a tight security model, most customers will have a hard time making it work, leading to temptation to switch vendors. If the network is configured loosely, the customer can make it work, so the customer will probably not change vendors. Only a few people in the security department will gripe about the security flaws.

What you are looking for here are devices that, despite their shipped configurations, can be configured to maintain appropriate security levels. Some features to look for in this area:

- *Ability to limit the services offered by this machine to the network.* If a machine has the ability to act as a file server or a router, for example, and you do not wish it to be a file server or a router, you need to be able to turn such a service off.

- *Level to which unnecessary software on the system can be removed.* If you need to turn off a service on a secured machine, you're probably going to want to turn it off as completely as possible, making it as difficult as you can for an attacker to turn it back on. One good way to do this is to delete the software necessary to support that service. Some systems permit careful deletion of core software. Others do not.

- *Ability to limit the source and destination network addresses of network service clients.* Wherever possible, a machine acting as a server should know which network addresses are allowed to receive a particular service and which are not, and it should be able to limit service only to those authorized addresses or ranges.

- *Ability to limit the privileges exercisable by programs providing a network service.* A common form of attack is to subvert a network service running on a server. Attackers can then run programs of their own choosing on the server. Some machines require service daemons run at the highest possible privilege level because they require a high privilege for some portion of their operation. Any attacker able to subvert these services would also be able to make use of these high privileges, perhaps by reading or writing critical files or running system programs. By having the ability to limit what programs can be run and the privileges that running programs are allowed to make use of, the damage that can result from an undetected flaw in a service daemon can be minimized.

- *Good security practices.* In particular, an operating system that allows all the functions described here should also make liberal use of them. Many operating systems allow different types of limitations on privilege, for example, but require the customer to rewrite system software to make use of them. You want to select an operating system that has been written with good practices in mind and takes advantage of them wherever possible.

- *Level of monitoring and logging of system and security functions.* While part of the battle is being able to resist attack, a very large part is knowing that an attack is in progress. A good network component should possess a flexible and reliable mechanism for notifying system administrators that an attack has occurred.

- *Ability to direct monitoring and logging messages to a secured log server.* A log entry is valuable only if someone reads it. If it is made and then erased before anyone has a chance to read it, it has no value. For that reason, a smart attacker moves to control local log files as quickly as possible. Logs that are mirrored elsewhere on the network are much more difficult to control and erase. Therefore a good network component should permit logging operations to be managed in a number of ways, including local logging, and direct logging to other machines and to other devices.

- *Ability to be maintained and upgraded in a secure fashion.*

Select components that are known to have successfully withstood known attacks. This seems at first like a straightforward requirement, but there are some hidden complexities:

- *What attacks are "known"?* As you are reading this, some fourteen-year-old is sitting in his basement saying to himself, "Gee, who'd have thought that would work?" after discovering a new way to attack across a network. The dynamic nature of these attacks means that constant research and study is in store for the defender. There is no way to completely avoid surprise, but your goal should be to minimize surprise and to minimize the effects a surprise can have. Fortunately, many other people are in the same situation. The Internet has many resources for the defender, but they change constantly and can be prone to mistaken conclusions and hyperbole.

- *How is "knowledge" of attack resistance obtained?* Simply asking the vendor may produce useful results, if you are lucky. More typically, you will get a useless answer, unless you ask the correct question of the correct person within the vendor organization in the correct way. It is worth the exercise to do so, however, because it shows vendors that customers are using security as a buying criterion, and that can only help. Another path is independent testing. The Internet can supply a wealth of information about component vulnerabilities, but the information is useful only if you can correctly interpret it. Finally, you can test vulnerabilities yourself, which is educational in the long run but time-consuming and open to testing mistakes in the short run.

- *How do you define "successfully withstood"?* Few manufacturers would say so explicitly, but their definitions range from "This attack will simply fail to work" to "At least the machine didn't crash when this attack was tried." Penetration-type attacks should completely fail to work as much as possible. For denial-of-service attacks, the machine should not crash at a minimum and should attenuate the effects of the attack wherever possible. Wherever possible, a machine should notify its owner that an attack was attempted.

Select components that are likely to withstand newer attacks. A system that is written with security in mind tends to have fewer problems with new attacks than one that is not. A vendor who detects a problem and then works to fix that *class* of problem throughout their system is what you are looking for. One objective way to detect such vendors is to look for those that release security-related patches regularly, without being driven to do so by a particular incident. A patch driven by incident response is better than no patch at all, but a patch driven by vendor conscientiousness is best of all.

Select components whose historical flaws are well known. Everybody makes mistakes, and operating system vendors are no exception. Select a vendor who admits problems and provides patches for problems on a regular basis. Look for vendors who find their own problems and then admit them and fix them. A vendor that has to be coerced into releasing patches and fixing problems is a vendor who will not support you when the crunch comes. It is important to remember that for some components a great deal of background information is available that does not come from the vendor, however. If the quantity and quality of the information is adequate, the component may be usable, despite the reticence of the vendor.

Select components whose newly discovered flaws come to your attention reliably and quickly. This is an extension of the "historical flaws" argument. A component about which you have a constant stream of information about flaws, tips, tools, tricks, and problems, both old and new, is going to be much more useful to you in the long run than a component which, while well built, you cannot investigate.

It is important that this stream of information come from a variety of sources, not just from the manufacturer. Having just one source of information about a product, even if it is a rich source, should be considered a danger sign. If people are using it, why aren't they talking about it? Even if customers are perfectly satisfied, there still should be newcomers with questions or informal testimonials out there somewhere. The lack of secondary sources is not proof that a product is insecure, but it is an indication that the forces that will help to keep it secure in the future are missing.

Some equipment, especially experimental devices, may be so new that they have not yet developed a following. Depending on how badly you need them, you should consider one of the these two courses of action if you find yourself a very early user of some piece of technology:

- Wait until it has been properly tested by others.
- Start testing it yourself, and announce the results.

Note that "Test it and keep the results to yourself" is not on the list. Throughout this book, you'll be urged to seek sources of information on the Internet about devices, software, and techniques. This information has been provided by people with experience who are willing to share it. You will benefit immensely from their willingness to do so, and so you should strongly consider building the same type of sharing somewhere into your organizational plan. It doesn't cost much and pays back tenfold or better.

Select components whose manufacturers have a history of responsiveness in determining and correcting flaws. In many ways, you are simply selecting for good customer service. If the vendor fixes other peoples' problems quickly and correctly and makes those fixes available to you, then you will have much better luck in configuring and operating the vendor's equipment for your purposes.

Take a quick look at the vendor's Web site. What? They don't have one? Unless there is something extraordinary about the component in question, drop it and look for another.

If the vendor does have a Web site, can you easily locate a technical or security-related list of frequently asked questions (FAQs)? Is the list a long one or simply a few token questions so that the vendor can claim it exists? Has the list been updated recently? Is there a means of downloading patches, and is there a list of what patches are related to security? Is that list regularly maintained? Does the Web site tell you things you didn't know? Does it tell you the things you need to know? Is there a way to request additional information? Do you actually get the information if you request it?

Component Categories

Thus far, we've been discussing a hypothetical network component as though it were a single thing, like a brick; once you pick the right brick, you just order a truckload and start construction. While network components do have many things in common in the way they are chosen, you need more than just a good brick. You need the right brick for the job. Understanding what the job is, therefore, is essential to choosing correctly.

For a typical corporate network, components fall into the following general groupings.

Border Components. These devices sit on the edge of your area of control and connect to components that you don't control. They are accessible to network traffic that you don't control and so are the logical target for attacks on your network. Following are examples of border components:

- Firewalls

- Routers to your Internet service provider

- Routers to your business partners

- Remote access servers

- E-mail gateways

- External Web and FTP servers

- DNS servers

Infrastructure Components. These devices are completely controlled by you. They are used for specific purposes in your organization. The functions they handle are functions that a wide variety of organizations might also want to perform, so they probably make use of software and configurations that are mirrored in many other organizations. Thus, they are susceptible to well-known attacks. Infrastructure components are generally maintained by a small group of people (in a corporation, this is often the IT department), though they may be used by a very large number of people in the organization. Examples of infrastructure components follow:

- Print servers

- Internal DNS servers

- News servers

- Time synchronization servers

- File servers

Business Components. These devices support functions, such as business-specific software, that are unique to your business. These components could be maintained by a wide variety of people and groups within your organization. Business-specific software actually performs the function your organization provides. A company that prints payroll checks runs payroll software somewhere. A company that handles airline reservations runs airline reservation software somewhere. Following are some examples of business components:

- Database servers

- Internal Web sites

- Research devices

- Business-specific software servers

Desktop Components. These devices are generally commercial desktop computers of varying power and quality. They may be centrally maintained, maintained by their users, not maintained at all, or any combination thereof. They vary greatly in software revision levels, configuration, and adherence to policy. They may be powerful enough to act as de facto infrastructure or business components, and they may be doing so without your knowledge or consent.

Fortifying Components

Once you've selected proper components for each part of your network, you'll need to fortify them. The question you should be asking at this point is "What does it mean to fortify a network component?" A component is fortified if the following conditions are met:

- All systems and applications software are at the most recent stable level.

- All known security patches have been applied to systems and application software.

- All required services that the component will provide have been defined in advance to a reasonable level.

- All other services that the component could provide in addition to the required services have been disabled.

- All required user-level and administrative-level access to this component has been defined in advance to a reasonable level.

- The system configuration for this component enforces the levels of user and administrative access requirements.

- All known steps have been taken to eliminate access to the system outside the required levels.

- The level of event monitoring required for this component has been defined in advance to a reasonable degree.

- Event monitoring has been configured in the requirements.

As you can see, there is a level of subjectivity to the definition. All components should be fortified to some degree. That degree is determined by your understanding of what the component is to do and how it is to do it, and what resources are available to constrain and monitor what the component can do.

A system can be fortified in two basic ways, unblanding and templating.

1. **Unblanding.** A generic, out-of-the box system (a "bland" system) is built according to the manufacturer's guidelines and then transformed, perhaps by a program, into a fortified system meeting the required specifications.

   Advantages: Easier to develop. Scales up to some types of templating. Requires no understanding of vendor installation process. Unblanding program can be as complicated as you care to make it. A sophisticated unblanding script can be run on nongeneric legacy systems, if you dare.

   Disadvantages: Must be run on a completely generic system for simple unblanding programs. As modifications increase, installation time increases. Each system configured in this way is potentially unique if mistakes were made or errors occurred during the unblanding process.

2. **Templating.** The system installation procedure of the vendor is modified to account for the changes necessary to fortify a given configuration of machine. The operating system is installed with all fortification in place from the start.

Advantages: Every system is identical. You'll get greater immunity from mistakes in the installation process. Once the template is developed and tested, installation requires no special security skills.

Disadvantages: A template is more difficult to develop than a simple unblanding script. Templating requires a detailed understanding of the vendor installation process or equivalent.

How will you know which one to select? Well, if yours is like most organizations, you'll probably end up following this path:

1. You fortify several machines by hand, complaining about the time it takes and the variability of the results and the skill level necessary to get good results.

2. As a reaction, you develop a simple unblanding script to speed things up. This will improve the situation and be quite satisfactory for a while.

3. As you need to configure more and more systems and add more and more changes to the unblanding script, it becomes unwieldy. You begin to investigate a template system. About this time you're also beginning to notice that some of your earlier systems are falling out of date. This will bother you but not quite enough to address it yet.

4. Your first pass at a templating system works for a while, until you discover a flaw that has affected all systems configured from template. By this time, no additional work has been done on the unblanding script because of the success of the template, so it has fallen out of date.

5. One faction in your organization favors returning to the unblanding script because it is safe and well understood. Another favors pushing forward with the template because it is fast and convenient. You'll cobble up working versions of both, but neither solution addresses the broken systems and the out-of-date systems.

6. About this time, the vendor releases a new version of the operating system, requiring you to rewrite both the unblanding script and the templating system. You do not have quite enough resources to do even one of these things, let alone both.

The best solution seems to be to learn from experience and pursue both strategies in tandem, using them to reinforce each other. This is somewhat more work at the start, but it pays off in the long run, because you won't have to throw away work or cover the same ground twice.

Customizing New Components

Customization Infrastructure Constraints

- The standard configuration should handle all known problems.
- The set of known problems will change over time. New flaws will be discovered, new patches will be released.
- The generic operating system base will change over time. Some of the releases will be incompatible with your current customizations.
- You should keep older systems consistent with new systems. A complete rebuild is not always possible to accomplish this.
- The difficulty of keeping systems consistent increases with the number of systems that are not consistent with the customization infrastructure you're building.
- You will rebuild the customization infrastructure several times before you get it right.

You can take any path you want to meet these constraints. One system that has worked well involves three related subsystems. The first is a means to build properly customized new components. The second is a means to determine whether a component is at the proper upgrade level. The third is a means to upgrade previously built components to the correct new level.

Much of the work of building the subsystems can be avoided by using software provided by the manufacturer or available from the Internet. Many operating system vendors offer pieces of this type of system, but unfortunately, as of this writing, no major commercial operating system vendors offer a complete system that is capable of addressing all the needs of a large, complex network running third-party applications in a robust security infrastructure. But a good system administrator can build basic subsystems from vendor-supplied software that will handle specific needs in reasonably short order. The keys to implementing this type of system successfully are documentation, attention to detail, and thorough testing, not intricate program architecture. You want to design the subsystems to interact well, to be robust, to be understandable to people other than the author, and to be scalable.

As we discussed earlier, the two major methods for customizing new components are an unblanding script and a template system. The best approach for customizing is a hybrid approach. What you want to end up with is a script that can be applied to a vendor distribution and that will produce a template that can be used to replace the vendor distribution for system installation. By doing this, the installed systems will be much more consistent, and you can avoid the problems of distributing and maintaining multiple versions of the unblanding script. More important, you'll avoid the problem of people who forget to run the unblanding script by providing them with no opportunity to do so.

This approach demands that you have a means to interpose yourself in the system installation process. If you purchase many machines from a single vendor, there is typically some way for you to make this happen. Some vendors are even designing for this, but it will usually take some research on your part to find out exactly how to accomplish it. It's worth the effort. If you are charged with managing and securing a large number of computers, you'll find that an understanding of the system installation process for the computers will pay for itself many times over.

Once you understand how you'll install your modified system, you then have to understand how you'll accomplish the modification. Designing the means of modification is very system specific, but the following guidelines will serve you well.

Guidelines for Building Templates

- You do *not* want to modify the template by hand. Avoid this trap no matter how strong the temptation. Use a script to convert the vendor distribution into your template distribution. This is less important for simple components, but it's always true for complex ones.

- Test, test, test, test, test. A hundred experimental reboots and rigorous testing in the early phases will save you hundreds of wasted hours when the template systems have been deployed. Try weird things: bad inputs, killing the program in mid-run, turning off the power to the workstation being upgraded. All these and more will happen to you in production.

- Be prepared to modify the template based on user criticism. In fact, aggressively seek out user criticism.

- Allow no applicable system to be built without the template. Aggressively adapt the template to whatever need exists. Every exception you make is a potential security hole.

- Don't worry too much about developing a templating system that can be used for multiple network component types. It is unlikely that your system will be usable for both workstations and routers, or for Unix and Windows NT systems. If you can share code, terrific, but it is much better to get a system that works well for a single component type than one that works badly for them all.

- Do set up a means for template developers working on different component types to coordinate their activities and share code, however.

Design your script so that it can be run many times on the same system without damaging the system. Each feature the script intends to install should be guarded with code like this (shown here in pseudocode):

```
install-feature(f) {
  if (already-installed(f)) {
    warn("Feature f is already installed.");
  } else {
    if (attempt-install(f)) {
      log("Feature f installed successfully.");
    } else {
      halt("Feature f installation was unsuccessful.");
    }
  }
}
```

By designing this type of logic pervasively throughout your script, you make it possible for your script to be run many times without damaging the target system. If it is run on a completely bland system straight from the vendor, it will install all the features it is supposed to install. If run twice, it will detect that all the features have been installed and do nothing the second time. Designing the program this way gives you good protection from problems while building the template and a good base on which to build your subsystem for upgrading old components.

It's also important to remember that your installation script must be able to handle a variety of different modifications. Some changes require the replacement of a file. Other require the careful editing of an existing file, or the modification of individual bits within a binary file. You need to make allowances for all of these.

Upgrading Old Components

This subsystem is a difficult one to get exactly right. Sitting at your desk, reading a book, it seems like a simple matter that can be handled in a similar fashion to the code fragment in the previous section. Look and see if the correct version of a feature is present. If it is, do nothing. If it is not, install the correct version. Nothing to it, right?

Well, unfortunately, the situation is likely to be a bit more complicated than that. Even if you are working with a collection of components all from the same vendor, unless you *and your predecessors* have been doing things correctly from the beginning of time, you're likely to be faced with a collection of different operating system versions, different styles of installation, and installations of varying levels of competency and correctness. There is only one known piece of software that can be expected to handle this complicated a problem, and that is the one running between your ears. Here are some rules of thumb for handling system upgrades.

> ### *Testing the "Upgradability" of Legacy Components*
>
> - Measure what you're up against. Don't try to solve an academic problem where anything is possible. Solve the specific problem you have.
>
> - Don't try to solve the whole problem. Look for a solution that will handle 80 percent of the work.
>
> - Once you've solved 80 percent of the problem, measure again. You may find something that will solve 80 percent of the remainder.
>
> - Solve the really stubborn ones by redesigning where necessary and installing a fresh system wherever possible. The thing that will clobber you in the long run is trying to defend improperly configured legacy sacred cow systems. Avoid it wherever possible.

Embedding these rules of thumb in a tool produces a yes or no answer to the question "Do I need to rebuild this system from scratch with the new template?" Much of the code can be borrowed from the template customization tool, if both are written with that in mind. Design this tool to be lightweight, self-contained, and universally distributed. If people can run it on their own machines and see that they get a poor score, they will approach you to be upgraded. If it is treated like a test that will be forced on people from the outside, they'll tend to resist and you'll have to compel them to upgrade.

The best answer is almost always to rebuild a questionable system from scratch. Unfortunately, there are times when you just can't do that. In those cases, you'll want to find a way to bring the security of a questionable machine up to a reasonable level without disturbing the configuration of the machine.

> ### *Upgrading Legacy Components*
>
> - Don't build an "all-or-nothing" type tool. Every hole you patch helps, even if you can't patch them all.
>
> - Wherever possible, make your fixes reversible. This is extraordinarily difficult in some cases, so if it is not possible, offer the option of skipping a nonreversible operation.
>
> - Before doing the upgrade, develop an acceptance test for the functionality of the upgraded system. Make sure that the current system passes the acceptance test completely before the upgrade is begun. Then make damn sure that the upgraded system passes it as well. The more thorough this test is, the less likely you are to have problems after the upgrade.

System Fortification

Now that we've discussed customizing the various network components you control, it is time to discuss what your fortification strategy will be. Obviously, the exact strategy will be different for each component type, but what follows is general guidance applicable to all types.

Early in the process, you should define the various levels of fortification that you wish to impose. There is a strong temptation to use definitions based on intensity of fortification, such as "light," "medium," and "heavy." This is not a bad scale, but you'll quickly find out that it is not going to be expressive enough to cover all the possibilities. You will need to build systems that are "sort of light, sort of medium" or "heavy except for this one area." A somewhat better strategy is to build your template generation system so that it can handle an arbitrary number of definitions and then build separate definitions to suit each purpose. "Light," "medium," and "heavy" are good places to start. So are function definitions such as "desktop," "border," and "infrastructure." If you can easily extend an existing definition to form a new one, then your templating system will grow to meet your longer-term needs.

Here are some starting points for various system definitions.

Desktop System

- Minimal restrictions on capabilities

- No users allowed service access

- Indefinite number of users allowed login access

- Indefinite number of users allowed administrative access

- Medium-strength user authentication required

- Minimal restriction on services; many types allowed

- Minimal logging

Infrastructure Server

- Medium restrictions on capabilities

- Many users allowed service access

- Limited number of users allowed login access

- Restricted number of users allowed administrative access

- Strong authentication required

- Heavy restrictions on services; only well-defined services allowed

- Heavy logging

Border Server

- Maximum restrictions on capabilities

- Maximum restrictions on services

- Maximum restriction on user service access

- Minimal (preferably no) user login access

- Restricted administration access

- Extremely strong authentication required

- Maximum logging

Configuration of the Operating System

The first step in fortifying a component is configuration of the operating system. System security and system administration cannot be easily separated, as they are highly dependent on one another. A properly configured operating system makes security modifications simple and painless. A poorly configured OS can make them impossible.

- *Make it easy to upgrade the system later.* Naive system administrators build their systems as though, once done, they'll never be changed. You want to make it easy to upgrade any system to a new version of the operating system.

- *Make each system as consistent with the others as possible.* Don't make each machine a unique work of art. If you have a hundred machines and they all look more or less the same, it is easier to train maintenance personnel, it is easier to locate problems, and it's easier to fix them if they actually are more or less the same.

- *Leave plenty of extra disk space.* When you configure a computer system for the first time, you are generally asked to allocate disk space for various functions. Be generous in this allocation. If you tune the available space to be only slightly more than you need, when you upgrade the OS you may find that you have slightly less than you need, and you'll be forced to rebuild the system from the ground up.

- *Separate the volumes that contain operating system data from the volumes that contain user data.* An operating system usually comes with a whole collection of programs that perform various functions as part of the central OS or as utilities. These programs remain the same until you upgrade the operating system. They are also a target for attackers. By segregating them onto their own volumes, you have another mechanism for protecting and monitoring them. If possible, make the volume that these programs reside on read-only.

- *Separate the volumes that contain system configuration data from those that contain operating system information.* Any computer contains numerous files that give it its "personality," defining what programs will be run on start-up, the name of the machine, the network address it uses, and so on. By keeping this information separate from the bulk of the OS information, you make it easier to upgrade the system (since the OS volume can simply be overwritten), and you make the system easier to back up (since the personality of the system is the only thing that differentiates it from the template, that and user data is all you really need to back up).

- *Separate the volumes that contain transitory system data from those that contain operating system information or system configuration data.* Many files created while a system is run are temporary ones, such as working data for programs, and transitory ones, such as log files. These should be kept separate, on a volume big enough to handle them. Also, remember that many operating systems are designed to keep writing to particular files (such as log files) indefinitely. It is important to find a way to rotate those out so that one file does not keep getting bigger and bigger until it fills the volume.

Applying Patches

Carefully collect all the appropriate vendor patches for the version of the operating system you are installing. When in doubt, it is better to apply a patch than it is to avoid doing so. Make a checklist of all the patches, ordering them carefully to make sure that they do not interfere with each other. The vendor should be able to provide an ordered list of patches or to certify that patches do not interfere with each other. Apply all the patches and verify that the system will reboot properly after you have done so.

Removing Unnecessary Services

Because you are building templates for specific types of machines rather than generic risk levels, you should have a pretty good idea of which services are needed on a machine and which are not. Knowing this is essential to performing the cornerstone task of network component fortification: turning off every network service that the component provides that is not related to the component's intended function.

Why do this? Simple.

> *An attacker cannot break into a system through a network service that isn't there and cannot be turned on.*

Obviously, the fewer network services your components provide, the fewer door-knobs the attacker has available to twist and the fewer doors you have to guard. The last part of that rule is important to note, however. It is not enough to simply turn off a network service.

> *Turn off a network service in such a way that the attacker has the maximum possible amount of work to do to turn it back on and the highest possible likelihood of being noticed while attempting to do so.*

What does this mean? Don't just delete the line from the start-up script, delete the software that it starts as well. Set the file protection on the start-up script so that an attacker can't read it or modify it. Think about the steps you'd have to take to reenable that service, and make the list of necessary steps as long and as complicated as you think appropriate. For low-risk machines, this might not be much, but for high risk machines you can use your imagination to come up with lots of surprises for an attacker. Just be sure to test the system before it goes into production.

Limiting Necessary Services

Sometimes you cannot turn a service off no matter how much you'd like to. In those cases, you want to limit how they can be accessed. There are a number of limitations that you can apply to services, among which the most common are the following:

- Network source address
- User authentication
- Time of day

Limiting services is trickier than disabling services, because a disabled service, by definition, is one that nobody should be using. A limited service is one that some people should be using some of the time, and your job is to draw the line. Invariably, some people will find themselves on one side of that line and be upset because they expected to be on the other side. Almost always, this means that they were denied access to a service that they felt entitled to receive, but once in a while every security professional encounters an indignant user who has discovered that he or she was permitted access to a service that should have been denied.

Another issue here is one of convenience. People generally consider it mildly "cool" to be allowed to access a network service that others are denied access to—until the third or fourth time they've had to type their password. An inconvenient service will inspire people to find ways to defeat the limitations by administrative pressures as well as technological ones, depending on who is inconvenienced.

The best way to deal with this problem is to apply subtle limitations wherever possible, that are not obvious to authorized users but severely hamper unauthorized attempts. This causes the minimum amount of friction with authorized users and reduces the amount of pressure in your organization to change security policies for the wrong reasons.

> *Design service limitations so that authorized users are as minimally inconvenienced as possible by the limitations.*

Access control lists (ACLs) are an excellent way to do much of this work. An ACL mechanism can be applied by an operating system, by general network utilities, and by specific programs themselves. The more ACLs applied to a particular network service, the more difficult it is for an attacker to defeat them all.

A good ACL mechanism has two important major features and one important minor feature. Major features:

- The ACL mechanism can accept an arbitrary-length list of network addresses, with wildcards and variable-length subnet masking, and permit or deny access efficiently based on that list.

- The ACL mechanism can notify the owner of the machine in some way about an attempted violation or successful access.

The important minor feature is that the ACL mechanism can be easily modified by an authorized user. Of course, an ACL mechanism that can be easily modified by an *unauthorized* user is worthless. But sooner or later, you'll need to change the ACLs you create.

Disabling and Deleting Unnecessary Software

Once you've turned off all unnecessary services and hardened the remaining ones, your system is practically impossible to break into, right? Your work is done and any further fortification is a waste of time, right? Maybe so, but what if you're wrong?

Remember what we discussed earlier: Your goal is to minimize surprise and to minimize the effects that a surprise can have. If you've done your job right in minimizing and hardening services, it would be surprising indeed if attackers could get into the system. But if they could, what would they find that they could make use of?

Operating system vendors configure their software to work for naive customers; that means configurations tuned for a "good first user experience" rather than a good security experience. To some degree, this practice makes sense. The security of your OS won't matter if people don't buy it because they can't get it to work. But in the world of the Internet, *somebody* has to fix the security problems before hooking these systems up to the Net. For the purposes of this discussion, let's assume that the person will be you.

Vendor-supplied security problems usually fall into these categories:

- *File permission problems.* Typically, these problems involve files that are readable by users who probably should not be able to read them, but sometimes it is the case that files or directories are writable by the wrong users. In some cases, file permission may even give additional system privileges to programs.

- *File ownership problems.* These problems are common to all flavors of Unix: a key system program is owned by the wrong user or the wrong group. This can lead to the "Trojan horse" problem: an attacker can gain access to that user's permissions and overwrite an otherwise "trusted" program with an untrustworthy one and have that program executed by a user with higher privileges.

- *System configuration settings.* The behavior of many system features is growing dependent on configuration files and databases that are shipped with the OS. Every setting should be analyzed against the security model under which the system should be operating.

- *Excessive installed software.* Why, for example, would an e-mail relay machine need a C compiler or program development utilities?

All these types of problems depend on the context of a given machine. What is the machine intended to do? What is it *not* allowed to do? If you have a well-understood context for the machine, the settings for these problems should be made as conservative as possible. For high-risk machines, the best policy is one in which all extra permissions and privileges are turned off and all extraneous software is deleted, except where a specific and well-thought out case can be made for leaving them as they were shipped from the vendor.

Deleting extraneous software, even from high-risk machines, can make that machine unmanageable. An alternative that can work reasonably well is not to delete the software but to make it inaccessible to anyone but the administrative user. If an attacker penetrates the system and gains administrative access to the machine, the absence of minor system utilities will not slow him down much, but the absence of the utilities to a maintainer may be a major handicap.

Sanitizing System Software

- Delete what you can.
- What you can't delete, restrict.
- What you can't restrict, log.
- What you can't log, avoid.

Conclusion

Having a good handle on the process of network component fortification makes the rest of the job of network security a great deal easier. But never forget that it is a process, not a one-time job. Today's fortified component is tomorrow's legacy security hole. Here are some general principles to keep in mind.

Principles for Network Component Fortification

- Test, test, test. Changes that you test successfully will probably work, with a probability that is related to the degree of your testing. Changes that you do not test will probably not work, with a probability that is related to your embarrassment when they fail.
- Design for testing. You can't think of everything up front, but if you design a means to test for problems, then you can see how exposed you are when new problems pop up.
- Be conservative. The more risky a system is, the more conservative you should become.
- Be consistent. The more the systems you install look like the systems you tested, the fewer surprises you'll have.

- Prepare for surprises anyway. Whether you do or not, you're going to get them. The more you can build systems that work correctly despite surprises, the more sleep you'll get at night.

- Design for change. Everything changes, usually sooner and at inconvenient times. If you don't plan for it in advance, you'll get bit.

Chapter

7

Personnel Security

IN THIS CHAPTER:

- Management Issues

- Hiring Process

- Trouble with Employees

- Firing Process

- Resignation Process

- Contractors

As discussed earlier in this book, security is a problem of people, not technology. Care must be taken with the people you bring into your organization. We've discussed this issue related to the security group itself, but what about the rest of the company?

It takes skill, motivation, and opportunity for an attack to succeed. The people in your organization, whether they are employees or contractors, members of the security group or working in other parts of the company, are the ones with the most skill and opportunity. If they have the motivation, they can be very dangerous to your network.

Part of keeping your network secure involves tailoring your personnel security policies to minimize the potential threat. You will want to set the following goals in your personnel security policy:

- Hire people who will not pose an undue threat.

- Make employees aware that security is taken seriously.

- Provide a plan for handling inevitable personnel issues cleanly and efficiently.

This portion of a security manager's job is rarely easy. If you walk into the office of the director of human resources with a list of demands, you're likely to be met with incredulity, outrage, or anger, but rarely with cooperation. Your HR department has plenty to worry about as it is, and the last thing they need is a bunch of hoops to jump through for some paranoid security nut.

Modifying your organization's HR policy to meet your security goals is a true test of how well management has bought into the concept of security as a process within your company. Because of that, you need to start at the top.

Management Issues

At some point during your tenure as a security officer concerned with personnel issues, you're going to have to do something like walk into the office of a powerful manager in your organization and tell him that he can't hire the brilliant young engineer he's selected because the kid's too much of a security risk. And the manager is going to blow a gasket.

This is not something you should do lightly, but when you need to do it, you want it to stick. Therefore, it's very important that you get all your ducks in a row with your management and the management of your organization before you take up such a challenge.

Hiring Process

The process of deciding whether or not to hire someone and exactly how you bring that person into your organization is where you can be the most effective in weeding out potential problems and setting expectations correctly. It's best to avoid personnel security problems by not hiring people who are likely to cause them. However, determining exactly who those people are with sufficient certainty is difficult. To complicate things further, there are many laws regarding hiring practices. Designing a safe and legal hiring policy is something a computer security manager can advise about but should not undertake fully without a great deal of thought and training. The role of security in the hiring process is most important during interviews and the first few months of an employee's tenure.

Interview Process

PROCESS DESIGN

Imagine that your organization wants to hire an engineer to work on your network. It is the most natural thing in the world to tell this candidate about your network and the various tasks it involves. You'll probably want to give the candidate a tour as well. This is all a normal part of the interview process, but it also can pose a threat to the security of your network. A smart intruder can learn a great deal from a walk through a busy machine room. Machines are often labeled with key information, such as network addresses. Network diagrams are often posted on the walls.

BACKGROUND CHECKS

A suite of background checks can provide a great deal of information about a prospective hire. These checks are relatively inexpensive, but they can take time, which is their biggest problem. In a competitive job market, if an offer is delayed because of a background check, you may lose the opportunity to make an offer at all. But the rewards of the wait are that you can eliminate a number of major problems before they happen. You should design background check levels to correspond with the sensitivity levels of positions being hired for. A heavy check would be for security people, systems administrators, and employees trusted with access to critical machines. A medium check would be for technical employees without critical access and for employees with access to confidential business information. A light check would be for employees in nonsensitive positions. But remember that employees are promoted and transferred. The assistant you did a light check on last year might be promoted to sysadmin next year. So any check you do should be heavy enough to give you adequate confidence about anything that person might do at your organization. Following are the areas you should cover:

- *Identity checks.* Is this person who she says she is? Does she live where she says she lives?

- *Employment verification.* Did this person work at all the places listed on his résumé?

- *Reference verification.* What do her references have to say about her? Are her references really who she says they are, or are they clandestine relatives and friends?

- *Law enforcement issues.* Any arrests, convictions, prison terms?

- *Financial issues.* Does this person have financial problems? Would he be a good candidate for a bribe because of those problems?

You'll need to get and record the candidate's permission to do a background check. Candidates with no skeletons in their closets will assent readily; the difficult cases will be scared off because they know they won't pass.

ACCEPTANCE/DENIAL CRITERIA

Background issues can be very sensitive. You need to know what criteria you can use to withhold an employment offer, and you must document your criteria and your process very carefully. If you find yourself in a lawsuit about background checks, the completeness of your documentation, the clarity of your criteria, and the degree to which you stick with the criteria are what will save you. So define an employment policy that simply and clearly lays out what will happen if candidates fail certain elements of their background checks and stick with it.

CONDITIONS OF EMPLOYMENT

Once you've made a job offer to someone, you can require them to meet certain conditions before they are allowed to become an employee. Typically, these conditions are related to HR issues, but you can apply a few yourself. For example, this is an excellent time to have people read, and sign as having read, the part of the security policy that pertains to them. The acceptable use policy also should be read and signed now, as should any nondisclosure agreements or proprietary information agreements.

Probationary Period

Employees, especially those who are to have sensitive access, shouldn't be given full access on their first day, as a general rule. A probationary period gives a new employee time to acclimate to the environment and to learn the quirks and details of the systems they'll be working on, without any danger of them accidentally destroying sensitive information or damaging systems. A probationary period also gives the security group a chance to see if the new employee tries to acquire sensitive access before being allowed to have it, which is a good sign of future trouble.

Trouble with Employees

There are several schools of thought about how to handle an employee violation of the security policy of your organization. Some people lean toward an approach that gives a severe warning the first time and dismissal the second. This is a reasonably fair policy, but to a person who intends to abuse the trust you've placed in them, it essentially means that they get a bonus free shot.

Alternative policies include immediate termination, which puts you in the unpleasant position of recommending the firing of the key salesperson, say, for a security infraction while your company is desperately trying to make the quarterly sales numbers.

The policy that seems to work best has these key points:

- A clearly worded security and appropriate use policy, which every employee reads and explicitly agrees to follow. This policy should lay out clear penalties for specific types of actions, all of which are substantial penalties, and not simply verbal reprimands. The policy should be fair and should require some effort to violate.

- An incident review board, whose members decide whether or not the employee is guilty of a particular infraction.

- The application of the penalty from the policy, based on the infraction.

If the policy is fairly worded, difficult to accidentally violate, and universally applied, not by an individual, but by a group, then the people who generally want to follow it will not have difficulty doing so, and the people who want to violate it will be quickly discovered and dealt with fairly. The danger here is selective enforcement of the policy. In that climate, people may feel that they can "get away with it" and may be more likely to skirt the edges of the prohibitions of the policy.

Firing Process

Sometimes, despite a great policy, you may need to let someone go because of a security problem. At other times, a person may be fired for reasons unrelated to security, except that the person being dismissed has special access to your network. A clear policy for handling the network security aspects of a termination is extremely important.

A good access termination policy has these characteristics:

- Universal and quick disablement of access

- Mechanism for terminated employees to retrieve or delete personal information from your network without endangering the network

- Means for gently but firmly conveying to terminated employees a sense that they would be foolish to attempt further abuse of the network

Exactly how these criteria are carried out will depend heavily on your HR and legal departments, and both should be included in the design of this policy. The case you want your firing policy to handle well is one in which a vital employee with special access must be fired according to the security policy, but the manager feels he or she needs to retain some level of access for a few weeks. If your policy can handle that situation, and your management backs up your solution, then you're in pretty good shape for the majority of cases.

Resignation Process

Handling a resignation is similar in principle to handling a firing, except that in a firing, the element of surprise is working in your favor most of the time. With a resignation, the resigning employee has the advantage of surprise. For this case, having an ability to cut off access quickly is not as important as the ability to review what that employee has done over the last few weeks. If the resigning employee intended to cause security problems, they've already happened by the time you become aware of the resignation.

Because a resignation is often a surprise, there will be added pressure to allow resigning employees to retain access for a few weeks, and a good policy has a means of handling this issue as well.

Contractors

Policies involving contractors are usually based on the concept of acceptable levels of risk. A contractor's relationship to the company is different from an employee's because the contractor's responsibilities and privileges are more explicitly spelled out and usually are for a single specific job, while the employee may work at many positions during his or her tenure with a company. For that reason, designing contractor access levels can be quite straightforward in most areas, because you can require more of a contractor in the form of nondisclosure agreements and legal paperwork than you typically can of an employee. Because of this, you can effectively select a level of protection that allows you to accept the risk of putting a contractor in most low to moderately sensitive positions. For positions of high sensitivity, you'll need to balance the need for a contractor against the potential of the compromise of proprietary information.

Chapter

8

Physical Security

IN THIS CHAPTER:

- What Are the Threats?
- Physical Security Basics
- Going Overboard
- Backups
- Denial of Service
- Electrical Power
- Telephones
- Access Control Logging and Log Analysis

Physical security is an important part of the overall security of your network, but it is one of the most misunderstood aspects of network security. All too often the image conjured up by physical security is similar to that of the *Mission: Impossible* movie, in which a team of agents sneaks into a computer center, climbing walls with suction cups, defeating laser warning grids, and hanging from the ceiling to evade ultrasensitive floor sensors. Very exciting, and all of it just to access a screen and keyboard that any competent designer would have disabled when all the security precautions were turned on but which was active nonetheless.

If you are in the sort of business where you expect black-clad spies to attempt entry through your enormous ventilation shafts, then you probably have entirely different sources for learning about physical security design than this book, and appropriately so.

What Are the Threats?

The rest of us face a number of threats to our networks that are much less colorful but much more troublesome on a day-to-day basis, among them:

- Employee tampering with equipment
- Improper access to backup tapes
- Accidental disconnection of production equipment
- Power circuit overload from unplanned equipment addition
- Power failure
- Water damage
- Theft

The most dangerous and damaging threats can also be the most prosaic. A friend of mine started an Internet e-commerce company in San Francisco. After a great deal of work, he managed to set up an interview with a major credit card company in New York City. He and his associates planned their presentation very carefully because a good demonstration of their technology would close the deal, and they had only a short amount of time. The man they were seeing was famously hard-nosed but gaining him as a fan would clinch a deal worth millions. They made a point of getting to the conference room early and setting up their equipment so that they could test and fix any problems. Everything worked beautifully, and they were able to connect to the servers back in their tiny office space in San Francisco. Unfortunately, just as they were being introduced to the Great Man himself in New York, the landlord of their building was letting painters into their machine room back in San Francisco. The painters moved tables around and threw protective sheets over the equipment, disconnecting the power cords so that they could get to the walls. When the time came for the demo in New York, the software, which had worked beautifully moments before, was stone cold dead. The Great Man had other meetings to attend and was gone before anything could be done to repair the damage. Their multimillion-dollar deal vanished as quickly as he did.

The design of any production network should include provisions for managing physical security issues. Many of these issues will be handled by other people responsible for the design of a computer facility, but a good network security designer will ensure that *somebody* has handled them correctly. In addition, network physical security designers should consider these issues:

- Access control to machine rooms
- Layered access to high-security areas within machine rooms
- Access logging and log recovery
- Visitor management
- Fire and safety issues related to secure facility access

Physical Security Basics

Some physical security issues, such as fire and safety, are far beyond the scope of this book. Others, such as access control, we will discuss at a high level, but the details are left for you to fill in as an exercise.

Your goal as a designer of a secured network is to create levels of protection that can support your security policy and provide reasonable protection against the threats that concern you. It is very easy to go overboard with physical security and worry about unrealistic issues, so you should be aware of this tendency and avoid it. Physical security can be expensive as well, so there can be a tendency to cut back too sharply and eliminate protection you need.

A good model for physical security is known as the *onion model,* or the layered approach. A representation might look like Figure 8-1. A security gradient is defined that covers everything from the outside world to the innermost security vault, and transitions (A, B, C, D) are defined that cover the protocol for moving from one level to the other. A simplified example of this in policy form follows.

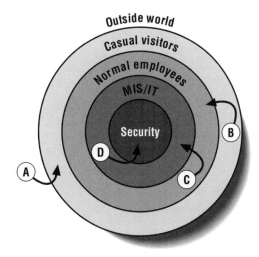

Figure 8-1: Onion model for physical security

Level: Outside world

Description:	Uncontrolled area surrounding the facility
Personnel allowed:	Anybody

Transition to Casual Visitors

Conditions: 8 A.M. to 6 P.M.
General business visitors only

Approved by: Receptionist

Conditions: 8 A.M. to 6 P.M.
Badged employees

Approved by: Receptionist

Conditions: 6 P.M. to 8 A.M.
Prescheduled appointments only

Approved by: Security guard

Conditions: 6 P.M. to 8 A.M.
Badged employees

Approved by: Security guard

Level: Casual visitors

Description:	Waiting area in lobby for visitors
Personnel allowed:	Approved by transition from **outside world** Approved by transition from **normal employees** Receptionist (normal business hours) Security guard (after hours) Maximum linger time in this area: 60 minutes

Transition to Outside World

Conditions: All times

Approved by: None required

Transition to Normal Employees

Conditions: 8 A.M. to 6 P.M.
                  Badged employees
                  Badged contractors

Approved by: Badge reader

Conditions: 6 P.M. to 8 A.M.
                  Badged employees

Approved by: Security guard (must be logged)
                  Badge reader

Conditions: 6 P.M. to 8 A.M.
                  Badged contractors

Approved by: Contract manager (letter must be on file with guard)
                  Security guard (must be logged)
                  Badge reader

Conditions: 6 P.M. to 8 A.M.
                  Visitors

Approved by: Security guard (must be logged)
                  Badged employee (must be logged, must escort)
                  Badge reader

Conditions: 8 A.M. to 6 P.M.
                  Visitors

Approved by: Receptionist (must be logged)
                  Badged employee (must be logged, must escort)
                  Badge reader

Transition from Normal Employees

Conditions: All times
                  Visitors
Approved by: Receptionist/security guard (must be logged)

Conditions: 6 P.M. to 8 A.M.
Approved by: Security guard (must be logged)

Level: Normal employees

Description: Area for normal business functions

Personnel allowed: Approved by transition from **casual visitors**
                          Approved by transition from **MIS/IT**

Transition to Outside World

Conditions: Emergency
Approved by: None required (alarm will sound)

Transition to Casual Visitors

Conditions: All times
Approved by: None required

Transition to MIS/IT

Conditions: All times
                  Badged MIS/IT/security employee

Approved by: Badge reader

Conditions: 8 A.M. to 6 P.M.
                  Badged nonMIS/IT employee (preapproved by MIS/IT management)
                  Badged contractor (preapproved by MIS/IT management)

Approved by: Badge reader

Conditions: 6 P.M. to 8 A.M.
                  Badged nonMIS/IT employee (MIS/IT escort required)
                  Badged contractor (MIS/IT escort required)

Approved by: Badge reader

Conditions: 8 A.M. to 6 P.M.
                  Visitor (MIS/IT or security escort required)

Approved by: Badge reader

Level: MIS/IT

Description: Business-critical computer equipment,
                        supplies

Personnel allowed: Badged MIS/IT/security employees
                        Badged contractors (with contract
                        manager and MIS preapproval)
                        Visitors (with MIS/IT or security escort)

Transition to Normal Employee

Conditions: All times
Approved by: None required (one-way door)

Transition to Security

Conditions: All times
             Badged security employee
             Badged employee (security escort required)
             Badged employee (preapproved by security management)
Approved by: Badge reader

Level: Security

Description: Core security systems plus core
                networking systems

Personnel allowed: Badged security employees
                       Badged employee (with security escort or
                       security management approval)

Transition from MIS/IT

Conditions: All times
             Record entry for correlation with exit
Approved by: Badge reader

Transition to MIS/IT

Conditions: Emergency
Approved by: None required (alarm will sound)

Conditions: All times
                Must correlate with entry or alarm will sound
Approved by: Badge reader

The idea is to describe the various places you want to apply physical security and then to describe the transitions between them and the conditions that will allow someone to make the transitions. For example, in the model, a visitor can walk into the lobby if the receptionist or the security guard allows it and then can go to the main working area of the building escorted by an employee. An MIS/IT or security employee must escort a visitor into the MIS/IT area, and no visitors are allowed into the security area. You want to model all allowed behavior. The general philosophy of physical security is usually a mix between the restrictive and permissive philosophies we've discussed elsewhere in this book. Within a security layer, you are governed by a more or less permissive model. Once you are allowed in that area, you can go anywhere you'd like within it (the exception here is visitors, who must be escorted). Between layers is a more or less restrictive model. No one can cross between layers except in an explicitly authorized manner (the exception here is the amount of difficulty you wish to impose on the transition mechanism—(will you install doors that only permit one person at a time, or will you allow "tailgating" of several people through a door on a single badge entry?) The higher the security level, the more restrictive the policy should be.

A real model tends to be much more complicated than a "simple" onion and looks more like Figure 8-2 (sometimes called the *garlic clove model* by people who like to cook). Once such a model has been constructed, you need to make the facility match the model: You must design the facility in such a way that it is extremely difficult to move between layers in any way other than the ways you are explicitly permitting.

Facility design can be more difficult than you might suspect. For example, you may have a badge reader on the door to your machine room that is supposed to permit entry only by specific people. So far, so good. Now, take a ladder and lift a ceiling tile on the outside of the machine room. If you were to climb through the hole in the ceiling, could you lift another tile and drop down into the machine room *without* having to use a badge? If so, then there is a way to make the transition

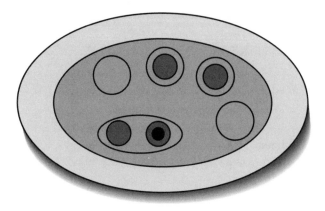

Figure 8-2: Garlic clove model for physical security

that has not been accounted for in your policy or in your construction. Can you lift a floor tile and crawl between the machine room and the security room? There is another way. Can someone outside your building wait for an employee to go out a locked door and catch the door before it closes and let themselves into a "secured" part of the building? Yet another way.

For the most part, network security designers do not take on these problems unassisted. There are companies and facilities designers that specialize in access control. But for a small to medium-size company that wants to build a reasonably secure facility, the money is often available for construction but not for expensive consultants. So a network security designer often finds himself entangled in these problems to some degree, either in terms of writing a specification for the consultant or actually doing the physical security design at some level.

As a designer, therefore, your responsibility is to carefully think through what you want and try to develop a reasonable design that both prevents people from crossing thresholds (as strong as is necessary for that particular threshold) and detects people attempting unauthorized level crossings (with a probability related to the importance of that threshold).

Going Overboard

Physical security issues seem to make people more passionate than computer security issues. They either want to build a fortress (physical security is something you can easily imagine and point to) or can see little or no reason for physical security measures when they are proposed (physical security obviously costs money).

Although the security measures you take on a computer system are quite real and do cost actual money to implement and test, they are not as tangible to most people as a big concrete wall or a door with a card reader.

For example, consider the transition in and out of the MIS/IT area described in the previous section. You might build the threshold perfectly, with real-floor to real-ceiling walls, no holes large enough to allow a person to crawl through, and laser detectors above the false ceiling to detect when tiles are lifted. But your walls are probably built from drywall and will yield easily to a crowbar or a sledgehammer. Does this mean that you should rethink the design and make the walls concrete or steel? The answer is "Probably not." If you think that the chances are good that an attack will come in that fashion or that what you are protecting in that room is so valuable that you simply cannot take the risk, then by all means, make the walls stronger. But for the most part, you want to design against people being sneaky; it's highly unlikely that someone next door in the accounting department will take a sledgehammer to the machine room walls to gain access.

Backups

A major concern of your physical security strategy should be backups. A proper backup will save you if things go seriously awry, but backups present a number of dangers as well. Consider your core intellectual property, which you have spent a great deal of time and money to guard on your network. It may be incredibly difficult to penetrate your network from the Internet, and gain access to the key system holding this information. It may be effectively impossible to sneak a copy of that information out across the Internet because you've done such a good job on your network design. But if a visitor on a tour can steal a four-millimeter tape cartridge (slightly larger than a box of matches) with a full backup dump of this key machine, slip it into a pocket, and leave without the theft being discovered, then all the network security is in vain. Or if the minimum-wage tape jockey who runs the backups for you is in the employ of your competitor and can "borrow" a tape, copy it, and replace it before it is missed, then your network security has a big hole in it.

Thinking pathologically about your backup systems is a very worthwhile endeavor and not something that should be put off. Everybody talks big about backups, but few organizations do them really well. Some questions you should consider:

- Have backups been done regularly?
- Were they done correctly?
- Are the backups usable?

- How are the backups stored on site? Are they vulnerable to casual theft? Who could steal them?

- Do you have a systematic way of noticing if a backup tape has been stolen?

- How difficult is it to locate a specific backup tape that is stored on site? When was the last time this capability was tested?

- How are the backups stored off site?

- Who can send or recall tapes from off site? What happens if that person is unavailable?

- What ensures that tapes sent off site are inaccessible by anyone but people in your organization?

- How long does it take to recover a tape from off-site storage? Are there procedures for emergency recovery twenty-four hours a day? Who must authorize emergency recovery?

- If there were a major disaster, are the key backups necessary to restore service on site, in off-site storage, or somewhere else?

- What object or knowledge, if any, other than physical possession of the tape, is needed to restore the files from the tape? Who controls that object or knowledge? Is there a potential for that person to abuse this control? What happens if that person is unavailable?

Denial of Service

Thinking pathologically about your physical security measures is often quite instructive. For example, consider the following questions:

- What access will you have to key areas (machine rooms, security areas, tape storage areas) if the badge access control system is out of order?

- What access will you have to those areas during a power failure?

- What access to those areas must you provide for fire safety that would jeopardize your security during a safety drill?

- Are there mechanical keys to the secure doors? Who has them? How are their uses logged?

A good way to deal with some of these questions is to equip doors with a fire safety bar, which allows the door to be opened without power but sets off a very loud, battery-powered alarm if employed. That way, you can design your system to "fail safe" in the event of a power problem (i.e., remain locked), but emergency crews still have an obvious way into the room if need be, and so do you. Remember that you must have a reasonably secure way to reset such an alarm if it is ever needed. It would not do to have someone use the fire safety bar and then immediately be able to cut off the alarm. A special key or something similar should be required.

The situation you want to avoid is the classic movie scenario in which a minor change to your access control system suddenly locks the key people out of the room from which the network can be monitored and controlled. Unless you're defending something life-threatening, such precautions are a good way to cause problems and unnecessary complications for your facility.

Electrical Power

When I was a college student, working in the Carnegie-Mellon University Computer Center, I learned a lesson about electrical power that was not taught by the school's electrical engineering department, of which I was a member. I was working on a class problem, using one of the terminals connected to the main student computer system (an ASR-33 Teletype, connected to an IBM 360/67, to give you an idea of how long ago this happened). The teletypes were electromechanical terminals, and they chattered noisily as they worked. They had quite stiff keyboards, and I was having difficulty with mine. I came to the end of the line I was typing and pushed the RETURN key quite forcefully. At that exact moment, there was a loud BANG!!! All the lights went out and the teletypes stopped.

For a moment, I wondered if it was my fault for being so forceful. Then, somebody near the window yelled out that a crane had fallen over outside. We all ran to the window to see. In the valley behind the science building was a large crane, which was being used to dismantle an old metal structure to make room for other construction. Apparently the ground had given way beneath one of the crane's treads, and the whole thing tipped sideways and fell over, cutting through a number of electrical cables in the process. What we discovered later was that the university had carefully designed the science building to have two redundant power feeds from different substations so that the building could continue if either feed was interrupted. A good idea, but unfortunately, both feeds ran on the same poles and were cut by the falling crane.

A few moments after I saw the crane, one of the Computer Center engineers came running through the terminal room and called me to come along. After a second I realized why and raced after him. The IBM 360 used a disk drive called a 2514. The 2514s were about the size of a small washing machine and used removable disk packs, which stored a few megabytes (quite a lot at that time). The disk packs were stacks of magnetic platters perhaps a foot or so in diameter and stacked one on top of the other, with about half an inch of space between platters. When you needed a particular set of files, you'd mount the disk pack on a drive and once it spun the pack up to a formidable rotation rate, you could see the disk heads sweep out over the platters. These heads floated on a cushion of air a tiny fraction of an inch above the platter in order to read and write on the pack. Occasionally, something would happen and a disk head would actually hit the platter, making a horrible noise and destroying the heads and the pack and sometimes much of the drive itself. The computer room had dozens of these disk drives running at any given time, with valuable scientific and administrative data on them. The machine room looked like a huge, very busy laundromat, with operators mounting and unmounting disk packs as the computer requested new ones.

The 2514 disks, we'd noticed, had a problem. A spring-loaded system was supposed to retract the heads if the power was cut off, but that system was not entirely reliable. If the circuit breaker popped and cut the power off abruptly, you had to examine the machine to make sure that the head retracted. Usually it did, but sometimes it did not. When power was cut, the rotational energy stored in the disk would keep the disk spinning and supply an air cushion to the heads for about 15 minutes. So you had time to get a special tool supplied by IBM and retract the heads by hand before they crashed on the platter and destroyed the disks, heads and all.

What I realized at that moment was that the power had been abruptly cut off on *all* the drives at once. The clock was ticking, and the machine room was three floors below where all the engineers' offices were, deep underground.

We raced to the stairwell and plunged inside, only to discover another problem. The university had wisely equipped every stairwell with light fixtures on the emergency power system. A centralized, generator-based emergency system, which would start immediately after a blackout, had seemed much more cost effective than battery-operated fixtures. But the system had never been tested, and it didn't work. We found the stairwell completely black. Our toolkits, with flashlights, were in the lab next to the machine room. We plunged down the stairs, feeling our way, and counting the floors. When we got to the right level, we crept along the walls from the stairwell to the machine room door.

There was a bit of fumbling as everyone felt for the machine room key on their key rings, but finally somebody got the door open and we made our way along the tape racks toward the lab. The operators, who moments before were busy running the giant mainframe, were now sitting in the pitch blackness wondering what to do. We located a flashlight by touch in the lab, and from that point, things moved quickly. We quickly moved from drive to drive, verifying that heads had retracted on some, fixing others. After several checks and rechecks, we tensely listened to each drive slowly come to a halt and sigh to a stop as the fifteen-minute grace period ended. When the room was silent and we'd heard no screech of a head crash, we knew that we'd been in time.

I learned several valuable lessons from that incident, lessons that have served me well ever since:

- A redundant system should be redundant at all levels, including the physical routing of cables, wherever possible.

- You won't know if your safety systems, such as emergency lighting, will work unless you test them.

- It's much better to test them in advance than it is to find out that they don't work when you need them.

- Crazy things happen, even when it's supposed to be impossible, so place safety equipment where you can find it in the dark.

- Systems that are supposed to "fail safe" sometimes don't. Hope that they will, but check anyway.

There are any number of questions you can ask yourself if you think pathologically about your power systems. Here are some good ones:

- Which systems should be on battery backup?

- How long do you have before your batteries are exhausted? How can you determine this in a crisis?

- The computers are on battery backup. Are the displays?

- What happens when the battery backup runs out?

- Do you need a generator?

- How many critical systems are on the same circuit? The same power strip?

- Do any systems that are supposed to be redundant share the same power circuit?

- Do access control and other systems "fail safe" or "fail open"? What do you do in either case?

When was the last time you had a disaster drill? Or tested your battery backup?

At one site I helped to design, I used to take customers and visitors on a tour of the facility and end part of the tour by turning off the main breaker for the machine room. The systems hummed on as the entire network ran off the batteries. It was very reassuring to me and to them that the system ran well enough that such a demonstration was casually possible. You may not want to go quite that far during a normal tour, but think about how close (or far) you are to (or from) the ability to do something similar, and consider what you could improve.

Telephones

The bane of every network security manager's life is analog modems. The widespread deployment of the Internet within companies has started to reduce their ubiquity, but analog modems connected to your desktop machines offer an unprecedented ability for attackers to break into your network. Consider this scenario.

> *An engineer on a tight deadline wants to work from home. Asking for permission takes too long and he's too busy to do it anyway. He remembers that the person in the cubicle next to him had a fax line before she was transferred to another department. The cube is unoccupied, so the engineer sneaks in and sees that the line is still active. He brings in a cheap modem from home and connects it to the fax line and his desktop PC. For the next two weeks, he works in his office during the day and from home at night using a popular PC "remote control" application. Because no one except himself knows about the line, he figures he's safe and doesn't set up a password for the remote control access.*
>
> *He completes his project on time and decides to take a few weeks of vacation to unwind. He forgets to turn off the modem before he leaves.*

If this had happened in your organization, you'd now have a modem that allows unauthenticated access into your engineering network just waiting to be discovered. A friend of mine, a respected Good Guy, has personally called most of (soon to be all) the telephone numbers in the 415, 408, 510, 707, 925, and 650 area codes (Silicon Valley and the San Francisco Bay Area), just to see what answered. The number of open, unauthenticated, *critical* systems he found was astonishing. Maintenance connections to routers, remote control applications just like the one described in the example, systems belonging to police and fire departments—the list goes on and on. His work was done with commonly available software and a couple of modems on a cheap computer. It could easily be duplicated by others and certainly has been.

Questions that you should answer with regard to your organization's telephone/modem usage follow.

- Do you have a stated policy on modem access to/from machines on your network?

- Are your telecom facilities people aware of this policy?

- Can an employee order an analog line capable of inbound calls without clearing it with the security department?

- Do you have a different, better-controlled, and better-monitored system to eliminate the need for such desktop modems wherever possible?

- Would your monitoring system notice a telephone number scan of your organization?

- How do you know that there are no modems connected to your network?

- Have you ever conducted a telephone scan of the numbers assigned to your organization, looking for unauthorized modems?

Access Control Logging and Log Analysis

Your organization has developed a wonderful system for managing the badges used to allow your people in and out of various parts of your facility. If you are like most companies, however, this system is run by a different part of the organization than the part responsible for network security. However, a failure of this system can impact network security, so there are some good reasons to think pathologically about it and ask a few questions:

- How are the access control system logs collected?

- How are they backed up?

- Do they log failed attempts?

- Who can change access control policy for a user?

- What approval is required?

- Can your access control system distinguish between an authorized employee and someone else holding that employee's badge?

- Do you have ways to cross-check entry into sensitive locations (such as by video recording)?

Chapter

9

Monitoring Your Network

IN THIS CHAPTER:

- The Shape of the Logging System
- What to Log
- Logging Mechanisms
- Time
- Sensors
- Logging System Design
- Log Management
- Log Analysis

The third part of the classic Greek recipe for successful engineering (analysis, synthesis, and evaluation) introduced in Chapter 1 is interesting and challenging. While a properly secured network must have the means for deterring attack, it is vital that it also have the means for detecting attacks. Without this component, you'll never know how well or how poorly the fortress you've built is actually repelling invaders.

In truth, you may never know exactly how well your network security is working. Part of the goal of an attacker is to bypass the monitoring and detection systems you have in place. If the attack is successful, you'll never see the attacker.

> **Goals of a Monitoring System**
>
> - Reduce the likelihood of an attack going unlogged to as close to zero as is affordable.
> - Increase the likelihood that the events logged for an attack will be recognized as an attack to as close to 100 percent as affordable.

Looking into the first goal, the question arises, "What causes an attack event to go unlogged?" Well, there are two basic possibilities:

- The event was of a type that your network does not know how to detect or log or chooses not to log.
- The event was logged or logging was attempted, but the log mechanism was tampered with by the attacker.

The first case is easy in principle to deal with: Simply log everything. In practice, however, this is difficult. At what level does the logging cease to have meaning? Log each packet? Each bit? How do we analyze such dense logs?

This is where the word "affordable" comes into play. There are two components to what you can afford here:

- How much will it cost you to develop and deploy extensive logging services within your network?
- How much will it cost you if an attack goes undetected?

The first is fairly quantifiable. The second is not. A successful attack may cost you nothing or it may put your company out of business. More than likely, the costs will fall somewhere in between those extremes. The security world uses the word "commensurate" to describe the relationship between the cost of what is being protected and the cost of the security system protecting it. It is usually expressed like this:

> **The cost of the security system should be commensurate with the value of what that system is protecting.**

Think about the security system guarding the Hope diamond, which is worth many millions of dollars. If the diamond is stolen, then the museum that lost it is out not only the cost of the diamond but also the respect of their contributors and fellow museums. It will not be trusted to host other exhibits of comparable value. So what they actually will have lost only starts with the cost of the diamond; it goes upward from there. In this situation, surely the security system for the diamond is worth some reasonable fraction of the cost of the diamond.

One unscientific, though common, test for the ratio is called the *Laugh Test*. It is simple to explain, though how it works is not. If you heard that the Hope diamond, worth (let's say) $100 million, was protected by a security system worth $100, your reaction would probably be to burst out laughing. At $1,000 and $10,000, you'd still laugh. At $100,000, you'd probably chuckle. At $1 million and up, you probably wouldn't laugh at all. But a trained museum security expert might continue laughing up to $10 million.

The flip side is the *Wow Test*. If you heard that the $100 million Hope Diamond was guarded with a $200 million security system, you'd probably say, "WOW!" At $100 million, you'd probably still say, "Wow!" Same for $50 million. At $25 million, you'd probably say "Hmmmm," and below that nothing, until you started laughing.

So based on a completely unscientific set of tests, the ratio of security system guarding to value guarded is most comfortable between 1 and 25 percent of the total quantifiable value. That is not the ultimate answer, but it gives you a place to start and a rough idea of what to expect. It also can be misleading, because the cost here is the total cost of security, including guns, gates, guards, and their pension funds.

The logging system we are discussing in this chapter would be just a small part of the overall network security system for a corporation. But how small?

> *It is much more likely that you will discover attacks and attackers through log analysis than it is that you will see them at the moment of the attack.*

Attackers know that they are likely to be watched, so they take pains to avoid being seen. It may be only the vigilance of the logging system that brings them to your attention. You can think of the logging system as the alarm system for your other defenses. Applying the Laugh and Wow Test ratio to that, and it would be reasonable to be spending somewhere between 1 and 25 percent of your total network security costs on logging and log analysis. Your mileage may vary, but if it is dramatically different from what is described here, you probably want to make sure that there is a good reason for the discrepancy.

The Shape of the Logging System

Earlier, we said that crucial events would not be logged if the system did not know to log them or if the logs were tampered with by an attacker. The second issue, tamperability, is the one that shapes a logging system most.

What enables an attacker to tamper with logs? Well, from an attacker perspective, there are two types of log entries to worry about:

- Entries that have already been made
- Entries that will be made at some point in the future

An attacker can tamper with past entries only if the logs are accessible to him.

> *Logs should not be accessible to an attacker.*

Many mechanisms can deny access to logs:

- The logs are kept on a separate machine.
- The logs are encrypted.
- The logs are stored in a write-only fashion.
- The logs are stored in multiple places.

Logs should be hard to tamper with, and tampering efforts should be easy to detect. This can be achieved in a number of ways:

- Cryptographically signing each log entry to detect invalid entries
- Monitoring the log entries to look for a sudden decrease in log size, indicating that log entries have been deleted
- Assigning a sequence number to each log entry and verifying that the sequence is unbroken
- A periodic check of different log storehouses to make sure that they are in synchronization

There are very good reasons for these antitampering safeguards. An attempt to break into the logging machine is a clear sign of intrusion.

Log entries that will be made in the future are another problem. If the attacker has penetrated a single machine, he may not be able to tamper with previous log files, but if he can modify the logging behavior of the system he's penetrated, the initial penetration may go unnoticed and he'll have time to look around.

The attacker has three basic choices at this point:

- Stop all logging.

- Allow only benign (from the attacker's point of view) logging.

- Force massive amounts of logging to hide attack activity.

As we discussed in Chapter 3, the goal of a defender is to require the highest possible skill of the attacker. As defenders, our goal therefore is to force the attacker to always have to choose the high-skill route to succeed.

> *The logging system should have some way of determining whether a machine has stopped logging unexpectedly.*

To be successful, the attacker must climb a hill of complexity and knowledge. To penetrate a machine without leaving a telltale sign on the central logging system, she must take control of the part of the logging system resident on the target machine and operate it in such a fashion that the machine continues logging events without registering the attacker's presence. There are still flaws in this system, but at this point, we've reached a plateau where the Laugh Test begins no longer to apply. You could stop here and still detect the bulk of attackers with the precautions we've applied. But the system is not yet safe against smart attackers or insiders. Smart attackers will deduce, as we have done, all the precautions taken to this point. Insiders will know exactly how the logging system works. If they see a way to defeat it, they may be tempted to try.

One way to rise above this problem is to require the logging system to log information about a session attempt, rather than just the success or failure of a session start-up. That way, log information is safely off the machine before the attacker can suspend or control logging. If an attempt does not correlate with a successful or failed session, an attack is probably in progress. By doing this, you'd require the successful attacker to use a nonstandard means of entry to the system, such as a buffer overflow attack on a network service, instead of the standard session login mechanism. But most attackers don't try to batter down the front door anyway, so while you've gained something, you haven't gone far enough.

One good way of approaching this problem is redundancy. Don't have just one logging mechanism on a system. Use several. That way, an attacker has to defeat them all at once. Don't simply log messages. Put sequence numbers on them. That way a missing message will stand out, and a reset of sequence numbers to the beginning without a system reboot being logged will indicate that the logging program has been restarted, indicating possible tampering.

How far you keep going up this path is a matter of judgment and budget. The important thing is that you have to think the issues through and make a call on how much time and trouble you want to invest to protect yourself and your organization in raising the skill level necessary for an attacker to be successful.

Right along with controlling the skill level is controlling the motivation level. The best defense of all is one in which the attacker says, "This looks too hard. I'd better look elsewhere" and attacks no further. If you can persuade your attacker to leave you alone, you have succeeded in defending your network.

There is a danger here, however. If you make your defenses too subtle, the attacker may not notice them and will continue. If your deterrence mechanisms get too personal ("Ha ha! You lose!!!" printed for a failed login attempt, for example), the attacker may take it as a personal challenge and continue. In that case, you've actually increased motivation to succeed. The best approach is to bore and deter the attacker at every turn.

What to Log

In an ideal network, you'd log every event possible so that you could analyze what happened and reconstruct what was going on at any given moment. You would record every packet, every command, every disk transaction, and be able to recreate the state of your network at any arbitrary time. It's a nice dream but impractical. Your logging system would be vastly larger than your production network and would consume far more resources—off the scale of our Wow Test.

> *The network should log any events necessary to detect known attack patterns.*

Clearly, if the network logs fewer events than that, attacks will go unnoticed and could become serious. However, the weakness is that it depends on the maintainers of the system to keep up to date on all current attack patterns. That is a difficult and in some cases impossible task. Your security organization must keep tabs on the state of the art in attacks, but no organization can know in advance all possible attacks.

Consequently, you'll need to rely on anomalous behavior from a system under attack. An intruder may have a new way to penetrate a system, but once on, they are probably going to want to do more than just quietly watch the system operate.

> *The network should log any events necessary to detect unusual patterns of access.*

Finally, consider the case of a compromised computer. If the attacker owns a machine, meaning that he can run any program as any user on it, he certainly has the capability of being able to tamper with the logging system. If the machine has been completely compromised, you cannot prevent tampering, but you can make it significantly more difficult by requiring that any tampering that is not very well done be noticed by the logging system.

> *The network should log information about the continued trustworthiness of the logging system.*

Logging Mechanisms

Having discussed much about what should be logged, we should think for a bit about mechanisms for implementing an organization-wide logging system.

Syslog

The most common network logging mechanism in the TCP/IP world is syslog. Syslog runs on all Unix systems, and many other operating systems, including Windows 95/98/NT, have adaptors to allow them to connect to the syslog system. There are several key pieces to the syslog system.

Syslog Daemon. This is a program that runs in the background on all machines using syslog. It serves several purposes:

- It collects messages from syslog-enabled programs on the machine hosting it and files them according to its rule set.

- It collects certain messages from the system that are not syslog enabled (such as kernel messages regarding start-up and some device problems) and files them as syslog messages.

- It listens on the syslog port (port 514/UDP) for messages and files them according to its ruleset.

Syslog Ruleset (usually in /etc/syslog.conf on Unix machines). This file contains directives to the syslog daemon that determine where various types of messages should be logged. Choices for logging are typically limited:

- Put a message into a file.

- Log a message to another machine via UDP.

- Write a message to the system console.

- Write a message to all logged-in users.

Some versions of syslog also allow you to run a program with the message as input.

Syslog-Enabled Programs. Because syslog is a standard facility in Unix, many Unix programs have calls to syslog built into them. This enables them to log various activities to the local syslog daemon, which can in turn forward them to the central logging server if configured to do so.

Syslog is the primary logging mechanism for most Internet-related equipment. Routers are generally configured to syslog their status, for example. This is both helpful and a problem at the same time.

Pros

- Universally available

- Standard implementation

- Available from nonprogrammable devices

- Is a read-only logging mechanism

Cons

- Unauthenticated protocol. Can be spoofed.

- Unencrypted transmissions can be eavesdropped by attackers.

- Unreliable UDP transmission mechanism. Not all syslog messages reach their intended destination even without attack.

SNMP

Another major logging mechanism is SNMP, the Simple Network Management Protocol. SNMP is a more recent development than syslog, but it shares a number of strengths and weaknesses with syslog. In particular, SNMP was developed as a means for controlling routers remotely, but its use has been extended to general-purpose computing devices as well. In many ways it is the flip side of syslog, which was originally used to monitor general-purpose devices but has been extended to monitor routers.

SNMP differs from syslog in one major area: It was designed to allow read *and* write access to the device being monitored. An SNMP-based system can be used to turn on or off various subsystems within the monitored device. Syslog is entirely passive. It generates logging messages but controls nothing. The only way syslog can be used to modify the state of a system is by a denial-of-service type attack, in which the logging system would be flooded with messages intended to fill up the disk, preventing other programs from running. SNMP can, if used properly, read and control many more aspects of system behavior. It is far more flexible and thus far more dangerous.

SNMP was also designed as a polling protocol. The central monitoring agent would make a specific request of the system being monitored, and the system being monitored would respond. This is fine for many types of network management, but it may be inappropriate for a security system.

SNMP does have an interrupt-based mechanism, known as a "trap," that allows a machine to make it known to its controller that something should be checked. This mechanism may be adequate for some types of event logging, but the bias in the SNMP design is for polling, rather than trapping, so there may be some difficulty in adapting SNMP to handle event-based logging.

Pros

- Universally available

Cons

- Weakly authenticated protocol.
- Attackers can eavesdropp on unencrypted transmissions.
- Unreliable UDP-based transmission mechanism.
- Primarily intended as a polling protocol rather than a reporting protocol.
- Can allow read/write access to device.
- Requires additional integration into system software.

Custom Logging Mechanisms

Oddly enough, there really isn't a third-place entry for system logging that is widespread, multivendor, multioperating system, and freely implementable. There are, however, a number of custom solutions that work within a single domain. Homogenous systems, such as networks that are all Windows NT or all Novell or all Macintosh, have means of informing centralized systems of a problem somewhere on the network. None of these systems scales well, and interoperating with such systems often involves a great deal of legal paperwork and money.

What would be helpful is a successor to syslog and SNMP that has been designed for the problems of running a large network and securing it. What might such a logging mechanism look like?

It would be widely and freely implementable. One of the advantages of both syslog and SNMP is that they can be added to anything without too much fuss and bother. This is not a technical consideration but rather a social one. Syslog is an extremely simple technology; SNMP is quite a bit more complex. But both systems do not require a license, are implemented by open standards, and source-code software for them is widely available on the Internet. A technology that is not available in a similar fashion will not become universally adopted the way these two are.

It would be secureable. What little security there is for syslog and SNMP was implemented essentially as an afterthought. By modern standards, the security of both mechanisms is minimal and easily bypassed. A new service would be designed so that its security could not be bypassed without a significant amount of effort.

Some areas in which better security would be helpful for logging mechanisms include the following:

- **Message Integrity Verification.** A logged message should be accompanied by credentials indicating that the sender was valid and that the message remains as it was originally sent. There are many cryptographic signature protocols for this type of verification.

- **Eavesdropping Prohibition.** All syslog and SNMP messages are sent in the clear, which means that someone who can listen in on a network connection with a sniffer can get full knowledge of whatever was logged. Encryption of the message would eliminate this capability, and by coordinating the encryption with the signature protocol, any problems related to a "replay" attack could also be eliminated.

- **Access Control.** A well-designed logging mechanism would have many ways of knowing which machines were allowed to log into it and would present minimal opportunities for abuse to machines that were not allowed access.

- **Denial of Service Attenuation.** One way that both syslog and SNMP can be attacked is to simply flood them with so many messages that the service cannot keep up, and valid, important messages are lost in the avalanche of meaningless ones. A well-designed logging mechanism would have ways to avoid this problem at best and detect it and send out an alarm on it at worst.

It would be reliable. As inferred in the previous paragraph, neither syslog nor SNMP are reliable mechanisms. The word "reliable" in this context has a specific meaning for systems running TCP/IP. Both syslog and SNMP are based on the User Datagram Protocol (UDP). UDP is known as a "connectionless" protocol. Implicit in its name is the reason why. The word "datagram" comes from the word "telegram." A datagram is more like a letter than a telegram in that once it is sent, it (usually) is carried along by the postal service and (usually) reaches its destination, where it is placed in the mailbox of (usually) the correct recipient and (usually) read. All of the "usually"s add up to the unreliability factor. The sender cannot guarantee that the transmission will reach its destination, and if it does, the sender has no way of knowing whether the recipient read the message or just discarded it. Also, like a letter, if two are posted at the same time, there is no way to know or guarantee which will arrive first and which will be read first.

The other major protocol used for data connections is called the Transmission Control Protocol (TCP). A TCP session is based on a connection, similar to a telephone call. If you call someone on the telephone, either the phone is answered or it isn't. If it is answered, you either speak to your intended recipient or you don't. If you do speak to the intended recipient, they acknowledge your message or they don't. In every case, you know for certain whether your communication has succeeded or failed. And the words you utter on the telephone are guaranteed to arrive in the same order you spoke them.

A well-designed logging mechanism would be reliable in the network sense as well as the normal sense of the word. Transmissions would generally get through. Where transmissions failed, there would be some mechanism to try harder to get them through. Where failure could not be avoided, the system would support notification of the failure.

It would degrade gracefully. The fact that syslog and SNMP are based on the "unreliable" UDP mechanism is not always a problem. In fact, simple mechanisms (such as printers) are capable of using syslog and SNMP exactly because they need not maintain a complicated memory of log transactions that have not yet completed. A simple device can typically handle only a simple logging mechanism.

A powerful yet universal logging mechanism would allow for such possibilities. It would provide a means for critical devices to have reliable, robust logging, for lightweight devices to have as much robustness as they can afford, and for failing devices or networks to allow as much logging as possible to get through.

It would be manageable. The biggest problem with syslog- and SNMP-based networks is handling network growth. It's easy to run a hundred-node network based on either system. Running a million-node network requires expensive software and massive machines or redundant designs and massive administration issues. And yet running a million-node DNS system is relatively easy. Why? Because DNS allows delegation of authority and syslog and SNMP do not. A million-node network can have a hundred DNS servers, each of which is responsible for ten subsidiary servers, which each handle a thousand end nodes. Or any other architecture that works.

A well-thought-out logging mechanism would allow for similar scalability. Delegation is one way of handling scalability and generally a very good one. Machines log to regional servers, which handle some issues and forward more important ones to a higher (and presumably smarter) node, so easy problems get filtered out and handled, while more difficult ones rise to the attention of somebody who needs to care about them. This would be a great boon for systems management, but a pure delegation model may not be appropriate for security, because it requires a high level of trust in the intermediate servers. Security would perhaps benefit by a delegation mechanism combined with a "fast track" to allow system administration issues to be handled locally and security issues to be routed centrally without the possibility of decryption.

Time

One issue that is very important in log gathering and analysis is that of time. Consider these log entries:

```
Jun 5 22:49:15 desktop.randomco.org login: user smith login ok
Jun 5 23:05:00 dialin.randomco.org login: user smith login ok
```

A security administrator at RandomCo looking at these two lines would wonder, "Why is user 'smith' logging in over a dialup line when he's here in the building logged into his desktop machine?" Normally, such a sequence of events would suggest that an investigation is in order. However, one implicit assumption in the two lines above is that both the "desktop" and the "dialin" machines know the correct time of day. If the machines are not in synchronization with each other or with the logging machines, these lines could mean anything, and it would take a great deal of time and effort to figure out what was really happening.

For that reason, a valid time source is essential to proper logging of information. And having every machine which might log to the logging system in synchronization with the time source can only help matters.

A widely used mechanism for this is NTP, the Network Time Protocol. NTP is a relatively simple protocol that allows a large collection of machines to synchronize to a central, trustworthy time server. The more network hops between a machine and its time server, the more inaccurate the synchronization will be. NTP has ways to compensate for this latency, but it is good for a logging machine to be reasonably close to a good time server.

One way to accomplish this is to make use of a dedicated time server. Time servers are network devices with Global Positioning System receivers attached to them, capable of speaking NTP. The GPS system is basically a hyperaccurate clock, and thus it provides an excellent time reference. Having a logging system with an independent time source removes a possible source of attack and allows your logging system to detect when NTP-based attacks are attempted by comparing "network" time to local GPS time.

Sensors

A variety of other mechanisms can be used to aid device-based logging. These mechanisms are typically called *sensors*. They provide a means for gathering information and integrating it into the logging system so that it can be acted on. The more sensors you have on your network, the more extensive your logging will be, thus, hopefully, improving your ability to spot trouble.

One example of a sensor is the NTP attack detection mechanism mentioned earlier. Having two time references is not enough. What you need is some part of your network that will (1) collect both times, (2) compare them, (3) detect a problem, and (4) report the problem to the logging system. The mechanism that accomplishes these things is a sensor for an NTP attack. A good sensor can detect several variations on attacks if appropriate, but the most important characteristic of a sensor is that it is reliable. The analogy is simple: You would not want a burglar alarm on your house with window sensors that gave false alarms 10 percent of the time, nor would you want one that failed to give alarms for 10 percent of actual burglaries. Nor would you want one that was easy to bypass.

Most sensors detect problems with the network being monitored, such as machines breaking or security issues. Some sensors should be built that detect conditions on the logging system itself:

- *Are the logs increasing monotonically?* In other words, at times A and B, where B is always after A, are the number of recorded log entries at B always greater than or equal to the number of recorded log entries at A, for any value of B? If this statement is ever false, which means that there are fewer log entries now than there were a moment ago, someone is tampering with your logs.

- *Is the logging system receiving all the logs that are being sent?* Some devices, such as Cisco routers, transmit a sequence number with each log entry for the exact purpose of detecting gaps. Every message from a particular router has a number that is incremented for each message. If your logging system has received messages 1, 2, 4, and 5, but you don't have a message with sequence number 3, then something is wrong and you are losing information.

- *Has any machine stopped logging?* As your network grows larger, it becomes very important to make sure that all of the nodes on it are logging correctly. A logging system that keeps track of who has logged and how long it has been since their last log message is a very good way to find machines that have dropped out for some reason. A machine that has stopped logging probably indicates a network problem or misconfiguration—but it may indicate an attack.

Logging System Design

A reasonable design for a logging system for a very large organization might look something like the diagram in Figure 9-1. The goal of such a design is to provide scalability for a very large number of monitored systems, a way to handle a

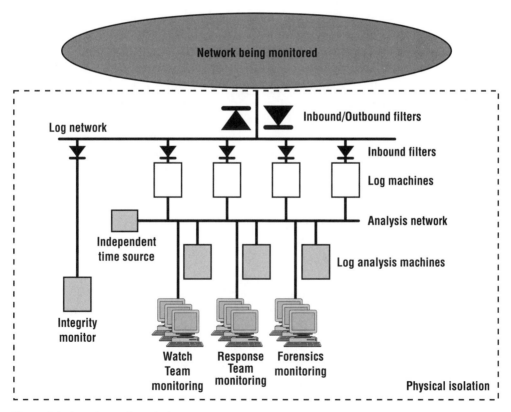

Figure 9-1: Logging system design

number of different logging mechanisms and a self-contained network that can be used by security and administrative analysts for their particular functions.

The physical isolation aspect of the design secures the hardware and networks from unauthorized tampering or inspection. Because a logging system is similar to an airplane "black box" (flight data recorder), it should be kept as separate as possible from the rest of the network. For that reason, this system has its own independent time source, which permits the logging system to be synchronized internally and not depend on external time.

The only connection(s) to the network being monitored are through inbound/outbound filters, which provide a very specific point of security policy enforcement. Typically, a logging system policy allows inbound logging traffic only and permits no outbound traffic at all. In theory, this could be accomplished by simply cutting the TRANSMIT wire on the network interface connected to the network being monitored, and no router is necessary. However, by placing a router at this point, you can handle a number of more sophisticated operations, such as network address translation and access control. Protecting your logging system from attack is one part of the job, but a router provides you with a means of knowing that your logging system is under attack, which is half the battle, by watching for access control list (ACL) violation attempts. Network address translation allows you to hide much of the detail of your logging system from outside scrutiny and to provide failover capacity for logging servers within the logging network.

Inbound filters allow you to supply each log machine with a specific security policy. Filters can be implemented in software on the machine itself, via packages such as ipfilter, or by cutting the TRANSMIT wire if that is appropriate. In some cases, both measures would be useful. Inbound filters at this point should be redundant to the outermost filter, but their presence as sensors gives you a means of determining whether your outermost filtering router has been compromised.

The integrity monitoring machine is connected to the log network in such a fashion that it can never transmit on that network, but it is able to listen to all packets crossing the network. The job of an integrity monitor is to detect unauthorized network traffic on the log network (which could indicate a penetration) as well as to keep tabs on all the various log sources to see if unauthorized logging is being attempted and to see if machines that logged yesterday are still logging today. Keeping this machine completely invisible from your log network and in physical isolation provides a nearly tamper-proof cross-check for your other monitoring systems.

Log machines collect the various log messages and organize them in ways that are useful to your data analysis efforts. They might store entries in a sophisticated database for later query or simply store them in a file.

Behind the log machines is the analysis network, which contains the various log analysis computers that process log entries and look for patterns that ought to be brought to your attention. Several sets of monitoring workstations can be used to view this information. You may wish to limit the viewing ability of some monitoring teams over others, so multiple sets of workstations may be used.

The number and power of each set of machines must be selected to fit your organization, your network, and your budget. At its simplest, this design would be a single router with a workstation behind it. For a very small network, that would be enough to get started. At the high end, you might have entire racks of logging and analysis machines and an operations center for the monitoring workstations. The idea is to provide your network with a monitoring subsystem adequate to the task.

Log Management

One aspect of logging system design that is often overlooked until last is the management of logs. For a large organization, overlooking log management can quickly become a major problem. Log management is the process of making sure that the logging system is stable and useful over the long run. For example, the syslog daemon is generally configured to write syslog messages into one or more files. These files will continue to grow in size until all available disk space on the machine is exhausted. Even if that has not happened yet, searching through the syslog files will become increasingly slow as the files grow in size. Eventually, the syslog mechanism will become unusable and may even crash the machine.

To make the syslog process stable, an external mechanism that manages the files created by syslog is needed. Typically, the mechanism involves a process known as "log rotation," in which old, full log files are moved to one side and new, empty log files take their place. On many Unix systems, this process happens when the log files grow too large. This is a functional solution for systems that have to contend with light logging, because it's better to have the last hundred days of full logs around in seven files than it is to have the last seven days of mostly empty log files. On systems with heavy logging or where the ability to quickly locate a log entry is paramount, this practice is usually replaced by time-based rotation, as illustrated in Figure 9-2 and 9-3.

Consider what the logging process looks like just before midnight (Figure 9-2). Logs are being written to a file for that particular day. At midnight, after log rotation, we should end up with a situation like the one shown in Figure 9-3. At midnight, the logging process is told to switch logging to a new file. The old file can then be processed, compressed, and archived. After sufficient time has passed, it may be removed from the machine. With this process in place, the logging system becomes dynamically stable. It seems simple, but there are some twists and turns to this process.

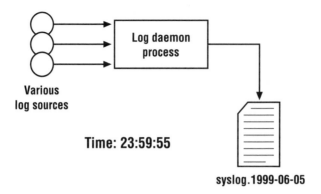

Figure 9-2: Logging process before midnight

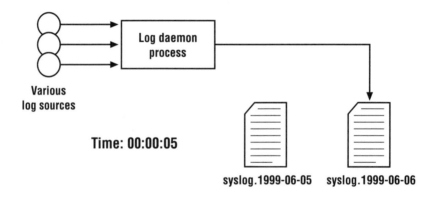

Figure 9-3: Logging process at midnight

It is difficult to get something to happen *exactly* at midnight. Unix systems are better than most other easily accessible operating systems for running programs at a prespecified time every day. This is accomplished by means of a system daemon known as *cron*. Cron has an accuracy of about one second. A job that is supposed to run at 00:00:00 can actually start anywhere between 00:00:00.0000 to 00:00:00.9999. This is not usually a problem, but a heavily loaded logging system may receive several dozen messages every second. This means that messages around midnight may end up in the file for the wrong day.

The log process may have possession of the file. The designers of the logging system have probably tried to create a mechanism that can handle heavy logging loads. This typically entails some design compromises. For example, the FILE-OPEN and FILE-CLOSE operations are usually quite slow compared to the FILE-APPEND operation on most operating systems. A logging daemon that worked like this

```
while (okToRun) {
  message = getLogMessage();
  FILE = openForAppending(logFile);
  append(FILE, message);
  close(FILE);
}
```

would be ideal for log rotation because it releases the file after every write. The problem is that such a process would be very slow in handling logging events and would run the risk of losing them. As a result, most logging mechanisms tend to be written like this

```
FILE = openForAppending(logFile);
while (okToRun) {
  message = getLogMessage();
  append(FILE, message);
}
close(FILE);
```

which allows them to run much faster and lose fewer logging events, but it holds onto the log file in a way that makes rotation difficult. As a result, logging systems usually have a means by which they can be told to close and reopen their files. This allows a log file to be switched with a minimum of trouble. But this process takes time also, so it too can result in a loss of messages (low probability, if done correctly) and misfiled messages (much more likely).

One way to handle this problem is to consider the logs written by the logging daemon to be "raw" logs and run them through a final cleanup and refiling to create "permanent" logs. Another is the judicious use of symbolic links to minimize the possibility of missed entries during the switchover. Finding a solution that works properly for your network will require some experimentation. Test and retest your solution until you've hammered out the difficulties and built something reliable before you put it into production use.

Having rotated the logs properly, you must also take care to back up your logs. A common situation is that an attack has been discovered, and you now want to look back to see what else the attacker attempted. To do that, you need a way to index your logs for retrieval, a way to roll your older logs to off-line storage, and a way to retrieve the off-line logs and find the appropriate entries as quickly as possible. The trick is not finding solutions for this problem—there are many commercial and freely available ways to back up computers—but to design your backup system into your logging system in such a way that the two are not working at cross-purposes and so that you can get commonplace tasks handled quickly and easily.

Log Analysis

Having collected a great deal of data from your network, you need to have ways to turn it into information you can use. A very good way to do this is to look for patterns in the logs. This is where the process of security that we discussed earlier in this book comes into full force. If you are applying the process of security to your network, you should be learning everything you can about the attacks to which you are susceptible. This library of attacks gives you the basis for your patterns. Your logging systems give you the insight into your network necessary to look for patterns, and your analysis systems give you the computing power to call your attention to any patterns that are seen in the log stream.

If there's an attack pattern that can't be disambiguated from your logging stream, the process of security says that you need to improve the quality of your logs. If there's an attack that is not detected by your library of patterns, the process says that you need to improve your library. It sounds simple, and in principle it is, but the practice is quite a bit harder. Nevertheless, the better your log stream, your pattern library, and your analysis tools, the better your overall security will be.

A good logging and analysis system sounds like a difficult and expensive proposition, but in fact it can easily pay for itself outside the security realm. Detecting a single log entry such as this one

```
Jun 4 15:15:18 router1.randomco.org 491: %CI-2-ENVCRIT: -12 Voltage
measured at -6.57
```

can often save you hours of downtime and missed schedules. This log entry says that a power supply on a critical router is failing. The router was bright enough to notice it and log the fact, but many organizations wouldn't notice the problem until the router failed, usually at 3 A.M., and then would take a couple of hours to figure out the problem and fix it. An organization with adequate system monitoring and logging can notice this kind of problem quickly and react to fix the problem much faster. A pattern analysis system looking for security problems would generally find patterns such as this one to be child's play, but the avoidance of a single major incident such as a core router failure can easily pay for the cost of the whole logging system.

Problems point out that the *timeliness* of the information is a critical factor in log analysis. Your logging system should be tuned to handle the following regimes properly:

- *Short-term patterns* have importance *right now*. Many network attacks fall into this category, as do imminent failure situations such as the router power supply failure.

- *Medium-term patterns* require some context for understanding. Some actions are not attacks if done only once, such as access to a public Web server. But repeat that same action a million times in the course of a day, and it is quite likely to be an attack. Denial-of-service attacks are usually medium-term patterns.

- *Long-term patterns* are where you will find evidence of very subtle attacks, as well as information regarding operational issues such as capacity planning.

By designing your logging and monitoring systems correctly, you can devote capacity to each different category.

> *Log analysis should never interfere with log collection.*

You should avoid having a single computer as your composite log/analysis machine, even though it is the most common configuration. If you build it this way, you'll always be limited by what you can do safely and rapidly enough. Break the problem into pieces, devote computing resources adequate to each piece, and make sure that the pieces don't interfere with each other, and you'll have a very powerful tool for operating and securing your network.

Chapter
10
Auditing
Your Network

IN THIS CHAPTER:

- Why Should You Audit Your Network?

- Types of Audit

- What Should the Audit Measure?

- Who Should Do the Audit?

- Expectations

One of the great things about science is that results are testable. If you design an airplane, you can build it and see if it will fly. If you create a new chemical compound, you can test it to see if it has the properties you think it ought to have. The cycle of analysis, synthesis, and evaluation has served science well for many years.

The methods of science don't always apply to network security because anything involving people is difficult to make truly repeatable, but a good idea is still worth following. There is no guarantee that a tested network is more secure than an untested one, but that is the way to bet. The better your tests and the more often you apply them, the more difficult your network will be to attack. To test your network, you need to develop an auditing process, and you need to follow through with the process on a regular basis.

The process is simple. It goes like this:

1. Audit the network yourself, testing everything you can think of.

2. Fix every problem you find.

3. Bring in an outside auditor and have them test everything they can think of.

4. Fix every problem they find.

At the end of this process, you should have a well-secured network. But though the steps are simple, the process can be quite involved. How do you audit your own network? What do you check for? What if the problems cannot be easily fixed? How do you find an outside auditor you trust? The four simple steps can easily consume a year's worth of time for a moderate-size network.

In this chapter, we discuss the various parts of a network security audit and how to get the most benefit from one.

Why Should You Audit Your Network?

Network security audits are not fun. They require a great deal of preparation, supervision, and management. The results of an audit are never good news. The tendency of an auditor is to give you what you're paying for, and what you're paying for is not "Everything's fine!" A good auditor will keep digging until there is something painful to report. So there's always going to be bad news at the end of the process, and that is going to require you to do something, probably something that you haven't budgeted for and don't have the people to undertake.

So why do an audit? There are a number of good reasons. The best is that an audit keeps you honest, even if you have no deliberate intention of being dishonest. An impartial, thorough audit takes away your illusions about the security of your network. Security is a difficult job to perform and a difficult process to explain to outsiders. It is the easiest thing in the world to rationalize to yourself that your network is safe. "Surely I've done everything reasonable here!" you might say. Or "No one would try that type of attack!" Or "I'll fix that next quarter," which is even more insidious. A heavy-duty security audit reveals your cherished assumptions to the cold light of day. Some of them may be correct, and you'll be vindicated. This time. Others may be foolishness in disguise. A good audit will give you experience for the future that is painful enough to be memorable but not so painful as to cause your company damage and loss.

Another good reason is that an audit provides an outside metric by which the quality of your security organization can be judged by your management. You can think of it as showing your college term paper to your parents. They may or may not understand the topic, but they can see that you got an A+ on it. They'll know that you did a good job, worthy of the tuition they're paying.

There's a danger there, however. The temptation is great to schedule only the kinds of audits you can do well on. But an audit that tells you what you already know is not going to be worth much.

Sometimes, though, an audit that tells you what you already know is worth quite a lot. A common reason for doing an audit is to support what the security group already knows: Something needs to be fixed. A management team will often believe what a third party tells them sooner than what their own employees tell them. They may even believe the internal team but want a second opinion anyway. An audit is a good tool for proving that there really is a problem.

Audits are generally valuable for several key reasons. First, they provide an unbiased look at your network that is outside the internal politics, scheduling constraints, resource limitations, and knowledge base of your organization. A good auditor is going to come in, look critically at what you've done, and give you an impartial reading of how well you've done it.

Second, an auditor has a formal methodology for conducting an investigation. This approach gives the auditor a process for grinding through the mountains of data, and it also helps you see the inconsistencies in what you have done. Even the best security teams miss little details here and there, and a formal, rigorous approach to analysis gives you the means to see and fix the spots that you might not see on your own.

Third, an auditor has a different perspective. A good auditor has analyzed dozens or hundreds of networks and has seen problems and solutions that you might not be aware of. For an auditor to be successful, he or she must come up with something shocking for your audit report. This gives the auditor a devious mindset that may not be matched in your organization. Thus, the auditor will have insights into the twists and turns of network security that may have escaped your own staff. That can only help. It also gives you a metric for knowing how well you've really done on the audit. If the problems found are straightforward, the auditor didn't have to work too hard and you did not do well. If the problems are devious and subtle, then you know you've covered the basics and the auditor had to sweat a bit to get something worth writing down.

Types of Audit

There are many different aspects of a computer system or network that can be audited. Following are typical areas:

- Network design
- Network implementation
- Host systems architecture
- Host security
- Physical security
- Disaster recovery
- Process and procedures

- Response time for problem resolution
- Emergency response
- Off-hours response

The key to any audit is the philosophical approach it takes to measuring the security of the network. The two most common philosophies in use today are *penetration study* and *configuration analysis*.

Penetration Study

A penetration study is a type of audit in which the auditor actually attacks the network under test. The auditor approximates what an attacker would actually do, such as scanning machines for network services, determining the versions of those services, and applying exploitation programs to attempt to use weaknesses in the services to gain access to the network. In effect, a penetration study is a game of capture-the-flag. If the auditor can grab the flag—penetrate the network sufficiently to compromise whatever it is you are trying to protect—then the network has failed the test. If the auditor cannot, then the network has passed.

Types of Audit

Zero-Knowledge Penetration. The auditor knows only the target. Every other bit of information used for penetration must be gathered by the auditor. This simulates attack by a complete outsider. In general, this type of audit takes a long time and costs a lot more.

Partial-Knowledge Penetration. The auditor already knows a lot about the target: the number of campuses, the phone numbers of dialin servers, the IP addresses of DNS, e-mail, proxy servers, and so forth. This type of audit is probably the most common penetration study.

Full-Knowledge Penetration. Involves an attacker with a map of the network, administrator passwords, and any other advantage you can give him. This audit simulates an attack by a knowledgeable insider. If your network can survive this kind of audit, it has impressive security indeed. Few networks can.

Zero-Effect Penetration. Places constraints on the auditor, restricting him or her from using any attack that will modify the target systems or that will degrade the service of the target systems. This kind of audit would be typical for a penetration study of a production system. You want the benefits of the test, but you don't want to disturb production.

Full Penetration. The auditor is allowed to modify the system, if possible, to prove that a penetration is possible by doing so, no matter what the cost to the target.

No-Holds-Barred Penetration. Any technique that could be used by the attacker is permissible. This could include bribes, social engineering, theft of documents, examination of trash bins, and much more.

Pros

- A successful penetration graphically depicts the problems in a network, improving the chances of funding for additional network security.

- A moderate penetration study, with focused goals and limited means of attack is reasonably inexpensive.

- A no-holds-barred penetration study closely resembles the way an attack is done.

Cons

- A penetration study measures the patience and skill of the auditor more than it measures the thoroughness of the defender.

- The more thorough this type of audit is, the more difficult it is to schedule. Penetration requires that a weakness be located and exploited, and several such cycles may be required to achieve the goal of the penetration. There is usually no way to know in advance how long it will take.

- The limitations you place on an auditor for this type of audit may be necessary to protect your network, but they can bias the results away from what an actual attacker (with no such constraints) might be able to achieve. This can create the impression that your network is more secure than it really is.

- A thorough penetration study requires that the auditor modify the network with backdoors (as a real attacker would). This changes the conditions of the test and decreases the security of your network. Since the goal of the audit is to become more secure, you must be comfortable with the idea of weakening the security of the network as part of the process of improving the security of your network.

- This type of audit requires that you place a great deal of faith in the auditor. By the end of the audit, the auditor will have a lot of sensitive information about and access to your network. You must choose an auditor who can be trusted with such information.

Deliverables

Minimal

- Report of success or failure

- Detailed description of what types of attack succeeded

Optimal

- Detailed description of the types of attacks attempted

- Detailed description of the attacks that could not be attempted because of audit constraints

- Description of exposures noted by the auditor

Maximal

- Suggested configuration fixes or software updates that would eliminate or minimize the problems noted during the audit

Configuration Analysis

In a configuration analysis audit, the auditor examines the network from the inside. Essentially, this audit is a highly detailed checklist. Every aspect of security is examined against the checklist and discrepancies are noted. If the number and severity of the problems found are low enough, the network has passed the audit. If there are too many problems, the network has failed.

This type of audit requires Full Access and Full Knowledge, as described for the penetration study. The auditor must look in every nook and cranny of the network. Because it is not a penetration study, the auditor cannot be required to crack the network to do so. One advantage of this approach is that the measurement can be done under your complete supervision. Another is that the measurement necessary is easier to schedule than that of a penetration study. Also, administrative access to systems can be granted for the duration of the measurement cycle and then changed so that the auditor has full access only for the minimum period necessary.

Components

Scoping. The auditor must come to understand the network design and configuration as well as the intent of the system (i.e., what it is supposed to allow, what it is supposed to prevent, and so on). With most configuration analysis audits, this basic understanding is crucial to pricing the audit.

Scheduling. A schedule for the audit must be developed. The schedule will include time on site for measurement and data collection as well as responsibilities and scheduling for the audit coordinators in the target organization. Audit coordinators are responsible for making resources and people available as necessary and for collecting some types of information (such as policy documentation) that must be tracked down in the organization.

Measurement and Data Collection. The auditor must collect enough information from each network component to permit off-site analysis of the component from a security perspective.

Interviews. People responsible for various aspects of the operation and security of the network are interviewed, as well as users of the network. Here, the auditor is looking for problems known by these people but perhaps not reported, as well as familiarity with policies and procedures.

Data Analysis. The data collected from the measurements and interviews is analyzed and a picture of the security of the network is developed.

Report Creation. A detailed report is created describing the network and any flaws or potential flaws that were uncovered during the data analysis.

Report Presentation. The report is presented to the target organization with discussion of any flaws and potential workarounds or suggested design changes.

Pros

- More thorough than most penetration studies.
- Measures the skill and thoroughness of your employees.
- Measurement can be done under direct supervision. That way, you know exactly what information about the network was exposed to the auditor.
- Authentication can be granted to the auditor only for the data collection phase; limited exposure.
- Can be done with little or no effect on production systems.
- Easier to schedule than penetration study.

Cons

- More expensive than most penetration studies
- Requires a highly skilled auditor, not just a tool operator
- Extensive measurement required
- Data are be taken off site for processing

Deliverables

Minimal

- Detailed report describing the flaws uncovered during the analysis

Optimal

- Discussion of ways in which the various flaws might be fixed or eliminated

Maximal

- Analysis of the design of the network
- Collection of resources from which updated software or knowledge can be gathered

What Should the Audit Measure?

Auditors vary widely in skill, technique, deliverables, and methodology. Audit customers vary widely as well. Because of this, you need to establish with the auditor what you expect from the audit. The best way to begin this process is to understand what you want from the audit yourself. Once you do, you'll be better able to select an auditor and better able to communicate your needs to the auditor.

> *The goal of a serious audit should be to reveal interesting and comprehensive information about the security of your network.*

Let's go through that statement a phrase at a time.

"Serious audit." Some audits are not serious but are done as a matter of due diligence. An example might be an audit that is required by a business partner as a prerequisite to doing business. In a perfect world, this type of audit would be done with exactly the same care that any other audit is done. But it is important to realize that, whether or not it is stated aloud, the goals of a serious audit and a due-diligence audit are very different. A serious audit is intended to reveal weaknesses in your security so that you can fix them. A due-diligence audit is intended to demonstrate that there are no serious weaknesses in your security. The amount of pressure you are likely to face from your management for each type of audit is significantly different. You can choose to treat a due-diligence audit as a serious audit if you like, but most security managers will ensure that one or more serious audits have been passed successfully before allowing a due-diligence audit at all.

"Interesting." The results of an audit are only interesting if you didn't know them beforehand. Paying someone to tell you about holes that you already know about is good for the auditor but not much good for you. If you intend to do an audit right, you should fix everything you possibly can first, and then see what the auditor will find. An unspoken rule of the audit game is that the auditor must find something. If you make it easy for an auditor to find large problems, then that is what your audit report will say. Make them earn their money.

"Comprehensive." You not only want to know what is wrong with the security of your network, you want to know everything you possibly can about it. The more interesting facts an auditor can reveal to you, the better off you are.

"Security of your network." A security audit is an audit of your security, not of your router performance or your skill in disk partition management. Auditors looking for something to write about will sometimes latch onto obscure technical issues in an effort to create the appearance of value in their reports. You want information about the security of your network. Anything else is padding, so make this clear to the auditor up front.

One common auditor complaint is that customers don't know what they want but don't want to be told what they will get. If you take the time and give some thought as to the kinds of metrics you want, and if you are open to the suggestions of the auditor as to a few others as well, then you'll get the most out of the experience.

One crucial aspect is knowing exactly what parts of your network infrastructure the audit should focus on. Different techniques (and possibly different auditors) may be appropriate depending on what you select. Some common areas of focus include the following:

- Connection between the Internet and your network
- Connections between your network and business partners
- Means used by employees for telecommuting purposes
- Internal network production infrastructure (DNS servers, file servers, mail servers)
- Internal business-specific infrastructure (database servers, process control servers)
- Desktop environment
- Processes and procedures
- Disaster recovery plans

You may select a very different type of audit for processes and procedures than you would for your Internet connection. Having one auditor do all your networks at one time will give you a small amount of value for a lot of machines. In some cases, such as your Internet connection, it may be more valuable to have a lot of information about a smaller number of machines, because those machines are in a critical area and subject to more attacks.

Another aspect of an audit is knowing which machines should be audited and which should not be. For a configuration analysis, you can select in several different directions, depending on what you'd like to measure. For example, you could audit for consistency: Do all of the machines within a given group live up to the same standard? Or you could audit for weakness: Given a selection of one machine from a number of different groups, rate them in terms of critical security issues. For a penetration study, you'll want to select in advance which machines, such as production servers, are off limits. For a configuration analysis, you'll probably want to eliminate duplicate configurations in favor of unique configurations so that you can get the broadest perspective possible on your network.

Who Should Do the Audit?

The selection process for an auditor can vary greatly, depending on the network being audited and your concerns about the security of that network. For relatively simple, straightforward networks, there are many different groups and individuals that can perform a useful and functional audit. For extremely complicated or sophisticated networks, your choice may be more limited.

In general, you'll have to choose auditors from one of these groups: independent consultants, security firms, and audit houses. In general, you want to pick an organization that is able to handle the level of audit you want, is able to handle the technical detail you need, is trustworthy with your data, is available for follow-through, has minimal formal ties with your business partners, and has minimal informal ties with your business partners or possible attackers.

The last two points are interesting ones. Sometimes you may find yourself in the situation of being asked to submit to an audit by one of your business partners. This is not a serious audit, as described earlier, so it should be handled with caution, since the goal of such an audit is to create confidence rather than to reveal weakness. However, if the auditing firm has a significant business relationship with your business partner, you could find that your auditor has been forced to reveal information of a serious nature to your business partner, and that could jeopardize your business relationships. It is up to you and your partners to negotiate what information is to be shared with other parties and at what times. If you choose an auditor carefully, you won't have to defend the release of information outside those agreements.

Informal relationships are more insidious, because rumors are so much harder to defend against than facts. And an auditing firm that has informal relationships with Dark Side attackers and allows information about customers to escape through that channel is not to be trusted with anything.

Take a look at each group of auditors and examine their strengths and weaknesses.

Independent Consultants

These are the most numerous of your choices for auditors. Independents can range from top-notch security experts either moonlighting or working for themselves and attackers looking for a way to social-engineer a target to poseurs who have downloaded some free software or read a book.

A concern with independents is that the ones who really know what they are doing also tend to be the ones with friends on the "dark side." By using them, you run the risk of an informal channel in which an otherwise Good Guy happens to mention a weakness of your network to a Bad Guy in a casual conversation over a beer, and that discussion leads to a security problem for your network.

Hiring independent consultants should therefore involve practices similar to hiring a security employee, even more stringent ones, if possible. Nondisclosure agreements, background checks, character interviews, and references are an important part of this process.

Pros

- Relatively easy to find
- Can be very cost effective
- Some significant talent is available

Cons

- Quality varies widely
- Trustworthiness can become an issue
- Consistency and audit standards difficult to guarantee
- May be an attack in disguise
- May be informal channel to attackers

Security Firms

A security firm is a company that specializes in security issues. They may be a collection of consultants, but more often their audit group is an offshoot of a larger, security-related business.

Usually, these organizations are private businesses, but some industry standards and monitoring groups maintain audit branches as well. Using an industry group can give you access to top-notch talent, but you must be careful if you don't want the results of your audit to become part of that group's statistics collection process. (Typically, groups that do this are very good about anonymizing such information, however.)

Pros

- This is their core business, so quality tends to be high.
- They've probably gone through the background checks for you. And if they haven't, that tells you something about the firm.
- They are probably up to date on the latest problems. And if they haven't, that tells you something else about the firm.

Cons

- Often oversubscribed
- Moderately expensive

Audit Houses

These would be the Big Six (or Five, or however many are left by the time of this publication) auditing firms. Some are developing groups for in-depth security auditing.

Pros

- Highly detailed reporting
- Strong on methodology

Cons

- Auditing methodology may not be flexible enough to tell you what you want to know.
- May not be as technically sophisticated as you need.
- Likely to be extremely expensive.

Expectations

What You Should Expect from the Auditor

Professionalism. Your auditor should conduct himself or herself with the highest level of professionalism at all times.

Caution. An audit should never involve any physical danger to the auditors, to the network or machines being audited, or to any people involved. An audit should never disrupt service in any way except with the explicit written consent of the organization being audited, well in advance.

Full Disclosure. Some aspects of a security audit involve some odd behavior on the part of the auditor. For example, an auditor will sometimes have lunch with participants to get information that might otherwise not be revealed. An auditor may attempt to bypass physical security in order to confirm some aspect of a problem. Your auditor should meet with you at the beginning of the audit process and describe, at least in general terms, what he or she intends to do; you should give your sanction, in writing, before the auditor does anything even slightly unusual.

Well-Written Report and Thorough Presentation. An auditor should create a well-thought-out report that is understandable and presents well-justified conclusions. Where appropriate, a presentation should be made, and the opportunity to ask detailed questions of the auditor provided.

Assurance That Your Data Will Be Treated Correctly. Before the audit begins, you and the auditor should come to a documented understanding about the storage, use, and disposition of any data, direct or derived, that is a result of the audit process. The auditor should take great pains to live up to both the letter and the spirit of that agreement.

Strict Confidentiality. Any information pertaining to your audit, even anecdotal information, should be held in the strictest confidence by the auditor and his employer.

What the Auditor Should Expect from You

"Safe-Conduct" Letter. You are paying the auditor to test certain parts of your security. He should be reasonably immune for the consequences of that testing. In order to ensure this, the auditor has every right to demand a written statement absolving him of blame for whatever you and he have agreed to allow.

Sensible Behavior. Every security auditor has had the experience of being followed around the building by an employee who did his best to warn co-workers that an audit was in progress. Such behavior only reduces the effectiveness of the testing. If you are going to pay the auditor to reveal interesting information about your security, you should agree with her in advance as to what is off limits and then let her go about her work unmolested.

Commitment Follow-Up. No matter how much advance warning is given, auditors rarely come away from an audit with all the information or access they were promised. If you say that you'll mail a copy of your security policy next week, then you need to do so.

Minimum Last-Minute Changes. Some changes are inevitable, but by the time the auditor shows up at your door, you will have gone through a long and possibly painful negotiation as to the scope and duration of your audit. The minutes when the auditor is cooling his heels in your office is no time to start changing the rules of the game. Also, you should recognize that the auditor's time is worth money. A last-minute major change in expectations should also be accompanied by a willingness to renegotiate the pricing of the audit.

Political Independence. If you are interested in conducting a serious audit, then the auditor is not a weapon against your enemies in another department. The auditor cannot be expected to take part in the internal politics of your organization, and attempting to have him do so only reduces the value of the audit.

How the Audit Should Be Conducted

This is a typical schedule an audit might follow.

Negotiation. Discussions about the scope of the audit and the goals. A rough network description is provided to the auditors.

Preaudit. Advance warning about any required information. Agreements about audit scheduling and access to personnel and documentation are made. A detailed network description is provided to the auditors.

On-Site Data Collection. Measurements are made on the network. Interviews of key personnel occur. Agreements to provide subsidiary information (such as documentation that was accidentally unavailable) are made.

Off-Site Analysis. Data from the collection phase are analyzed. Subsidiary information is received. A detailed report is written. A presentation is scheduled. The audience for the presentation is characterized so that the auditor knows the level at which to speak.

Presentation. One or more presentations occur, tailored at the groups interested in the results—for example, an executive overview, a management presentation, a technical overview, and a detailed technical presentation. The customer can ask questions about the audit process and results.

Reaction. Your organization reacts to the audit typically by addressing the various issues at a technical level, sometimes by refuting the auditor's conclusions, though contentiousness should be read as a possible sign of trouble within your organization.

Follow-Up. The auditor is available for additional measurements or to confirm that particular actions were handled appropriately.

What You Should Do About the Audit Results

Develop a plan to address any action items. An audit does you little good if you don't listen to what the auditors told you. You need to assign people to confirm the various problems, investigate fixes to the problems, and then apply the fixes.

Carry out the plan. A schedule and milestones are very important here. Fixes tend to fall in two major groups: Those done by a conscientious security administrator during or immediately following the audit presentation and those that lapse for weeks or months. The sooner you fix all the problems, the easier it will be to move on to more interesting problems.

Schedule a follow-up audit to verify that all the items were addressed. A follow-up audit can be expensive, but it gives your team a deadline to work against, which can help in prioritizing the fixes.

Chapter

11

Quantifying the Value of Security

IN THIS CHAPTER:

- Perception of Value
- Process of Explaining Security Issues
- Measurements

Pity the poor network security manager. Ask him what his department does and you'll get a list of things like—but not limited to—the following:

- Protect the network from attack.
- Ensure that changes to the network which might affect security are properly handled.
- Ensure that the services the company deploys are properly designed with respect to security.
- Keep track of the ever-changing threats against the network.
- Ensure that the network is protected from threats.

Now, go to the other side of the building and pick a manager at random from some other department. Ask him what the security department does, and you'll probably get something like: "It, uh, keeps us secure?" Take that same manager out for a few beers and ask again, and there's a good chance that what you'll get is "They give me grief, that's what they do! I want to put up a simple Web server, and the damn security guys are all over me about how I can't do this, and I can't do that!" Or words to that effect.

To work back to something we discussed in Chapter 5: Security is a matter of perspective. One of the biggest difficulties faced by a security team is that the only place to see how well the team is doing is from within the team itself. Everyone else has a worse perspective. There are a number of reasons why this problem comes up so frequently with security departments.

The security process encourages its practitioners to keep their mouths shut. Because the business of security takes place on many levels both technological and social, it's difficult to know who to trust and what to trust them with. As you quickly learn, the safest course is often to keep your mouth shut and your ears and eyes open. It's much harder to reveal a secret if you are silent. Unfortunately, this can sometimes apply to areas where speaking up would make a large positive difference in how you do your job.

Note that this issue applies primarily to people actively working in the trenches of the security field. As you move further away from handling day-to-day security issues, such as in upper management or in consulting, the problem can become exactly the opposite. What every consultant sells is himself, first and foremost. In the next half-dozen articles you see quoting some "noted security expert," you'll find that the expert is almost always a consultant, not a front-line security worker. This is not to denigrate the skills of consultants but rather to point out that the rules by which they succeed are different than the rules by which a corporate security team composed of employees succeeds. A consultant thrives if people call her on the phone and want to pay her fees. That means that she must be known, and one of the best ways to become well known is to become controversial. Another is to be entertaining. This is true of not just the security field but of almost any field.

There is a key point to consider here, though. If a consultant tells interesting war stories about previous clients that give away information that should really have been kept under wraps, what will he tell his next clients about *you?* An "indiscreet security professional" is not an oxymoron yet, but it certainly ought to be.

If you're doing your job right, the results are largely "negative," anyway. If you own an office building, it's nearly impossible to measure how many times you are not broken into because you station a guard in the lobby all night. The best you can do is to measure how many times the neighboring buildings are broken into and extrapolate from there. Making that measurement is not trivial, but the number of times the police are called to various buildings is usually a matter of public record.

With computer network intrusion, the ability to do comparative studies is almost nil. Go ahead, pick a company that you consider to be your peer in size, business, network, Internet connectivity, and anything else you feel is relevant. Pick two or three. Then call them and ask them how many times their network was broken into last month. If you get even one useful response, consider yourself exceedingly fortunate. As a rule, companies announce a network penetration only when they are forced to do so by other circumstances, because a front-page *Wall Street Journal* article reporting that XYZ, Inc., was broken into is sure to make the stock value for XYZ drop considerably.

Consider also that they may not even know they've been penetrated. Their security may be much worse than yours and their monitoring may be non-existent. Given all of that, finding comparable statistics on your own is nearly impossible.

Some organizations, such as a few insurance companies, and some security organizations are beginning to compile statistics, but these measurements are in their infancy. And even so, they suffer from the same problem: Most organizations won't report a break-in even for statistical purposes because word of it might leak to the wrong people (read "the press").

The results that aren't "negative" are often difficult to understand. As we've discussed elsewhere, watching someone defend against a network attack can be quite boring for casual observers. What they expect to see is flashing lights, vivid graphics, and possibly machines exploding in a cloud of sparks. What they get, even under the most dramatic of circumstances, is much less interesting. While a change in Cisco router logs might speak volumes to a trained security engineer, an untrained observer doesn't have the background necessary to understand the difference between a log entry with a label of %SEC-6-IPACCESSLOGP and one with a label of %SEC-6-IPAC-CESSLOGDP.

The results that are easy to understand are often quite sensitive. We're not talking about a video game, after all. Granted, many attacks are simply kids fooling around, not corporate espionage, but there are few companies, if any, who want to see a major news story about fourteen-year-olds penetrating their network. If such stories become common water-cooler talk in an organization, they soon find their way outside to more sensitive forums for discussion.

Another aspect is self-preservation. Consider a situation in which Company A blocks a tenuous attack that appears to come from Company B, their arch-rival. If the security group reports this to their management and it is true, they'll be heroes. But if they are wrong, all the blame will descend on them. And they know exactly how difficult it is to prove, beyond a shadow of a doubt, to nontechnical people who are not well-versed in computer and network security that what appears to be an attack really is one. So even if the evidence is reasonably convincing and reasonably easy to grasp, the tendency of a security group is to block it and watch it but not to escalate the situation unless the evidence becomes completely overwhelming and indisputable.

The upshot of all of these issues is that your security group may be working night and day to protect your network, but nobody else knows what they do, how they do it, or why.

Perception of Value

Marketing people are fond of saying that perception matters more than reality, especially when it comes to explaining to engineers why their sensible modifications are being postponed so that the product can be reengineered to have a more colorful exterior. The truth is somewhat more complex and subtle, of course. Perceptions do matter, especially in the short term. In the longer term, actual performance can matter more than perception, but there is no guarantee, and deciding what is long term versus short term can be very tricky. And having a long term outlook is useful only if your organization survives long enough for it to apply.

For those reasons, any serious security effort should include a plan for making sure that the value of what is being done is brought to the attention of the people who pay for it. We are not talking about ways to dress up a poorly performing group so that it appears better than it really is. What we are discussing is a set of tools for demonstrating the value that is inherent in any good security team, value that may not be obvious to outsiders without explicit demonstration. A well-run, smoothly functioning security team should be appreciated. Your goal, therefore, should be to create a situation in which your team is given credit for everything to which they are entitled credit. No more, no less.

To see that your group is properly appreciated, think a bit about what it takes to make someone appreciate something.

Business people will appreciate something if they

- can see it.
- can understand it.
- agree that it is valuable.
- know they couldn't do it as well themselves.
- can show it to their boss.
- can get their boss to understand it.
- can get their boss to agree that it is valuable.

Any solution that successfully addresses the issues in the list will find no difficulty in being embraced by a business as a vital part of their organization. Let's discuss these issues specifically.

"See it." Yes, you're absolutely right. It's impossible to demonstrate to anybody how many times your network was *not* penetrated last week. But there are many different things you can show about your security, such as reports specifying how many computers are being monitored; what types of attacks can be detected; how many attack detections happen per day, per week, per month; the average time of response to each incident.

And for any of these items, you can also show trending. How did your routers score this week versus last week, versus the week before? How many new attack signatures were added this week? Trends are not only interesting, they're vital for both setting expectations and showing how well you are living up to expectations.

The flip side is also worth considering. If you *don't* make some particular useful piece of information visible, then you cannot be appreciated for having collected it. Some facts are not directly useful or relevant for the lay person, but any piece of information that you've taken the trouble to collect ought to be represented somewhere in your report structure, even if it is combined with many others to form a composite fact. And if you have information that is not relevant to your monitoring and never contributes to a larger picture of your security, then why are you collecting it in the first place?

"Understand it." As with any information display, there are two types of understanding that are critical here: *implicit* understanding, or the degree to which the display makes the viewer aware of both the question being asked and its answer, and *contextual* understanding, the background necessary to understand what the information on the display really means. If you had a graph showing a declining trend in frobistals per hour (Figure 11-1), even though your graph design is clear, the viewer will be left in the dark until he knows the context—what a frobistal is and what ranges of frobistal activity are normal, excessive, and inadequate.

The design of effective information displays is a topic far larger than can be covered here, but you should keep two key principles in mind as you design a report or a display that is intended to prove to your management that what you are doing is worthwhile.

> *Minimize unstated context.* In Figure 11-1, the graph is worthless unless you understand what a frobistal is. Consider the graph in Figure 11-2. Someone looking at that graph knows that there was a

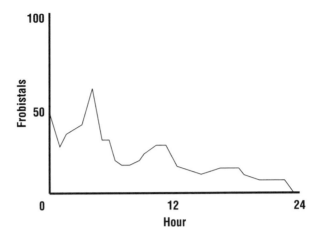

Figure 11-1: Frobistals per hour—poor context

problem in the morning, California time, but that it wasn't too serious, that it mostly went away before lunch time, and that it was almost completely gone by the end of the day. They still don't know what a frobistal is, but they know that they probably don't need to worry too much about the frobistal rate now. You can imagine a more elaborate graph that would show other interesting information, such as a better indication of trends, and you can even imagine a legend that would define "frobistal." Any of these features would be helpful to this graph to make it more quickly understood.

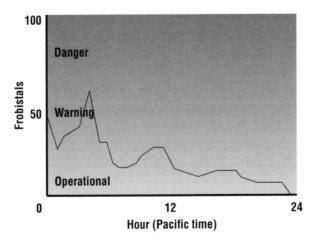

Figure 11-2: Frobistals per hour—better context

The principle of minimizing unstated context says that you should design your displays so that they contain as much context as is necessary for your target audience to quickly understand what you are trying to say. To understand why this is important, imagine that you're explaining to your boss a problem illustrated by Figure 11-2. You spend fifteen minutes carefully explaining the problem and how the display relates to it. He asks for a hard copy of the graph, which you supply. He then takes it and forwards copies to his boss and the president of your organization with *no* other explanation, or at best, a minimal one. If your display is unclear, you could suddenly have a bunch of irate executives demanding an explanation. If you've used a fancy Web-based reporting system, where the context is just one mouse click away, you're out of luck because you can't click on a sheet of paper. Your goal, therefore, should be to create reports that can be understood with the shortest possible explanation by someone only slightly familiar with the problem. You may create more complicated reports for yourself and your team, but don't depend on them for continued funding.

Minimize unnecessary ink. Having just implied that your reports should contain entire dictionaries of background in your reports, this principle implies the exact opposite. You should use every bit of "ink" necessary on your report to make the message of the report clear in the mind of the viewer and not one bit more ink than that. "Ink" of course, refers not to an actual chemical substance but to the details (be they physical or electronic) that distinguish your report from a blank page.

These two principles form a sort of feedback system. If you live up to both, then you'll write management reports that serve their purpose. If principles fall out of balance, then you'll end up with a cluttered display that nobody bothers to look at or a sparse one that nobody understands.

> *Create management reports with all and only the information necessary for them to be understood by people two levels of management above you in 30 seconds or less.*
>
> *For complicated issues, assume that you are also allowed one easily remembered paragraph of explanation. Write the paragraph and make sure that anyone who can see the report can also see the paragraph.*

"Agree that it is valuable." Wonderful reports do you little good if your audience doesn't know why they are valuable. The best way to ensure this perception is to design good reports and then test them with your audience. A common mistake in this process is to go to your audience with a blank sheet of paper and ask, "What do you want to see?" Instead, ask yourself, "If I were my boss, what would I find valuable in a report like this?" and develop a rough draft. Then merge your mental simulation with reality by checking with your boss and seeing if he actually does find it valuable. Repeating this process for many different types of reports and several iterations each will get you much more useful feedback and help you educate your boss about what you do as well as helping him educate you about what he wants.

"Knows he couldn't do it as well himself." This is a somewhat odd phenomenon that occurs in technical organizations more than other companies. Many engineers and technical people who have risen into management have a tendency to dismiss tasks they themselves know how to perform as being worth less expenditure of resources than jobs they know they can't handle. Oddly enough, this tendency is almost entirely unaffected by the person's workload. The fact that the person complaining, who may indeed be competent to perform the task, has no time available to take that task on is mostly irrelevant.

A common and unfortunate way for security people to handle this reaction of managers is to be extremely secretive and cryptic about what they do in the hopes of creating the impression that their jobs are much harder and much less understandable than they really are. Taking this position can work for a while, but it tends to make all justifications for security issues a matter of faith: "Trust me, it's hard!" It's as much a mistake, in the long run, to make a security task look harder than it really is as it is to make it look easier.

A much better choice is to find ways to play to the time issue. By not disagreeing with the notion that another person can handle the job but instead pointing out how many man-hours are expended on the job and possibly even soliciting additional help from other groups, you can often turn a potential critic into a supporter. At worst, this happens for no other reason than that the person does not wish to have his group distracted from their goals by having to work on your issues. At best, it offers the technical manager insight into how much actual work is being done, and when their mental estimates correspond with your actual estimates, they can develop an appreciation for your ability to know what you are doing as well.

"Can show it to the boss, can get the boss to understand it, can get the boss to agree that it is valuable." These three issues are actually a much deeper issue than they appear to be at first. A very powerful strategy for being successful in any business venture is this: "Make anybody who partners with you successful." Success in the security business, as in many others, looks something like this:

- What you are doing works.
- People who support what you're doing find more and more reasons to want you to keep doing it.
- People who do not support what you're doing find fewer and fewer reasons to want to stop you from doing it.

The way you achieve that is by developing strategies that get your job done and by developing explanations for the strategies that convince others that you're doing the right things, and by developing reports that enlist those people as proselytizers for your cause.

Process of Explaining Security Issues

Underlying the issues of appreciation is the issue of expectations. In many sections of this book, we discuss how the expectations of people not directly involved in computer and network security are wildly different from what can actually be built and operated. So if you look at the criteria for appreciation in the previous section and think of each one on a numeric scale, many of them start not at zero but at a significant negative value, because of expectations.

Prior expectations can work against appreciation.

Let's talk for a moment about a process you can use to explain to other people what you've done.

- Set expectations correctly.
- Meet expectations visibly.
- Exceed expectations usefully.
- Present information theatrically.

It sounds like something out of a management handbook, but sometimes even those books have something valuable in them. This process can be applied to any aspect of security value quantification.

Set expectations correctly. Any piece of security reporting, whether a graph, a talk, or an automatically generated report, should show the audience not only what you've done but how what you've done relates to what you could or should have done. Consider the usefulness of this statement—"We blocked ten denial-of-service attacks last month"—versus this one—"We blocked ten denial-of-service attacks last month compared with nine the previous month. Organizations comparable to ours detect an average of eleven attacks like this per month." The context of the data is as important as the data themselves.

Meet expectations visibly. Set a measurable scale of "reasonability" and then show your audience how you rate on the scale. As with the setting expectations example, you need both historical trend information and comparison information. Comparison information in security is notoriously difficult to come up with, but you might consider the partnership technique explained earlier. Go to security conferences and actively seek out people from organizations like your own. Explain what you are looking for, and offer to partner with them for the purposes of exchanging sanitized security statistics. It takes only a few for the effect to be felt positively, and your partners will find the exchange as valuable as you do.

Exceed expectations usefully. Once you've set the stage for your audience to understand how your department can be successful, you actually have to *be* successful by your criteria. One thing you should never do is make up criteria to make your group look good. Actively solicit opinions about the criteria you select, and ask your advisors to try and think up ways to misinterpret them. If your security group looks as if it is doing a good job according to a reasonable number of difficult-to-dismiss measurements, then your potential critics will not have very much to latch onto.

Present information theatrically. It's easy to take this point much too far or to dismiss it too easily. I've sat through far too many presentations where the speaker buries the key point on a minor slide in unreadably small fonts, and I've been at a few where the presenter is so overwhelmingly bullish about his topic that you find it difficult to take anything he or she says without a grain of salt. Learning to convey information to your audience so that they will remember it, appreciate it for the reasons you think they should appreciate it, and understand the point you are trying to make is an important part of any job, and, compared to forensic analysis of a stack-smashing attack or understanding cryptographically protected virtual private net-working, it's relatively easy to learn. There are classes you can take and books you can read, and you have endless opportunities to practice, if you want to take them. If you can learn to give four short, satisfying presentations about what you do per year, few obstacles will stand in your path to success.

Measurements

Now let's look at some of the things you can quantify in your reports.

Attacks

- How many total declared attacks occurred over a time period?
- How many attacks were suitable for pursuit of the attacker?
- How far did the pursuit go?
- How many attacks of a particular kind occurred over a time period?
- How do the attack numbers compare with those of similar organizations?
- What were the most popular attacks?
- Characterize the mix of attackers (browsers/campers/vandals, spies/saboteurs, insiders)
- How is the attack mix changing over time?
- How does the attack mix compare with those of similar organizations?

Defenses

- How many types of attacks do we know how to detect?
- How many types of attacks do we currently know how to defend against?
- How have our defenses changed over a time period?
- How many transitions to "possible attack" alert status occurred?
- How many transitions to "definite attack" alert status occurred?
- How many of the transitions were justified by the attack post-mortem?
- How many attacks were handled by the passive defenses?
- How many attacks required human intervention?

Security Organization

- Shift coverage
- Skill set coverage
- Attacks per shift
- Mean time to respond to an attack
- Mean time to respond to a change request
- Mean time to respond to a security review

Third-Party Audits

- Time since last full audit
- Serious issues raised by last audit
- Issues responded to since last audit
- Number of outstanding issues from last audit

Education

- What sources do we monitor for new attack signatures?
- How has that list changed over time?
- Which sources are proving the most useful?
- What training has the security group focused on over a time period?

Data for any or all of these issues should be collected as a routine part of your security process. If you can build from the data a short status report presentation for the people who pay the bills of your organization on a regular basis, you'll make your professional life and that of your team a lot easier.

Chapter 12

Preparing for an Attack

IN THIS CHAPTER:

- Getting Started
- War Games
- Post-Mortem Analysis
- Developing a Response Plan
- Personnel
- Safety Equipment
- Survival Pack Contents
- Choosing Hiding Places
- Set Your Own Ground Rules

> *The worst time to invent a policy is when you need it.*

To this point, we've discussed the steps you should take to prevent an attack from being successful. With any luck at all, those fortifications are all you'll ever need, and you'll be able to sleep well at night.

But . . . let's suppose for a minute that those precautions aren't enough. Let's suppose that, even though you've done all the things you're supposed to do to protect your network, there is still a way in that you hadn't thought of or protected against. Now, picture yourself coming into work one day, and one of your security team members comes running up to you, frowning with worry, with a message that someone has broken into your network.

What will you do then? What *exactly* will your next action be? If you don't know, then you still have work to be done.

Getting Started

What you need is a plan. An "In Case of Network Penetration, Break Glass" plan. There are a lot of ways you can create such a plan. The most obvious is to sit down with this book and perhaps a few others and write a plan. Then you march in to your team, pass out copies, and say, "Make it so." That might work just fine.

Let me suggest another way: Play a game. Make it simple at first. Hide a handful of files in interesting places around your network. Don't work too hard to hide them, and don't do anything dangerous to your production systems. Then announce to your team that you've done so, and them to to find the files. Set a time limit. Less than a day is a good choice, leaving time to discuss it afterward while it is still fresh in everybody's minds. Take notes as your team goes through the exercise.

When the fun is over, have the debriefing session. Here are some of the things that you want answers to:

- What was the biggest frustration you had in solving this problem?

- What additional logs would have helped you solve the problem sooner?

- What additional tools would have helped you solve the problem sooner?

- Who took charge of the hunt, and why?

- What utility programs did you use in the hunt?

If you've never done this kind of exercise before, you will learn quite a lot from the first one. Summarize the things you've learned, and implement the ones that you can quickly.

Once you've put a few of the suggestions into practice, do it again. Play another game. Make it harder this time, and start it without warning. Perhaps, if you like, declare the most popular utility used in the first game to be off limits in this one. Say that it has been "contaminated" and cannot be trusted.

Run through the exercise, and keep track of what you see happening. At the debrief, ask the same questions as before and few new ones:

- What did we do better this time?

- What did we do worse this time?

- Did the changes we made to the system help or hinder us, or did they have no effect at all?

Create a summary of your results of both games. Then, and only then, sit down with this book and those other few and start to write an attack preparation plan. If you've made the games challenging and interesting for your team, when you discuss your plan with them they'll be very attentive and interested and will have many useful suggestions.

War Games

The idea of holding a training game is not a new one. Military organizations have been testing their organizations this way for much of human history. Games like chess were devised to teach battle strategy. But for most businesses, the idea of a war game as a means of policy design and testing may be unfamiliar.

A war game is a valuable exercise at several levels:

- It exercises your existing policies and procedures.

- It helps to point out where your policies and procedures fall short.

- It familiarizes your staff with your policies and procedures at an applied rather than an intellectual level.

- It familiarizes your staff with the tools at their disposal and the systems that they are protecting in conditions that mimic very closely an actual security problem.

The last point is very important. The United States Marine Corps has a saying that is applicable to network security:

> *Train the way you fight. Fight the way you train.*

The defenses that keep attacks from happening are important, but you must assume that one day, an alarm will go off and you will need to react quickly and correctly to protect your network. A war game allows you to practice your responses and to test and improve them so that you can focus on the situation rather than having to invent policy in real time.

There are three levels at which you should consider holding war games:

Theoretical Level. A theoretical game is one conducted primarily in the minds of the players. Think of it as a game of Dungeons and Dragons. Gather your people together in a quiet room, with adequate whiteboards and sketchpads. Assign the following roles to some of the participants:

- *Recorder,* whose job it is to take notes on what is said and done

- *Systems judge,* who rules on whether or not your current network and computer systems can fulfill what you ask of them during the course of the game

- *Game judge,* who rules on whether a move was adequate and who determines when the objective of the game has been reached or whether the game has stalled

Pose a simple problem and then work through the problem with your group. It will take a few tries before your team gets the hang of gaming in this fashion, but it can be both fun and instructive. The systems judge and the game judge can be the same person if participants are limited, but in a more complicated game, that may be asking a lot of a single person.

The systems judge responds to actions players take with the computer and network systems. For example, if a player asked for a search of log files for a specific type of record, the systems judge would rule whether or not the record was in the log files. In a more complicated game, the systems judge might require that the player attempt login to the logging server, which may or may not be denied based on the game, and then would provide more specific answers to the record question. Keep it simple at first so that all participants can become accustomed to the gaming style, and then increase the complexity to keep the game interesting.

If the systems judge is a surrogate for your computer systems, the game judge is a surrogate for the real world. The game judge rules on moves such as "and then we have him arrested," determining whether enough evidence has been gathered, whether law enforcement has been notified correctly, and so forth. For simple games, the game judge can be any member of the team. For more complicated games, this role will evolve to become the *game master,* who creates the problem and provides the systems judge with any required background material needed to carry out the game. As your group becomes more skilled at these games, the role of game master should rotate among the team members, who each create interesting games based on your systems.

It's helpful to keep this type of game light, fun, and fast paced, and yet work through real problems. Games can be won by the team if the problem is solved within the allotted time or by the game master if the problem cannot be solved because of a significant weakness in the network, computer, or procedural infrastructure. A game that cannot be solved (or can be solved trivially) but results in no insight into your systems is an impasse and results in both sides losing. Your goal, as manager of the team, is to review games beforehand and try to avoid the ones that will result in an impasse.

Small, clever rewards can be given to the winners. The rewards are symbolic, but symbols can be a great motivator if used correctly.

Practical Level. This type of game uses your own systems and thus requires no systems judge. A member of your team is designated the Fox. This person makes a significant but not dangerous change to your network. The remainder of the team are the Hounds, who must find the change and safely fix it in a specific period of time.

The role of the game judge in this case is to review the proposed change *before* it is made and verify that it is significant (i.e., it is not a change that would happen in the course of normal use of your system or one that would be of little educational value) and relatively harmless. During the game, the game judge's role is to monitor the behavior of your systems and any trouble reports and to call off the game if the gaming change is causing unexpected problems. The game judge is also the person who authorizes the proposed fix so that inappropriate modifications are not made to your systems as a result of overzealous gamers.

Some variations that can make the game more realistic, more interesting, and more engaging for the players:

- *How the change is announced.* A real attacker does not typically attend your staff meetings and announce that a change has been made to your system. But attackers do sometimes brag to each other and to their victims. Obviously you cannot use an underground bulletin board to announce your drills, but a little imagination can make your exercise considerably closer to reality. Any extremely realistic announcement should be cleared in advance with the game judge, however, and all such announcements should contain a code word, which changes from game to game, to ensure that the game isn't mistaken for a real attack.

- *Clues.* If your system is adequately logged and protected, it should be very difficult for an attacker to make a change without leaving some clues. You probably do not want to go as far as doctoring your log files to supply clues for an exercise like this, but you can simply make up clues and announce them at the beginning of the exercise as a given. As your games grow more complex, you may choose to add false or misleading clues to approximate real situations.

- *How the game is scheduled.* A theoretical game should be scheduled in advance with all team members because it is, for all intents and purposes, a meeting, and should not interfere with other activities. As your practical games grow more realistic, you can add some elements of surprise to them by announcing them with no advance warning (except for the Fox, of course). Considerable realism can be gained by starting a game in the middle of the night or on weekends, but there are obvious consequences to doing this too often or without buy-in from your staff or management.

- *Who is the Fox?* Normally, the identity of the Fox will be known in advance by your team, unless you've taken pains to keep it a secret. For that reason, in a normal game, you'll probably want to keep the Fox separate from the Hounds during the course of the game so that body language and facial expressions do not give clues that would not exist in a real situation. A very realistic and somewhat disturbing game variation that can be played after your team is familiar with the Fox and Hounds exercise is one in which you quietly select the Fox well in advance of the game, allow her to make the change, and then do not announce her identity. The Fox is then part of the Hound team and can cooperate or deceive as circumstances permit. Variations on this include games where the Hounds know that a traitor may be among them and where they have been led to believe that the Fox is not among them. Because this game depends on abusing the bonds of trust between your team members, it should not be played too often, but it is important to play it from time to time so that all team members are aware of the concept of a defector in their ranks and any potential real-life defectors are aware that the team has been trained to spot such problems.

- *Variations on a theme.* There are many different ways in which you can make games more difficult. The trick is to make them more interesting and educational as well. One good way of doing this is to run several exercises in a row with more or less similar changes. The first game would be run as normal, but the second would be run with the most popular and useful tool of game 1 being out of bounds; you could simulate that it was compromised or untrustworthy in some way. The goal here is, of course, to train your team in ways to cope with attacker-induced problems as well as different ways to solve the same problem.

Unlimited Level. This type of game is the most dangerous. You designate a small group of your people as the Red team, the remainder as the Green team. The job of the Red team is to attack and the job of the Green team is to defend.

There are many possible variations on this game:

- *Zero knowledge.* The Red team must prove that they were able to learn any feature of the system they chose to exploit from the outside, rather then from their knowledge of the system as insiders. The goal here is to develop a good picture of what information can be deduced about your network from the outside.

- *Full knowledge.* The Red team is allowed to use any information and authentication they have at their disposal as members of the security team. The goal here is to learn how effective your mechanisms for tracking internal and high-privilege users are.

- *Jumpstart.* In this variation, the assumption is made that the attackers have the ability to bypass some important safeguard, regardless of whether or not that ability can be justified technically. An example would be to assume that the attackers have the ability to avoid being blocked by the packet filtering provisions of your routers. The goal here is to determine your vulnerability if a major component of your network hardening is suddenly ineffective.

- *Complete.* A larger part of your organization, beyond the security team, is involved. The goal here is to test how readily important information passes between your security team and the rest of the company and how well the various groups interact.

- *Warm.* Some changes are allowed to be made to your systems by the Red team, but those changes must be reviewed by the game judge before they are made. The Red team uses restraint in making changes so as not to affect the production aspects of your network.

- *Hot.* No constraints. All safeguards are off. The Red team is free to do anything they believe they can accomplish. This is obviously the most dangerous variation and will require full management buy-in, careful planning, and complete indemnification for the Red team members.

This game is similar to, but not exactly the same as, a penetration study, which is a common form of network auditing. The difference here is that the game is being played by the defenders, not so much to prove that a hole exists as to improve their knowledge of the systems they are defending. A penetration study is performed by an outside agency, a third party, whose only goal is to write a report indicating that a successful penetration has occurred. In that case, the penetrators learn a great deal about your network, but you, the defenders, learn relatively little, except that a hole was uncovered. In an unlimited game, the defenders learn a great deal about their systems, and no outsiders learn anything.

Post-Mortem Analysis

You can learn from a war game through several basic tools:

Careful Note Taking. During the entire game process, the judges and you should be scrupulously taking notes on everything you observe. You'll get a sense for what is important after several games and several post-mortems, but for the first few, you'll want to be fanatic about keeping notes. It will become clear that everybody saw the game slightly differently, so your notes are what will keep you focused on what you saw and heard.

Participant Logs. For complicated games, especially ones in which actual modifications may be made to working machines, a participant log is an absolute necessity. In particular, any machine change should be noted and brought up during the debriefing session so that you can decide whether or not it needs to be undone. Players should also make special notes of any difficulties they encounter, technical, procedural, bureaucratic, or otherwise.

Post-Game Debriefing. After every game, you'll want to gather the players together in a single room and work through how everything went. You'll collect the logs at this time, if appropriate, and get an initial sense of how all the participants evaluated the game. Make this short and sweet: Post an agenda, and work through it quickly. But make sure that everyone is encouraged to participate and contribute. The final agenda item should be to create an action item list.

Action Item Summary. Based on the debrief and the collected notes, you'll want to write up an action item report detailing exactly what, if anything, should be done as a result of your experiences with this game. Like all action items, yours should have the names of responsible parties associated with them and times for their completion. Action items can include changes to the systems, changes to procedures and policies, and anything else that requires someone to actually modify something. If possible, action items should be tracked and in future games (or real incidents), you should note whether the changes improved or reduced the effectiveness of the systems to which they were made.

Post-Game Summary. The action item summary concentrated on what should be done. A summary of the debriefing session, with a reference to the action item report, should concentrate on what was learned in the game. Both should be distributed to all participants in the game and filed for later reference.

The post-mortem analysis should become a regular part of your routine and should be the one part of every war game that is *exactly* the same as what you'll do when a real incident comes along. The better you get at this process, the better your defenses will be.

Developing a Response Plan

Playing a few rounds of the simplest games will give you a good feel for what to do in the event of an attack. But even though games give you a good sense of what will work and what won't, games aren't enough. A game will train your people to respond more or less correctly to situations they've been exposed to, but you need to develop a response plan that gives them a framework for responding to any security situation, including ones that catch them by surprise.

One of the things you should have learned from your games is that people can get very excited in situations where they are expected to defend something. An attack in progress is disturbing and threatening and invigorating, all at the same time. Time is critical, and you don't know the extent of the danger. In the case of computer security, the danger is probably not life-threatening, but it is real enough. Correct action must be taken quickly to minimize the damage.

Mistakes can cost you time and money. If you were off site and called in during such a situation, probably the first thing you'd want to know as a manager would be who was in charge of the situation. Therefore, your first order of business in writing a response plan should be to determine a means by which your team can designate a leader themselves. You could define a path from "all is well" to "we have a problem" and back to "all is well" that automatically assigns appropriate responsibility based on the current state of affairs. A good way to do this is to define states that cover all the conditions you expect to encounter and then define actions that must be taken.

The next few pages contain a simplified example of such a plan, showing the structure and the transitions between each state. For those of you with an analytical computer science background, it has been designed like a finite state automaton (Figure 12-1).

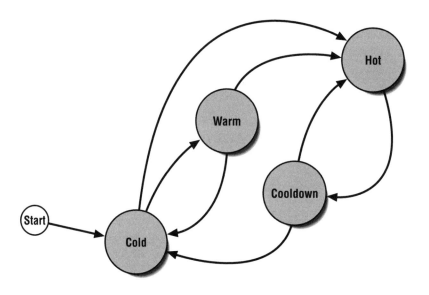

Figure 12-1: Finite state model for response plan

Condition: Cold

Definition: Normal state of affairs; no threats detected

On duty: Security Watch Officer

Priorities: *Watch Team*
      Monitor systems and logs for activity.

Transition to Warm

Declared when either (a) a significant attack is in progress or (b) evidence indicates that an attack may have gotten past the outer defense perimeter.

Declared by: Security Watch Officer

Approved by: No further approval required

Actions Required

- Log transition to Warm condition.

- Call Response Team Manager to station.

- Initiate investigation of attack or possible penetration.

Transition to Hot

Declared when it is immediately apparent that a major penetration has occurred and rapid response is required.

Declared by: Security Watch Officer

Approved by: No further approval required

Actions Required

- Log transition to Hot condition.

- Call Response Team Manager to station.

- Call Forensics Team Manager to station.

- Call additional Watch Team Members to station.

- Response Team: Initiate blocking action against attacker.

- Forensics Team: Determine time, extent, source of penetration.

Condition: Warm

Definition:	An attack is in progress or unconfirmed evidence of a penetration has been discovered.
On duty:	Security Watch Officer, Response Team Manager
Priorities:	*Watch Team* Continue monitoring for activity. *Response Team* 1. Confirm attack or penetration. 2. Decide whether to go to Hot condition.

Transition to Cold

Declared when it has been confirmed that the triggering condition for escalation to warm was in error.

Declared by: Response Team Manager

Approved by: Security Watch Officer

Actions Required

- Log transition to Cold condition.

- Log reasons for transition to Warm status.

- Log reasons why Warm-to-Hot transition was not required.

- (Optional for Response Team Manager) File request for Watchstander procedural review regarding this incident.

Transition to Hot

Declared when sufficient evidence of an attack has been accumulated.

Declared by: Response Team Manager

Approved by: No further approval required

Actions Required

- Log transition to Hot condition.

- Call Forensics Team Manager to station.

- Call additional Response Team members to station.

- Call additional Watch Team members to station.

Condition: Hot

Definition: A serious attack is in progress and/or a penetration has been confirmed.

On duty: Security Watch Officer, additional Watchstanders, Response Team Manager, additional Response Team members, Forensics Team Manager, additional Forensics Team members.

Priorities: *Watch Team*

Continue monitoring for additional attacks.

Response Team

1. Safeguard the functioning of the production network.
2. Safeguard the network against additional attack.

Forensics Team

1. Determine the extent of any penetration.
2. Determine the method of penetration.
3. Determine the source of penetration.

Transition to Cooldown

Declared when all parties agree that the incident has been contained and sufficient damage control work has been accomplished so that no reoccurrence is likely.

Declared by: Response Team Manager

Approved by: Security Watch Officer, Forensics Team Manager

Actions Required

Log transition to Cooldown condition.

Condition: Cooldown

Definition: A major security incident has occurred and is now believed to be under control.

On duty: Security Watch Officer, additional Watchstanders, Response Team Manager, additional Response Team members, Forensics Team Manager, additional Forensics Team members.

Priorities: *Watch Team*
1. Continue monitoring for additional attacks.
2. Release additional Watchstanders from duty as soon as feasible.

Response Team
1. Complete any actions necessitated by incident.
2. Conduct Response Team debriefing.
3. Write Response Team Incident Report.
4. Release additional Response Team members from duty as soon as feasible.

Forensics Team
1. Complete any actions necessitated by incident.
2. Conduct Forensics Team debriefing.
3. Write Forensics Team Incident Report.
4. Release additional Response Team members from duty as soon as feasible.

Transition to Cold

Declared when all action items relating to the incident have been completed.

Declared by: Response Team Manager

Approved by: Security Watch Officer, Forensics Team Manager

Actions Required

> Log transition to Cold condition.

Transition to Hot

Declared when an indication that the transition to Cooldown was premature or in error.

Declared by: Response Team Manager

Approved by: No further approval necessary

Actions Required

- Log transition back to Hot condition.

- Recall all personnel to duty stations.

- (Optional for Response Team Manager) File request for procedural review of Hot standdown handling of this incident.

Personnel

Three teams are involved in the response plan: Watch, Response, and Forensics. The Watch Team was discussed in Chapter 9. Their role is to monitor your warning systems and defenses and to handle normal day-to-day operations, as well as to handle very simple security incidents.

The Response Team is tasked with immediate handling of much more critical situations. Their job in a crisis is essentially to determine what you will do *right now*. They are in charge of the overall response to an incident. This includes a preliminary assessment of the means used by an attacker to penetrate your network, if possible. The roles and duties of the Response Team will be discussed in much more detail in Chapter 13.

The Forensics Team has the job of damage assessment and recovery. They examine your infrastructure in great detail after an incident and determine which machines were contaminated and how badly and which systems must be rebuilt and which, if any, can be repaired; they confirm or determine what the method of penetration was (if that has not already been determined by the Response Team) and if it has been adequately closed.

It may seem to you, after reading the response plan, that an awful lot of people must be involved for this type of defense to be workable. To some degree that is true. You cannot implement this type of defense with only one or two people. But keep in mind that we are defending a reasonably large organization, which requires a defense commensurate with what is being protected, which implies a moderate-size security organization.

On the other hand, you don't need dozens of people, either. A perfectly good example is likely to be not very far from your home: the volunteer fire department. The volunteers are people who work at other jobs but have undergone training and participate in drills so that, in the event of a fire, the small number of full-time fire fighters employed by your community can operate as if there were many, many more. A small number of full-time security people can be augmented by others from your organization whose primary role is elsewhere but who fill in as part of the security team when needed.

Safety Equipment

One of the reasons businesses and schools have fire drills is to familiarize people with what to do, where to go, and how to cope with the situation. Another reason is to make sure that evacuation has been planned correctly. Are there fire extinguishers near places where they might be needed? Are they fully charged and functional? Are too many people scheduled to go down the same stairwell?

Computer security drills such as the ones discussed at the beginning of this chapter are done for much the same reasons. At the end of each drill, you do a post-mortem analysis that covers what you learned from the drill, what problems you discovered, and what worked well. You develop a list of action items and then attempt to accomplish each of those items before the next drill (or real incident). Part of what you learn, especially if you play the versions of the game where certain pieces of critical software are contaminated, is how difficult it is to restore trust in a contaminated system and how difficult it is to operate in a situation where your basic tools are unavailable.

If you design a building, you are required by law to distribute safety equipment of various kinds around your facility so that they will be easily available in the event of an emergency. Your computer network is probably as complicated as your building is, and it certainly is of similar importance. You should be able to do the same thing on your network: Place caches of important software where it will be available to your security team in the event of an emergency.

There are two basic kinds of caches you'll need to concern yourself with:

- An exposed cache is one that resides on a machine that may be a target for attack.

- A protected cache is one that is kept in a safe place until needed and is not accessible to attackers without physical access to a part of your facility.

Exposed caches are generally the most useful, but they are also in the greatest danger of alteration. They should be hidden on each system in such a way that they will be known to the members of your security team but not apparent to intruders. Following are some concerns about hiding a cache like this:

- *How do you unpack it?* For example, you may choose to hide your cache of software in the form of a system archive file. If that is the plan, how will you know that the tar program that you use to unpack the archive has not been contaminated?

- *How do you prevent it from being spotted by an attacker?* Clearly, a directory called /emergency-tools containing copies of system software is not the right answer.

- *How do you determine whether the cache has been tampered with?* If the attacker can replace your safe tools with his own compromised ones, then the advantage goes to the attacker.

What you are looking for here is not a guarantee, because there cannot be one on a system that has been thoroughly penetrated by an attacker. What you are looking for is an acceptable level of risk. If you can place a cache of tools on a machine, and the cache does not draw the attention of an attacker, then you have a capability that may allow you to recover quickly from situations where the attacker is expecting that recovery will take a significant amount of time.

Survival Pack Contents

What do you want in your cache? Well, first you want tools that are minimally dependent on other parts of the system outside the cache in order to work. For example, you would not want dynamically linked program binaries, because contamination of a single system library could affect any dynamically linked program, including your "safe" ones. Beyond that, you'll want the following tools:

- *Basic tools:* a shell listing directories, listing running processes, searching for files, editing files, changing file permissions

- *Systems administration tools:* file system backup and restore utilities, network access utilities for at least simple file transfer, file compression/decompression utilities, utilities for examining the state of the operating system

- *Security-related tools:* advanced file checksums, file comparisons, signature lists

You will almost certainly want to add a few tools of your own to the cache, but you want to avoid complicated tools and tools whose capture could give the attacker an advantage. The point here is not to give yourself a full environment as much as it is to give yourself a bare minimum of trustworthy tools to work with.

Having selected a list of tools, you must assemble them into a package. Consider the environment you'll be using them in. Everything on the contaminated system is suspect. Your "survival pack" is the only set of programs you trust. What you want under such circumstances is a single directory with all the tools in it. Then you can set up your trusted shell, point your path only at this single directory, and operate in reasonable safety. You can easily create such an environment on a test system and debug its setup carefully before you commit it to use.

Once you have the survival pack in the shape you'd like it to be in, you can pack it up for distribution. You have a number of choices here, roughly categorized into these options:

- *Be cautious.* Create a simple package that requires only one or two simple utilities to unpack (Figure 12-2).

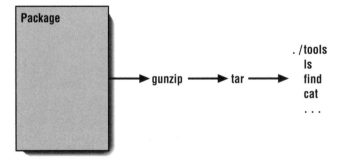

Figure 12-2: Simple survival pack

- *Be slightly paranoid.* Create a more complex package, one that requires one simple utility to unpack (such as tar) (Figure 12-3). Place copies of this program in different places on your target systems and give them nonthreatening names that don't attract attention. Embedded within the outer package will be all the utilities necessary to unpack a complete package, as well as an inner package.

- *Be extremely paranoid.* Create a self-extracting package that requires no external software to unpack, perhaps requires a password, and logs a message to some central authority indicating that extraction has been attempted. Or better yet, burn the package onto a CD-ROM that you can mount and use directly.

What you might want to consider is creating all three survival packs, and putting them on your target systems. If an attacker discovers them, he'll have to waste time unpacking them, defeating your precautions, repacking them, and eliminating any traces that he was there. That means that he spends more time on your systems and performs more activity, thereby increasing his risk of discovery. Or he simply deletes your packages, in which case you're no worse off than as if you'd done nothing, and you have a measure of the thoroughness of your opponent.

You want to keep a record of an advanced checksum of all of the various forms of your survival pack. Having a program *inside* the package that appears to be

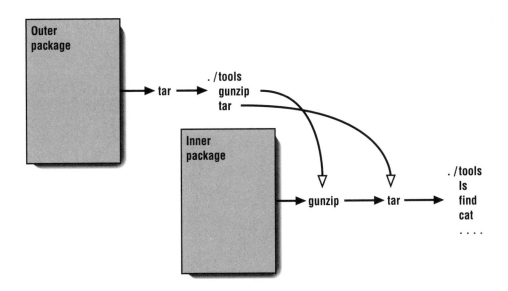

Figure 12-3: Complex survival pack

something else but that verifies the contents of the package is also not a bad idea. Utilizing all of these tests to verify the integrity of your pack before using it should be part of your forensics checklist.

You also might want to leave a set of tools in a hidden directory outside any package on each machine. If the attacker is using an automated tool to compromise your machine, it will not know about the location of the clear package (unless you allow the location to become common knowledge) and will not modify it. That way, you'll have access to safe tools that much faster. If the clear tools are modified by the attacker for some reason, then you've learned something about the attacker.

Choosing Hiding Places

There is no simple rule I can provide for locating a hiding place that will not be found by attackers, yet will be easily used by you. The reason for that should be obvious: Attackers will either read this book as well, or will quickly deduce the rule from other systems that apply it. There are some guidelines that will allow you to select your own hiding places, however.

> *The best place to hide a needle is in a pile of needles.*

. . . especially if the searcher doesn't know that there is anything special about one of the needles. You could hide a survival package by placing it in a special directory with extremely restrictive permissions and a special nonsense file name. In fact, chances are good that such a technique would work against many attackers. But if you hide it this way, you are calling attention to this special file. What you really want is for the attacker not to know that it is special. So you might consider hiding it in some place where there are a lot of obscure files, giving it a name that matches the other file names, and giving it similar protection. Of course, you want to make sure that you don't cause it to be used accidentally by the attacker (or anybody else). And you want to make sure that it doesn't stand out simply because of its size: One really large file in a directory of small ones is usually a sign of something unusual.

> *Hide by misdirection.*

Your attacker will attempt to make his files look like something they are not but in a way that will cause you to ignore them. You can do the same thing for yourself. If you create a file called `/var/tmp/scratch0359`, an attacker may simply assume that it is a temporary file and not worth looking at. You have to be careful with such a strategy, though, because one useful attack technique is to look for interesting things in dump or scratch files. But if you cause your survival package to look like something harmless and uninteresting then it might be treated that way by your opponent.

The more the merrier.

There is no reason for not having multiple copies of your survival packages on each system, each copy hidden in a different way. If your bookkeeping system is up to it, you could even have packages hidden on different systems in different locations. The difficulty with hiding a package in the same place on every machine is that once one package is discovered on one machine, all of the packages in similar places on other machines are known as well.

Of course, like safety equipment, your survival packages must be inspected regularly to verify that they are up to date and haven't been tampered with. A deleted or modified package indicates potential intrusion, so this signal should be added to whatever system you use for monitoring your machines. Another good reason for having several copies of your survival packages on each machine is that you can check some but not all of them on each machine. That way, if an intruder manages to see what files you are looking for in your periodic checks, you won't give away all of them.

Set Your Own Ground Rules

The attitude you want to adopt in defending your systems is that they are *yours*. Your attacker is fighting on your turf, and you should prepare your turf accordingly. Cached weapons such as the survival packages are one approach. Another is altering known signatures. If you have, for example, Sun workstations running Solaris and you've installed from a standard Solaris distribution CD, most of the files you install will have a similar modification date, which is the date the CD was created. Many attackers know this, and when they penetrate a specific machine with automated programs, their programs will set the modification or creation dates of their files to match yours. But this is *your* system. You own those file times, not the attacker. So why not change them all to something you choose? An attacker with automated tools may not notice, so her changes will stand out. An attacker who does notice will have to modify her attack, wasting valuable time and improving your chances of detecting them.

There are many other similar things you can think of and do. All of them should be well tested, of course, but the more you make the rules of the game *your* rules, the harder it is for the attacker to win the game. You want to set the game up so that the attacker has to play by your rules and your rules favor you winning and her losing. The more hurdles the attacker has to jump over, the more likely she will be to give up and go home.

Chapter
13

Handling an Attack

IN THIS CHAPTER:

- Exciting, but Not Fun
- Thinking Pathologically
- About Attacks
- What You Can Do
- What You Should Not Do
- Response Team
- Priorities During an Attack

You've built a fabulous team and designed a state-of-the-art security monitoring and management system. Then one morning, the big red "Attack" sign lights up. Your people scramble to their posts like a well-oiled machine, monitor the attacker, track him back to his source, and notify his Internet service provider (ISP), as well as law enforcement. The ISP cooperates fully with you and the FBI, and unmarked cars silently approach the suspect's house. Agents burst through the doors and windows, taking the attacker completely unaware. His equipment is captured before anything can be deleted, and crack FBI computer forensics technicians extract a wealth of incriminating information from the machines. Those data, combined with your excellent logs of the entire event, lead to a speedy trial and a swift conviction. One more Bad Guy is off the streets.

If only it worked that way. Even once, so you could tell your friends. All the other security people would be so jealous. Unfortunately, the reality is more like this.

You build the best monitoring system for your network that you can afford. But you're having a hard time locating people to staff your security team. Because of this, you've got a hole in the Saturday midnight to 8 A.M. shift. Just as you leave for the big Friday night party to celebrate your brother's anniversary, the battery in your pager goes dead. You don't notice this. Your Friday night shift operator sees some odd traffic but does not react to it because it isn't definite enough to be declared hostile. He leaves at midnight, and half an hour later, the attack begins in earnest. Your logging system notices an anomaly and pages you, but your pager doesn't work. The attacker gains entry, trashes your logging system, and installs a backdoor program for later access. You return home from the party at 2 A.M. and fall into bed.

You're woken by the morning shift operator, who has noticed that the logging system is broken. You drive in, groggy and unhappy, to fix it. About noon, you start suspecting that it was not a system failure but an attack, and you start searching for damage. About 9 P.M., you find a few trojanned binaries, and you call everybody in to start searching for more. You work throughout Sunday, but your company has a big deadline on Wednesday, so about 2 P.M. on Sunday, you have to suspend your forensics and get the system administrators to work rebuilding the compromised machines, destroying the evidence trail in the process. You think you've cleaned up the trojanned machines, but you're not sure, and you never will be. Because the logs are gone, you don't know how the attacker succeeded in penetration, and you may never know.

Exciting, but Not Fun

It would be very nice to be able to say here that if you follow the suggestions I've made in this book, everything will go well for you and you'll have no significant problems. It would be nice, but it would not be realistic. The reason is simple: people. You are defending against people who wish to attack your network. Attackers will be nasty, devious, and clever. They will try very hard *not* to be predictable. They will look for weakness in your defense, and they will try to exploit it.

But attackers are not the only people involved. There are people on your side, as well. Your own people will be difficult to hire, difficult to manage, difficult to train, will not perform perfectly. They will be clever, as well, and sometimes too clever for their own good. And sometimes, they'll be dumb. They will make mistakes and not notice or correct them. And once in a while, they'll turn from Good Guys to Bad Guys, and it will take you too long to notice.

Computer scientists are accustomed to what in any other endeavor would be an unreasonably high standard of perfection. A programmer can easily create a "machine" that will perform some operation ten million times and do so the last time exactly as it did the first time, with no wear and tear, no fatigue, and no deviation from plan. This can give them something of a blind spot to physical systems and systems involving people. But the real world is sloppy and messy, and things often don't work the way they should twice in a row, let alone a million times. Add to that natural variability the possibility of human deceit, and you can end up with a very difficult situation to manage.

It is possible to create reasonably reliable systems from unreliable "components" such as people, however. What it takes, first and foremost, is the recognition and acknowledgment of human unpredictability. In the computer security business, this cognizance is sometimes referred to as the ability to think pathologically. Not everybody can do it well, and it is difficult to train people to develop the skill, but once you're good at it, you can design and manage the teams and systems that you'll need to protect your organization from attack from without and within.

Thinking Pathologically

What follows here are some principles that will move you in the right direction. There is no good way but experience to prove some of them, but if you keep them in mind, you'll be much more likely to design your operations properly and react correctly in a crisis.

> *Murphy's law rules.*

Murphy's law, if you don't have it tattooed on the inside of your eyelids, is "Anything that can go wrong will go wrong." This is why many engineers tend to be pessimists. What it means for network security is that you *cannot* design a system that will keep out all attackers. It just isn't possible.

But while you cannot guarantee that you can beat Murphy, you can work around him statistically. You can make it unlikely for your attackers to succeed. You can make it improbable that a battery failure will prevent you from being notified of a problem. You can make it probable that your people will carry out the attack reaction procedures you've defined. The way to do this is to use the process of security, which is at the heart of this book (refer to Chapter 1 and the box in Chapter 4).

"Thinking pathologically" is difficult to learn but well worth the effort. It means learning to see your system as a collection of interlocking components and then imagining what would happen if one component failed to work as it was supposed to. Suppose, for example, that your packet filters suddenly stopped providing protection. Or suppose that someone learned the "secret" password for a particular account. Or suppose that the person working your night shift was really unhappy in his job and wanted revenge. Or suppose that an engineer trying to meet a deadline turned off some inconvenient protection mechanism.

Learning to think pathologically is an endless process and is both educational and disturbing. Some people compare this kind of thinking to looking several moves ahead in chess, but it is more than that. A more accurate chess comparison is not thinking about winning a normal chess game. If you've done your design correctly, you've already won any legitimate game that is played by the rules. Thinking pathologically about chess would mean asking yourself questions like "What if that bishop suddenly had the ability to move like a queen when you weren't looking?" In chess, which has rules, moving a bishop like a queen would be cheating. In computer security, which has no rules, it would be normal.

> ### *Your automatic defenses will detect and handle the boring attackers.*

If this statement is not true for your network, then you should carefully review the design of your defenses. Another way to phrase it might be that your automatic defenses, the configuration of your routers and computers and network components, should be designed to counter all attacks you are aware of. And you should make a serious and ongoing effort to be aware of as many as possible and extend your defenses to cover any new ones that come to your attention.

The defenses should inform you that an attack was attempted and give you as much information as possible about the source of the attack. As part of their routine duties, your security watchstanders should be able to use the information to contact the management of the source network used by the attacker, inform them of a problem user at their site, and request further action on their part. Routine requests like this from a single organization will not have much effect, but as more organizations operate in this fashion and the requests to ISPs and other network management organizations increase, the pressure will help to reduce the number of places that serve as comfortable homes to attackers and thus help reduce the number of attacks you must face.

The attacks that will concern you more than the routine ones are the ones in which the attacker can challenge your defenses and find a way in that you have not considered. Your goal, as a defender, should be to relegate the largest possible fraction of the attacks you face to the "boring" category and to develop ways in which you can minimize the risk of any other types of attack going unnoticed.

> *It usually takes a long time for you to know that you are under serious attack.*

The movies have spoiled it for the computer security business. People have been taught that a computer intrusion is detected by a grim technician wearing a communications headset, sitting in a dimly lit command center deep in the bowels of your company. A red flashing display alerts him that there has been a security penetration in sector 9, and he watches as the intruder graphically shatters layer after layer of defenses. "He's into the central core!" the technician cries, as a laughing icon appears on the main viewscreen, says something clever, and then the room goes dark (or consoles erupt in a shower of sparks).

I, for one, would love to work in *that* industry (although I'd still probably insist on fuses on my consoles so that they wouldn't set the room ablaze every time something interesting happened). When someone asks, "What did you do at work today?" it would be so much more fun to be able to tell that story.

The real story is much less colorful, much less noisy, and sometimes much more frightening to the trained observer. Watching someone detect a computer intrusion is very much like watching someone balance a checkbook on the computer. There are bursts of typing, some puzzled looks when the numbers don't add up, some more typing, perhaps some consultation with others in the room. Eventually, it may reach the point where people become agitated and start swearing and running around, but that generally takes a very long time.

The reason is that a smart attacker doesn't come through the front door, guns blazing. He tries to slip in through the seams of your organization, where several different systems come together but don't fit exactly. Noticing a good attacker is much like finding out that you have mice in the house. There may be very slight clues, which you ignore. As the mice grow more confident and gain more access in your house, they grow bolder. The clues become more obvious, and one day, you put it all together and suspect that there's a problem. Proving that there really are mice is harder, and catching them and proving that you've eliminated them all and the means they used to get in is harder still.

A perfect example is the famous case of the intrusion into the Lawrence Berkeley Laboratories computer noticed by Clifford Stoll (detailed in his excellent book *The Cuckoo's Egg*). The penetration was noticed because Cliff was writing a new program to handle the accounting of computer use for his organization. When the old program and the new program were compared, there was a $0.75 discrepancy. Cliff began to investigate this difference in results, and the investigation led him to discover a network penetration. The trail eventually led to (what was then) East Germany, Soviet spies, and the United States Strategic Defense Initiative program (commonly known as Star Wars), and it may have resulted in the death of one or more foreign agents. (The penetration methods used by Stoll's attacker are now considerably more than a decade old. Many of the problems have been fixed in subsequent operating system releases or software updates, but security auditors are still finding many machines on the Internet vulnerable to some of them.)

Chances are good that Stoll's adventures were more colorful than you are likely to see today. But the manner in which he discovered his attackers is a textbook example of the way you are likely to find yours. No bell will ring, no laughing icon will suddenly appear on the screen. You will probably see them first in a minor discrepancy, and then you will spend a great deal of time investigating to see if it is a real problem or not.

> *You will waste much of the time between your first clue and your eventual conclusion that you are under attack.*

It is inevitable that you will waste some of the time. In an odd way, the amount of time you spend doubting that an attack is possible can be a reflection of how well you've done your job in designing and building the network. If attacks are typically turned away by your outer defenses and do not reach inside your network, then you will be likely to rationalize internal anomalies as other types of problems instead of security problems. If your defenses are weak, and attackers penetrate frequently, you are much more likely to come to the correct conclusion quickly, because in that situation, almost any problem is likely to be rooted in an attack.

But large computer networks are complicated and cantankerous and are fraught with minor troubles, and you will almost certainly see minor problems every day that are not caused by intruders. So you will exhaust many other possibilities before you seriously entertain the idea that an intruder has penetrated.

Another issue that can cost you valuable time is that the discrepancy may be noticed not by your security team but by some other part of your organization that is comparatively untrained in spotting computer security problems and much more likely to assume other causes. For that reason, it is very important that you have plans for the following actions:

- Training other parts of your organization to spot potential security problems
- Providing those groups with a reliable means of communicating the problem to you
- Handling the inevitable false alarms that will result

- Distinguishing a real problem from a false alarm

Handling these tasks well can give you many more eyes and ears for detecting problems quickly within your organization. Handling them badly can create a barrier that blocks you from information you may need to react properly and solve the problem quickly.

> *The chance that your people will act quickly, accurately, and correctly is directly proportional to the amount of training and practice they've had and inversely proportional to the number of other (nonsecurity) tasks they are responsible for.*

When your people face a real attacker for the first time, they should feel, as much as you can make it, as if it were just "more of the same." Sure, they'll be excited and will know that it's no drill, but if you've made a good plan and they've been trained in it, the routine parts will take care of themselves so that the security team can work on the hard parts.

The day your team has to deal with its first serious, no-holds-barred attack situation, they should already have the following:

- Thorough understanding of the network they are protecting

- Thorough understanding of the systems and tools at their disposal for implementing that protection

- Thorough understanding of the plan they will use to work through the attack situation

- Experience of as many simulated attacks as possible, using the plan as a guideline

- As few other pressing tasks as possible distracting them from their security work

The last point is an interesting one. In the past, organizations seldom had many full-time computer security people. Typically, a person with another full-time job (often as systems administrator) also had security responsibilities. Nowadays, this model can still work for very small organizations or organizations in which the computer network is not central to the way the organization does business. But for a company that cannot work without their network in reliable operation, computer security should not be a sideline. Although the participants need not all be full-time computer security employees (see the discussion on volunteer fire fighters in Chapter 12), there should be a core team of people who do nothing but prevent and prepare for security problems in any network of reasonable size and importance. One of their jobs is to assemble the rest of the team and train them.

If you can manage this, then you and your team will handle attack situations in relative calm and with reasonable skill. Not that it is entirely bad for the situation to get a little tense. In the short run, a little adrenaline rush can sharpen senses and help you to think more clearly. In the long run, however, adrenaline and excitement and the fatigue that comes from them are conditions you want to avoid.

> *A small number of false alarms in a given period is good for training.*

As with most things defensive, it is better to be a little too careful than not quite careful enough. Your outermost defenses and your watchstanders should be handling the bulk of the attack attempts, so the team of people you've built to respond to serious attacks will need some stimulation to keep them familiar with their jobs. An occasional anomaly to investigate and a reason to increase your operational tempo can help keep a team from feeling that things are too quiet.

If things *are* too quiet, you should be asking yourself two questions:

- Do I believe that everything is working properly? Should I be suspicious of the fact that no one has gotten through the defenses enough to trigger a serious alert? Has no one tried to do so?

- If the defenses are in good working order, then should I be scheduling a drill?

Bear in mind that it is entirely possible that you could *never* be in a situation where an attack was serious enough to warrant scrambling your security team. If you are doing a superlative job applying the security process to your outer defenses and are guarding a network that is not particularly attractive to intruders, then you may never see a real attack get through to the core organizational network. Does that mean that your defenses are perfect? No. It means that you are lucky. Does it mean that you won't see a serious attack tomorrow? You might. As many a Las Vegas gambler has learned the hard way, luck has no memory.

> *A large number of false alarms in a given period is bad for training.*

Too many false alarms indicate that something is wrong with the way in which you are discriminating between possible attacks and real attacks. This alone is not a problem, but if it is training your people to expect a dud each time they rush to stations, their ability to respond properly in a real crisis will be dulled.

Another consequence of a large number of false alarms applies in the volunteer fire fighter model of staffing. If you keep pulling your part-time team members off their "real" jobs to handle situations that turn out to be false alarms, it won't take long before their management will begin to react to the drain on their resources. If your volunteer fire fighters are called away from their jobs to handle a situation, their coworkers and management will want to hear "the full story" afterward. If too often there is no good story to tell, everyone will grow more cynical and more convinced that the security system is a waste of time and money, regardless of the facts.

Even if you are fully staffed and need no volunteer fire fighters for your active defenses, this effect will occur, though it will be less pronounced. For that reason, you need to have a plan that will call up your response team in the appropriate numbers at an appropriate time so that you, they, and all concerned can feel that the situation is being handled intelligently and appropriately.

> ### *Coming up to an attack from a cold start is bad.*

In Chapter 11, we discussed a possible plan of response to an attack that called up the various teams in order and quantity of their usefulness. Your organization needs such a plan to work effectively under attack. This plan should provide answers for the following questions:

- Who is in charge of the attack response at any given time?

- Who decides to increase the amount of response? What approval is necessary?

- Who can decide that all is well and that the amount of response can be decreased? What approval is necessary?

- How and to whom are duties assigned?

- What are the priorities for the duties? Who is allowed to change those priorities?

- Who speaks to management?

- Who speaks to the press?

- Who speaks to law enforcement?

- Who speaks to other network organizations?

- How is new information assimilated by the group?

- What is the standard of proof for a new piece of information?

- How are notes and logs taken?

- How is an attack declared to be "over"?

This plan will be different for every organization and every response team, but one must be written and practiced if the team is to be effective.

About Attacks

Thus far, we have discussed issues about your team and its response to an attack. Now let's talk about issues related to the attacks and the attackers.

> *Most attackers are smart enough not to be easily trackable.*

Eons ago, at the dawn of the modern Internet (say, about 1995), an attack method would be discovered by a bright Bad Guy and used by him only, kept as a closely guarded secret. After a few months, the inventor would tire of the secrecy and brag to his friends about the technique. The smartest of his friends would carefully attempt to duplicate the attack, and some would succeed, after a great deal of trial-and-error effort. In this way, new attacks would slowly percolate through the fabric of the Internet underground.

A fact of life on today's Internet is that the process has been greatly accelerated and streamlined. An ability to attack is not enough. Now the people who create new attack methods also create simple and easy-to-use tools that can exploit the methods. These tools spread across the network in days rather than months, so you can find yourself under serious attack on Friday from Brazil by an attacker using a technique that was perfected on Monday in Bulgaria.

This proliferation of tools has led to the rise of what is known as a "script kiddie." These are young kids, almost always boys (in fact, the gender of Internet attackers is so overwhelmingly male, of all ages, that the terms this book uses for a generic attacker are masculine, rather than feminine or neutral), who may not be expert in the ways of the Internet or even computer programming and usage but are perfectly capable of locating exploit scripts and running them. To the defender, they can appear as brilliant, capable attackers, as long as the attack is being handled by the program. Once the script has done its job, the attacker can change from brilliant technician to bumbling fool, as the script kiddie takes control of the attack and types commands appropriate to other operating systems or other situations.

Make no mistake, a script kiddie can be a dangerous attacker. He is, by analogy, a child with a fully loaded machine gun. Having a machine gun makes him more powerful than most soldiers throughout human history, except in situations where judgment and experience are required. That is a large exception, but one of little comfort if he gets off a lucky shot that hits you.

Not all of the power of exploit scripts is in their ability to finesse the defenses of the unwary. Much of the art of Internet camouflage has been coded into some of these programs. The person running a sophisticated exploit script can often mask the source of their attack very well indeed. In fact, some scripts can create attacks (especially denial-of-service attacks) that are all but untraceable.

Combine exploit scripts with the easy availability of free demonstration accounts on many ISPs and on-line services, which require little or no identity confirmation (and what little may be required is easily forged), and it does not require much of an attacker to be set up with many untraceable paths to the Internet.

> *Many ISPs will give you some cooperation until you make it clear that you want to pursue legal action. Then they will clam up and require a subpoena. Sometimes legal action is implicit in what you ask for.*

ISPs that have long been a haven for attackers are slowly responding to pressure from other Internet organizations to provide trace information for attackers, but the pressure has been relatively light compared to the volume of attacks, because many organizations do not pursue attackers. As we discussed earlier, some amount of pursuit is helpful, because it brings these issues to the attention of the ISPs and their management.

An ISP can do many things to assist you in locating an attacker if they are willing to help you and if they've taken the trouble to set up their systems in a way that is effective for this type of tracking. The majority of attacks come through dialup lines, because that is the best way for the attacker to remain anonymous. By carefully logging the source of an attack and making sure that your log times are well synchronized to the actual time of day, an ISP can often locate the user who was connected to a particular IP address at a particular time. If this user is a normal, paid-for account (which is unlikely), the ISP can often take action or at least log a complaint against the user. If the user account is a temporary one, then the ISP may be able to locate the telephone number from which the call originated, if they have specifically designed their systems to log this information. If you can persuade the ISP to give you the originating phone number (which is unlikely without a court order), then you must persuade the telephone company to give you the customer name and address for the phone number (which will definitely require a court order, although sometimes a trip to the local branch of the library for that region will suffice).

Unfortunately, ISPs often resist helping without court orders and can abruptly become very bureaucratic and stubborn when it becomes clear to them that you are asking for information regarding a particular subscriber at a particular time. This is not surprising, because an ISP has everything to lose by cooperating with you to locate an attacker without a specific court order. Assuming that the attacker used an account with a free trial period provided by the ISP, the resources used by the attacker have already been discounted by the ISP as overhead. They give away free disks as a means to attract new customers and plan on a certain amount of wasted time with no follow-up subscription. The use of their network by an attacker does not consume any resources that the ISP had not planned to waste anyway. So at best, they gain nothing, and at worst, they can be sued by a potential client for invasion of privacy, lose subscribers, and get bad press if they cooperate with you without specifically being ordered by a court to do so. The attack you report may be a big deal to you, but they get many reports per day of this type of abuse, and most of the larger ISPs have evolved a combination of minimal activity, lack of interest, and legal bet-hedging to deal with it.

An ISP will often help a business partner much more effectively than they might help an organization with which they have no prior relationship, however. So if you are tempted to call an ISP for help, finding out if you have a relationship with them of some kind before you call and being prepared to exploit that relationship for the purposes of your investigation can often be helpful.

ISPs that do not give away free trial subscriptions can be very helpful when tracking down abusers of their systems. The best approach, when dealing with any ISP, is to treat them like fellow security professionals and let them take care of the situation in their own way, if they can. For "casual" attacks, this approach will accomplish about as much as any other approach.

> *Your chances of an easy arrest are effectively zero.*

For more serious attacks, however, you may want to go the extra mile and attempt prosecution. That means that you'll have to worry about the following issues:

- Locating the attacker

- Collecting enough proof that he did it (himself, not someone using his account, for example)

- Not breaking the law yourself in the collection of such evidence

- Finding a lawyer familiar enough with the Internet and Internet-related law, such as it is, to take the case

- Convincing the lawyer that there is sufficient proof to make a good case

- Finding a court that is sufficiently familiar with the Internet and Internet-related law that can understand the case

- Convincing the court to issue an order allowing the appropriate law enforcement agency to act

- Locating a person at the appropriate law enforcement agency who is sufficiently familiar with the Internet and Internet-related law

- Convincing this person to pursue the case, which usually involves proving that a tangible loss of $25,000 or more has been sustained (You can't typically claim your time or the time of your employees as the loss. The attacker has to come reasonably close to walking into your office, taking $25,000 while you weren't looking, and running out, in order to clearly satisfy this requirement.)

- Getting the legal official to execute the court order and arrest the suspect in such a fashion that any corroborating evidence (such as the contents of the suspect's computer) is not destroyed

Your mileage may vary, of course, but if it does, the chances are excellent that it will be more complicated, not less.

Your chances of an easy conviction are effectively zero.

If you do manage to get this far, the next step is the courtroom—or more precisely, the endless succession of law office conference rooms that lead to the courtroom. It is not impossible to get a conviction for computer crime, but it definitely helps if the alleged perpetrator did something that was well publicized, threatened public safety, and/or stole a very large, tangible amount of money through the commission of his particular act of network abuse.

The problem here is that the things that normal criminal cases depend on, such as

- evidence that you can put on a table in front of a jury
- a jury that understands the issues involved
- a judge who understands the issues involved
- laws that deal sensibly with the issues involved
- witnesses at the scene of the crime
- the scene of the crime
- an object that was stolen or a person who was abused

are all missing or incomprehensible to a lay person in a computer crime case. You are attempting to prove, for all intents and purposes, that the soul of the attacker traveled through the ether and stole a bit of the essence of the soul of the victim. It might be possible to do so, but it will never be easy.

> **Every interesting case will involve an international component.**

Add to the foregoing issues the likelihood that an attacker will relay through or originate from a network outside your own country. This is not accidental. It is often done for the exact purpose of making a prosecution seem obviously impossible to the victim. If your ability to obtain court orders and prosecute in your own country are very, very limited, your ability to obtain and execute court orders in another country are even more restricted.

What You Can Do

> *Skilled is the general who can sap the enemy's will to fight, so they lay down their arms before the battle has begun.*
>
> —Sun Tsu, *The Art of War*

After reading the problems in the previous section, you may be feeling that there is little point in pursuing an attacker through legal means. That is an understandable sentiment, but in fact, there are several valid things you can do that may discourage this attacker and will probably discourage future attackers.

If your outer defenses are well crafted, the attacker has already developed a sense that you know what you're doing. Chances are good, therefore, that they will see their ability to sneak in through a hole that you did not close as "moving to the next level." Even the most experienced attackers tend to think along this line, because a good attack experience for the attacker is much like a very complicated video game. It is, to them, challenging but rewarding.

You can use this to your advantage. What attackers are looking for, consciously or subconsciously, is a feeling of exultation when they outwit you and slip past your defenses. This feeling is their reward for the hard work and patience that went into finding the hole in your defenses. Your goals as a defender should therefore be the following:

Deny attackers the feeling of satisfaction. If you are facing an attacker who has slipped by your outer defenses, this will be hard, because you've already given him one good experience in leaving a hole for him to enter by. You've made one mistake. Perhaps you've made a second one, by taking a long time to notice the attacker. You cannot afford a third mistake. Once you know that an attacker is in your system, devote all your time and energy to frustrating him, flushing him, and closing the mode of entry.

Subtly convey to them that no such feeling will ever be forthcoming. Video games always have a way to succeed, to move to the next level. Sometimes finding that way is devilishly hard, but the game always has subtle ways of enticing you to keep playing. Because of this, the amount of concentration and effort that a player will put into a game is staggering. But game players want to be able to try alternatives and see which ones work. Whether they work or not, the player wants instant feedback. You can deny feedback to the attackers by denying them the ability to work unmolested. Cut off their connection to your network. Frustrate them at every opportunity. They've already won level one of the game. Convince them that level two is the network equivalent of slamming their head against a concrete wall and then waiting two hours for the privilege of doing it again.

Make the situation "real" to them. Video games are "immersive" fantasies. Players learn to block out other distractions and live only within the world of the game. Your goal, therefore, is to ruin the illusion that allows attackers to immerse themselves in the game and convince them that their actions will have real-world consequences. This must be done subtly. An overt threat will not be believed unless you can back it up. (Though it is quite satisfying to call and have the parents of an attacker knock on his bedroom door and tell him to cut it out, it is rarely possible and never safe.) Do everything you can to convert their feeling of "YES!! I got in!!!" to one of "Uh, oh. Maybe I've made a *very* big mistake."

> ### React quickly and decisively.

The faster you react, the more competent you'll be in the eyes of the attacker. The more competent you are, the more nervous he will be about continuing the attack. Remember, you're not playing chess, where there are clear rules and you can see the position of all the pieces on the board. If you adopt a conservative "plan, move, wait for countermove" approach, you're playing the game the way the attacker wants it played.

Also, remember that security systems can be "coevolutionary": A slight improvement of offense begets a slight improvement of defense, which improves the offense, and so forth. Or to use a more rural analogy: If you want to stop deer from jumping over your garden fence, you don't raise the height of the fence gradually, because all that does is train the deer to jump a little higher each time. What you do is put up a very tall barrier all at once so that the deer don't even try to jump it; they give up and go away.

> ### Expend the attacker's time and energy. Frustrate him. Bore him to death.

As we discussed earlier, you're not likely to get much legal satisfaction from the ISP the attacker is using. But you may get them to cut off the account and kill the attacker's session. Doing this will not usually endanger the attacker, but it will slow him down somewhat, as he now has to shift to another account and possibly another dialin number. He may have many of these accounts in reserve, but creating new ones takes time and effort. Every one you use up expends some of the attacker's time to replace. Each time you can put an inconvenience in the path of the attacker, try to do so. Your goal is to sap his motivation to continue the attack, but you should be careful not to annoy him in a way that will actually increase his motivation to succeed.

The way to do this is to be dull and consistent. This is harder than it seems. Your people will want to engage the enemy in battle and defeat him soundly. They'll want to humiliate him. If you take that approach, you'll create an enemy, giving him a grudge to settle and the will to do so. Your problems will increase, even if you do win a round or two.

If you can drain the fun out of the attack and destroy the attacker's motivation to continue, then if he is attacking for those reasons, he'll soon tire of not enjoying the game and move on to somebody who will play with him. If the attacker is motivated by revenge, then by impersonally blocking and frustrating him, you may force him to respect your defenses a bit more. While there's certainly no guarantee of it, revenge is often fueled by rage and contempt of the target, and creating more respect for the target (you) in the mind of the attacker may defuse some of his anger and allow him to withdraw. Revenge is an especially tricky motivation, however, and one of the most dangerous, so treat it with great caution. Finally, if your attacker is motivated by money (he's being paid to attack you), then your only recourse is to make him earn his pay. If you are going to be a target, then you want to be a really expensive target.

> **Create doubt in the attacker's mind.**

Above all other things, you want your attacker to think that you are bigger, stronger, more powerful, better staffed, and more knowledgeable than you really are. If you've made a mistake and left a hole in your defenses, it should be one that an attacker can respect rather than a simple one that you should have found on your own. Your actions, once you know that a penetration has occurred, will either give the attacker pause or give him reassurance that he understands you correctly. If you can remain an enigma to him, you will make him fear you and worry about what you have learned of him. If you put a face or a voice to yourself, then you'll shrink back to human dimensions and become someone he can deal with.

What You Should Not Do

> **Don't get personal.**

Don't let the attacker know your name. When an attack begins, it is an attack against your organization. If you allow it to become so, it can easily become an attack against you personally or some of your people. In a serious attack, it is not at all uncommon for key defenders to be personally harassed by anonymous phone calls, by credit card or bank account abuse, or even by personal visits at home. A little research on the Internet and other places can turn up a wealth of information about anybody, and that type of knowledge brings with it the power to intimidate. You could assign false names to your people so that any attempt to look them up will fail. This must be done carefully, though, because you could find yourself bringing the wrath of an attacker down on an innocent "civilian" by the wrong choice of names. Also, if the attacker is deep enough into your network, he will be able to see the names associated with each account, so care must be taken there as well.

Don't insult him or his intelligence. Remember that your goal is to bore and block the attacker. If you do communicate with him, calling him names only strengthens his resolve. Suggesting that he's stupid only gives him more motivation to prove you wrong. Be dull. Be boring. Be repetitive. Fail to rise to his provocations if they occur.

Don't try to make him angry. The sentence that should strike fear into your heart is one that you may hear in your own operations area: "If we do X, that'll show the little creep!" or something to that effect. All that does is make him come back harder and more subtly. In this situation, be like the turtle. Pull your sensitive parts into the shell, button up, and sit tight. If you let him make you mad, and you turn that anger back around, you will have given up whatever advantages you have.

> ### *Don't motivate the attacker.*

All these points apply to your automatic systems as well. In some places, it has become common to "customize" various programs so that, for example, several failed login attempts give the message "Guess again, LOSER!" or something to that effect. That type of message is an annoyance to legitimate users, and it can be a goad to the attacker. Better to simply terminate the connection. That's just as effective and much more implacable.

An interesting exercise is one in which you attempt to penetrate your own systems and take notes and screen shots of the sessions. Afterward, you and your team go through each failed attempt (presumably, you've dealt with any successful attempts already) and ask yourself questions: How can I make this failure more boring? How can I make it less personal and less interesting? This helps not only to deplete the motivation of your attacker, but to teach your team to cultivate the art of boring the attacker to death.

> ### *Don't counterattack.*

This point is somewhat controversial. Many people feel that it is legitimate and even ethical to attempt to counterattack someone who is attacking you. I disagree. I feel that it is not only the wrong thing to do but the dumb thing to do. Here's why.

You cannot claim to be acting in self-defense. Under certain circumstances, such as being mugged, for example, you can legally fight back and damage or possibly even kill an attacker if you perceive your own life or health to be in danger. There is little likelihood that a network attack will threaten your life personally or the lives of your team or anyone in your organization (though I grant you that it is more complicated if your network operates hospital life support systems, for example). You know this for certain, but you don't know what effect a counterattack will have on your attacker. Given that, your motivations for a counterattack are not likely to be considered legally sufficient. That is important for you to think about, even though you may not be able to prosecute your attacker (for reasons discussed earlier). If you counterattack, he may be able to prosecute you.

You could be counterattacking the wrong target. One common form of attack is "misdirection," in which attacker A has a grudge of some kind against organization B. To cause trouble for B, A attacks organization C, while making the source of the attack to appear to be organization B. So from C's perspective, it appears that B is attacking them, even though the attack is really originating with A. If C counterattacks B, A's intentions are carried out.

You are giving your attacker grounds for legal action. A perfectly reasonable, subtle, and nasty attack scenario is one in which an attacker goads you into attacking him by attacking you. You do so and disable his computer systems. He then turns around and sues your organization for interfering with his business. He will probably have carefully collected logs accurately documenting what you did. His logs will completely agree with your own. He will also have carefully collected documentation proving that he could not possibly have been the attacker who triggered your wrath but that he certainly was the victim of your wrath. Yes, you might win. But unless your judge, jury, and lawyers are all trained computer security experts, you probably won't; you'll end up writing a check to the Bad Guy who attacked you while looking like a Bad Guy yourself.

You cloud the legal issues of your own defense when you do so. We have already discussed how difficult it is to make a case against an attacker. If you have enough information to counterattack, you have a good chance of actually making a case stick. But if you counterattack, then you are transformed from victim of an unprovoked assault to one of many combatants. That mess will be much more difficult to sort out in court.

You risk bad publicity. "Big Nasty Company attacks local travel agent" is not a headline your management or board of directors will appreciate. It is, however, an angle that many news organizations will find appealing on a slow news day.

You are now making a personal attack on the attacker, giving him even more motivation to respond. See the first two principles in this section.

You may be creating an international incident. The Internet goes everywhere, or nearly. If you are attacked and are considering a counterstrike, you don't know whether your target is in the same legal jurisdiction you are. Consider what would happen if, during peace talks to settle a war, a company on one side attacks a network that turns out to be part of the military or industrial infrastructure of the opposing side, and the attack becomes publicly known. For that matter, is an attack by one military network on the Internet against another an act of war? I don't know, and I doubt that the system administrators of either side would, either.

You risk personal liability. If there is legal fallout to a counterattack and you didn't get written authorization from your management to execute the counterattack, you may be held personally liable for damages.

The idea of striking back is appealing, but the reality is messy. Granted, you could use attacker techniques to hide your identity and strike in secret, but if you do, don't *ever* tell *anybody* about it.

Response Team

Having discussed much of the philosophical considerations of coping with a serious attack, we can now turn to the organizational side and discuss how you can structure your security team to cope with such an attack.

If your Watch Team supplies first aid for your network security problems, your Response Team members are the paramedics of your organization. They are responsible for taking charge of the situation and stabilizing it so that it does not get any worse. The Forensics Team (see Chapter 14) are the doctors and diagnosticians of the group, providing you with an in-depth analysis and solution.

The key individual in a Response Team is the Response Team Manager. This person will be responsible for most of the decisions that must be made quickly in the event of an attack. He or she should be

- very familiar with the design of your network.

- very familiar with the operation of your organization.

- very familiar with the defenses of your network.

- very familiar with the monitoring systems used in your network.

- experienced in the ways of computer and network security.

Such a person will be difficult to hire directly, because the general skills are not commonplace and the knowledge specific to your organization can come only from within it. You can conduct a lengthy search, but the best approach is probably to hire from within your group. Find a likely candidate and then train this person by sending him or her to classes and seminars; have the candidate train your organization by conducting drills and classes. In point of fact, you'll want to groom several people, if possible, because a single candidate may not be appropriate and cannot be available twenty-four hours a day in any case. Having a small number of response team managers gives each of them someone to have lunch with, talk shop with, and impress with new knowledge and new skills.

It sounds expensive, but if you think in terms of insurance, it really isn't. The cost of a single unchecked security incident, in time and opportunity lost as well as cost of investigation, recovery, and in the worst case, public exposure and subsequent loss of public confidence, is far worse than the cost of maintaining such a team.

The first order of business in a security crisis is to locate a Response Team Manager (RTM) and put him or her in charge of the situation. In many organizations, all the managers or their equivalents are available by pager and cell phone as much as possible, and one of them is available at all times, day and night, year-round. For extensive network operations in which the network must be available at all times, you may wish to run round-the-clock security operations so that a designated RTM is on site at all times. In other cases, having RTMs who can be contacted day or night is adequate. You want to avoid a situation in which a long lag occurs between contacting an RTM and having him or her be able to begin action. You want to equip the RTMs with a means for securely connecting to your network from their homes and a telephone connection adequate to their needs so that they can take charge of the situation immediately, hold a conference call if necessary, get the ball rolling, and *then* leave home for the office if that is required.

The membership of a Response Team underneath the manager can vary widely depending on your organization, its function, and its network. The key characteristics of a manager are

- ability to take responsibility for the situation.

- ability to work well under pressure.

- ability to analyze a situation correctly and rapidly.
- ability to coordinate technical specialists and arrive at a solution.
- technical familiarity with the systems, techniques, and procedures involved.

The key characteristics of the Response Team members are

- technical mastery of some portion of the system appropriate to the task.
- ability to work well under pressure.
- ability to communicate well with the Response Team Manager.

The Response Team Manager should probably be an employee who is significantly focused on the job of being an RTM, while the response team members can be volunteer fire fighters, technical contributors within your organization who work at other jobs but can be called on for security purposes if need be.

Priorities During an Attack

The question you don't want to hear your team ask during the first moments of a crisis is "What should we do now?" You need to develop a plan well in advance and practice it with your whole team so that everybody will know what must be done. Of course, every organization is different, every network is different, every security team has a mix of different skills, and, given Murphy's law, somebody important will probably be out sick or on vacation during your moment of crisis.

Because of that, a good way to provide a general response plan for an attack is to decide not who will handle a specific task but what are the most important tasks at specific times. Then you can plan for your specific situation and assign roles and backups as appropriate.

What follows here is a general response plan that works for many circumstances.

Phase 1: Confirming the Attack

At this point, the Response Team Manager (RTM) has just been called into the situation. The Security Watch Officer (SWO) has declared an emergency and handed over to the RTM. The RTM's immediate duty is to verify the emergency and confirm the escalation decision by the SWO.

Priorities

1. *Receive quick briefing on the situation.* The SWO reports, quickly and concisely, what was found that triggered the alert. During the briefing, the RTM makes notes on what information sources might be able to confirm that a problem really exists.

2. *Examine other information sources for confirmation.* After the briefing, the RTM immediately looks for confirmation of the problem. The goal here is to avoid scrambling the rest of the Response Team until the incident has been verified. The RTM examines router, server, and sniffer logs and anything else pertinent to see if the penetration report appears to be valid. The RTM changes nothing and does not use privileged access to perform this examination, just in case the compromise is widespread.

3. *Confirm the decision.* If the RTM finds sufficient evidence or feels that it is justified, he or she confirms the attack.

4. *Scramble the appropriate personnel to handle the response.* The RTM scrambles the appropriate Response Team personnel. This should be a well-oiled mechanism, simple to initiate and adequately practiced.

Phase 2: Attack Response Preparation

At this point, the attack is confirmed and Response Team members are available and ready to begin the investigation. The goal of this phase is to get enough information to be able to act decisively and with a reasonable probability of correctness.

Priorities

1. *Acquire a suspect.* Based on the information you have and whatever other information can be gathered quickly, you try to determine where the penetrator is coming from so that you can cut him off.

2. *Decide on a state of lockdown.* Cutting an attacker off may or may not be appropriate, depending on the situation. If the attacker has penetrated only slightly, you may want to monitor and record his actions. If he has compromised administrative privilege across many machines, you may want to halt the entire network. Or you may choose something in between.

3. *Verify the integrity of all information sources.* One of the most important things the Response Team must do is to verify that all logs and logging machines have not been tampered with by the attacker. The logs are likely to be the source of any significant information about the attack, so if they are compromised, the attack is extremely serious. If the logs are intact, then the Response Team can have greater confidence that they are dealing with the situation realistically.

4. *Locate all contaminated systems.* The Response Team must begin a rapid survey of the network and begin making a list of machines that may be contaminated. The goal is to produce an early estimate of the extent of the contamination, which will be refined by the Forensics Team.

5. *Locate the means of entry.* This is an early estimate of the way in which the attacker may have gained entry into the network. Later information developed by the Forensics Team may reinforce or replace this estimate.

6. *Scramble the Forensics Team.* Now that preliminary information has been gathered, the Forensics Team can begin in-depth examination of the systems, data, and network to confirm, deny, or elaborate on the early conclusions.

Phase 3: Lockdown

At this point, you have an estimate of how, when, and from where the attacker penetrated your system. You know how seriously you wish to treat this attack, and you've planned a response to it. Now you begin to implement the response.

Priorities

1. *Verify the integrity of essential infrastructure systems.* You cannot lock down your network until you trust the lock you are using. You must verify that the core systems that you are depending on to apply the lockdown are stable and trustworthy.

2. *Brief the Forensics Team on the early results.* The Forensics Team will be performing the in-depth research and analysis on this intrusion. They must be brought up to speed so that they can begin to analyze the information already collected and develop new information. Their first goal is to confirm or deny your initial conclusions and to make sure that your response is adequate.

3. *Deny the attacker additional access to the network.* Based on initial conclusions, you will deny all access to your network from the source network of the attack. The size of the block should be chosen carefully but be sufficiently conservative so that the attacker cannot simply switch to another machine on the same network and continue. All attempts at communication from the attacker network should be logged for later analysis.

4. *Close the apparent means of entry.* This closure can be temporary (such as denying all inbound traffic to a particular service) or permanent (such as repairing the hole, if you know how to do so). All attempts to access this service should be logged for later analysis.

Phase 4: Stabilization

At this point, you've blocked the attacker, and he may respond. You are monitoring for that and are prepared to enhance your lockdown (up to and including taking your network off the air in an extreme situation). Your Forensics Team is hard at work analyzing the situation. The goal of this phase is to make sure that the attacker has no further influence over your network.

Priorities

1. *Receive preliminary briefing from the Forensics Team.* The Forensics Team should be ready to report whether your preliminary conclusions were adequate or whether there is more to this attack than was originally noticed.

2. *Monitor for secondary means of entry or contamination.* The attacker is now probably aware of your blocks and may be reacting. In addition, automation embedded in your system by the attacker may be reacting as well. You need to monitor for all such activity and decide whether further action is required.

3. *Apply any additional lockdown required.* If further action is necessitated by the attacker's actions or the forensics reports, you should take it.

Phase 5: Cleanup

You can enter this phase when you are reasonably certain that the attacker has no further access to your network and that the means and scope of the attack are understood. You now focus on any activity necessary to returning your network and systems to full operational status.

Priorities

1. *Verify the integrity of essential business systems.* Up till now, you've focused on core systems because those are the ones that allow an attacker to take control of your network. Now you must verify that the business systems, the ones that actually perform the functions that are the reason for the network's existence, are in good working order and uncontaminated.

2. *Receive final report from Forensics Team.* The Forensics Team should have confirmed and possibly even duplicated the attacker's means of entry and analyzed the attacker's modifications to determine any secondary means of entry. They should have developed an attack signature, which can be used for additional verification of the extent of contamination.

3. *Apply any additional lockdown required.* The Forensics Team report may point to a final round of lockdown.

4. *Rebuild any contaminated systems.* Working in conjunction with the Forensics Team and any systems administration groups required, any contaminated systems should be rebuilt. Ideally, the contaminated systems should be taken completely off line immediately and rebuilt off line. If that is not possible, then they should first be purged of obvious contamination and closely watched for reinfection or self-infection.

5. *Verify correct operation of the network and all systems.* As rebuilt systems come back on line, the entire operation of the network, including logging and monitoring, should be reviewed to make sure that everything is working as it should be.

6. *Develop a workaround for the attacker's means of entry.* If the attacker exploited an unintended hole and the hole can be closed, that is all that is needed. If the attacker compromised an existing and required service, then a plan must be developed to resume that service without permitting further exploitation.

Phase 6: Restart

At this point, all attacker entry mechanisms are believed to be closed and all compromised systems are rebuilt and tested.

Priorities

1. *Lift any nonattacker-specific blocks.* You will probably want to leave the attacker block in place for awhile to monitor possible subsequent activity. The attacker may simply be biding his time to reactivate a hole you have not yet caught. A full block of all traffic, with logging enabled, may help you to spot the hole.

2. *Verify normal business operation.* Confirm with other parts of your organization that all systems and services are now working properly.

3. *Stand down Forensics Team.* Their work is done, unless reactivated by you. Volunteer fire fighters will need to return to their other jobs as quickly as possible.

4. *Pursue appropriate action against the attacker.* Contact the ISP or network administrator, or take any other action you deem appropriate.

Phase 7: Monitoring

You enter the final phase of the attack response when you believe that all problems have been resolved and when all general blocks have been lifted. The Response Team, or part of it, will remain on duty for a short while longer, but most team members have been stood down.

Priorities

1. *Watch for subsequent activity from the source network or to the attacker means of entry.* Monitoring should continue under Response Team supervision for at least a day, if possible. The attacker may be in another time zone or may be waiting for you to go to sleep. Providing Response Team shifts to monitor the network for a full day after restart gives you a quick way to reactivate the full team if there is a subsequent problem.

2. *Integrate monitoring into normal Watchstander activity.* The monitoring for subsequent attacker activity should be turned over to the Watch Team. In addition, the Watch Team should be instructed to review any attacker-specific blocks after a comfortable period of time (several weeks at least, but the length of time can vary depending on the size of the block and the source systems) if no subsequent suspicious activity has been detected.

3. *Stand down Response Team.* They've worked hard and deserve a rest. But make sure you can reach them by pager . . .

Chapter

14

Forensics

IN THIS CHAPTER:

- Getting Started
- The Art of Investigation
- The Clean Room
- Analyzing the Contaminated File System
- Analysis Tools
- What to Look For

The worst-case scenario is in effect: You've been penetrated. You think you've stabilized the situation and now it is time for damage assessment. What do you do?

Well, what is it that you want to know the most in this situation? Unless there are unusual circumstances, the facts you want to find are the following, in order of priority:

- How were you penetrated?
- When were you penetrated?
- What else has been compromised within your system?
- Who attacked you?
- Why did they attack?

To some people this order might seem a little odd. Why, for example, is the identity of the attacker fourth on the list, not first? If this were a murder, identifying the murderer would be the foremost priority, would it not?

Perhaps so, but a computer attack is not a murder. The victim of a murder is dead and nothing can change that. Your computer system may or may not be disabled by the attack, but you can always resurrect it if you know what to do. Assuming that your business depends on the use of the computer system and that a company that has gone bankrupt has no means for further investigation, then the first goal of your investigation should be to determine whatever information you need to keep yourself in business. Following is another way of stating your priorities:

- Restore the normal operation of your business.
- Ensure that you cannot be penetrated by the same means again.
- Prevent the attacker from attempting other means of attack.

Consider, also, what is likely to be successful. You *will* find a way for your business to return to operation; that is almost inevitable. You control the means for doing so, because at worst, you can flush the contaminated software and restore from a very old backup tape. (You *are* making regular backups, aren't you? And storing them in a safe place? And occasionally verifying that they are still good?) Or you can reinstall the vendor-distributed software and build everything back up from scratch. If you can find an easier way that you can be confident of, you'll do that. But one way or another, you'll get those systems working.

Finding and identifying the attacker is much more complicated. Unless the attacker is very careless, you'll need to track him back through other networks and perhaps telephone systems. You may need to get court orders and involve your lawyer in recovering evidence from Internet service providers, on-line services, or the telephone company. And even after doing so, the evidence may lead nowhere. So you may never know who attacked you or why.

You'll do the best you can, and if you pursue the trail of evidence correctly, you can get lucky. Good can prevail over evil, especially if evil is stupid or careless. As this book is being written, the alleged writer of a pervasive e-mail-borne virus has been apprehended because, while he did a very clever job in writing the virus, he signed his name to parts of it and other parts were traceable to his home computer. So it is possible to get lucky and actually nail the Bad Guy. Try for it. But don't depend on it.

Getting Started

You have one or more computers that you believe have been penetrated, and you want to examine one and find out how it has been compromised. You believe that the rest of your network is safe for the moment, perhaps because you've turned off your Internet connection or disconnected the modems. Where do you start?

The immediate temptation is to dig right in and look at the damaged machines. But that is not where you should start. The place to start is in your office supply closet. Get a nice, clean, fresh notebook and pen (not pencil) for yourself and every member of your team.

In any technical lawsuit, the person with the most documentation wins.

Gather the members of your Forensics Team together in a conference room, away from the computers and equipment under investigation. At this point, you are likely to notice something unusual happening. You may find that all the members of your technical staff who have the slightest relevance to the problem believe that they are or ought to be a member of your Forensics Team. Believe it or not, this can be a good thing, if you use it wisely.

Step 1: Take charge of the situation. If you are the person who is supposed to be in charge of the crisis, then make it clear to everybody in the room. If you are going to have to fight for control of the situation, now is the time to do so, before anybody touches any equipment. You want to avoid the situation where many people independently go off and do different things, stepping on each other's toes (and evidence) with no coordination.

Step 2: Explain why the investigation *must* be done your way. If your people disagree or if your management will not back you up, now is the time to find out. You should not proceed until you've gotten a reasonable consensus from the people you need to have on your side. If you are the right person for the job, you've probably laid the groundwork for this scenario, so consensus should not be difficult to achieve.

Step 3: Give the excess troops something to do. This step can be tricky, and for good reason. Before you take this step, ask yourself the following question: "Could this have been an inside job?" In other words, could someone on your staff be responsible for the problem you are now facing? Did someone working for you have the skill, the motivation, and the opportunity to cause the problem? At this point, you don't have enough facts to know for sure, so you need to make an educated guess. If you guess wrong, you may be placing the attacker in charge of the evidence. So be cynical, and guess conservatively.

If an inside job is a possibility at all, then you may rightly wonder why it is necessary to give the troops something to do. Human nature being what it is, people want to be included in a group, not excluded. And computer programmers being who they are, many of them will feel that they are as capable as you when it comes to investigating the situation. If you include them in the group and set them tasks that are at worst harmless and at best useful, then you minimize the possibility of any rogue actions.

What can be done safely by these people will depend on their skills, their temperament, and the situation, as well as your sense of whether or not the perpetrator is among them. Here are some possibilities:

- *Ask them to go home immediately.* This is the safest course of action but will require management buy-in. Depending on your level of paranoia, you can just send them home and proceed, or you can escort them, one at a time, to their offices to pick up personal belongings (lightweight stuff, such as coat and car keys) and then walk them to the door. Be sure to tell them that this action is for their own protection as well as the company's. And make sure to disable any mechanism that would allow them to connect to the company network from home.

- *Ask them to write a statement.* Depending on the situation, this could be a chronology of their last ten minutes of computer activity or a report of any suspicious incidents that they may be aware of or a list of theories they have as to the cause of the problem.

- *Have them turn off their computers in a safe way.* If you have a lot of compromised machines, it may be dangerous to keep them operating. One way to deal with this is to turn them off. However, you cannot rely on the normal shutdown procedure for a compromised machine, because the machine may be modified to take some action on shutdown. For that reason, it may be necessary to halt the machine abruptly and without warning. One good way to do this is to simply pull the power cord from the back of the machine. As a rule, technical people will not do this unless you specifically instruct them how and why it is necessary.

In all these cases, you are enlisting their help to solve the problem, not accusing them of anything. Stress this both overtly and subtly. Even if it is an inside job, the chances are very small that everybody is in on it. So you need to conduct your investigation in a way that encourages the most cooperation and results in the minimum amount of alienation and interference. If you act like a concentration camp commander investigating an escape attempt, you will get exactly the cooperation you deserve.

Step 4: Start logging what you do. With the excess troops taken care of and out from underfoot, adequate management buy-in, and all temporary measures for stabilizing the situation in place, you are left with the core Forensics Team, in whom you can place some level of trust. Now the real work begins.

The first thing you should do is instruct your core team on how you want the investigation conducted. Issue the notebooks to the team members and ask them to sign and date the first page. These notebooks are to be a personal and professional diary of everything done by each member of the team until the investigation has been completed. Each new entry should have a date and time entry beside it. Because the situation is now stable, at least theoretically, an exact synchronization of time probably won't be necessary, but it may not be a bad idea to have everyone set their watches in reasonable synchronization with yours. It may sound like something from a spy movie, but if you need to reconstruct a sequence of events later, a significant clock skew could make a mess of it.

The notebooks should remain with their owners while they are working. If an investigator needs to leave the facility for any reason, she should give her notebook to you, and the fact should be logged in both your and her notebooks. Be sure to give the person some scratch paper and a pen to write with while she is off site. You never know when a good idea will strike, and it would be a shame to lose one because there is nothing to write on. If possible, copy the scratch notes into the notebook when the investigator is next on site. If that is too difficult, just staple the scratch paper onto a page in the notebook.

The notebook should be used to record not just facts and actions but speculations as well. It's very easy for a good thought to be lost in the press of events, so a quick note on the spot might save hours or days later.

Step 5: Set the ground rules. It is very important to make your expectations clear about personal conduct at this point in the investigations. You need to determine and communicate answers to the following questions:

- Will this be a 'round-the-clock investigation? If so, how will we be handling shifts? How will we be handling meals? How will we be handling family issues?

- Who is second-in-command? You will not be available twenty-four hours a day. If you are not available for some purpose, who can stand in for you?

- Who is allowed to know about the investigation? Who can we talk to? Who should we not talk to?

- If we find something, who should we tell first?

- Who talks to the press?

- Who talks to law enforcement?

• Who talks to management?

Bringing up these topics proactively and answering them before the questions are asked will keep your team's mind on their collective jobs and make everyone a lot more comfortable with a stressful situation.

Step 5: Assign tasks. If you were to just tell the team to start investigating and then look at the situation an hour later, you would most likely find one person working and everyone else reading over that person's shoulder. Investigating that way is a waste of time, and time is not on your side. You need to break the investigation up into pieces that can be handled concurrently and assign team members to each piece. The choice of tasks will depend on the situation, but here are some major tasks to consider:

Safety

• *Enhance monitoring.* You think the current situation is stable, but it may not be. This person will devise some means of monitoring your network for additional trouble and then keep an eye on the results.

Restoration of Service

• *Locate and test backup tapes.* Backup tapes may be off site or may not be correct. This person will locate several sets of tapes (most recent, last week, and last month are a good place to start) and verify on a clean machine that the tapes are usable. Remember that the attack may have been designed to erase backup tapes when mounted, so you need to do the verification in a way that is not susceptible to this type of problem.

• *Begin planning to bring the production systems back into operation.* Which machines need to be fixed first and which can wait? What special changes to the production environment have happened recently that may not be on older backup tapes?

Investigation

• *Build a "clean room."* You've got a bunch of computers that need to be examined. To do that, you'll need a safe way to examine them without destroying evidence. This person will create the means to do so.

• *Determine the date of the initial attack.* If you know when the attack took place, then you can know which backup tapes to restore from and how long you have been exposed.

- *Determine which machines are compromised.* Compromised machines cannot be trusted and must be rebuilt, so if you know how many have been damaged, then you have a much better idea of how long it will take you to become operational again.

- *Determine which files have been compromised.* This is sometimes difficult, because the attack may target the utility programs you use to measure such things, as well as the date stamps on the filesystem itself; you will probably need to be quite clever. Remember, however, that if any file is compromised, you must rebuild everything from safe archives before returning the machine to production. Never assume that you've found all the compromised files.

- *Determine how the initial penetration occurred.* If you rebuild the system but don't fix the hole, then another attack at the same spot will be successful, as well. This person needs to look at the system from the various perspectives of an attacker (and remember that one such perspective is internal, because the attacker may be within your organization) and see what weaknesses are visible to be exploited.

- *Determine what holes have been added.* The penetration may have been difficult to arrange and very limited in scope, but probably the attacker was able to parlay the hole into much better and easier access to your network. You cannot fix the first hole and leave created ones open.

- *Analyze logs for anomalies.* Hopefully, you have lots of event logging turned on. Someone needs to sit down with the logs and see what they say. If you've done the setup correctly, then the story of the attack is buried in the logs somewhere, and someone has to sift it out. Remember, however, that the attacker knew you were logging and wanted to eliminate the logs that tell the story. So you've got to see whether the logs have been damaged and make sure that your reading of them does not destroy them or interrupt the logging process.

- *Analyze the network for anomalies.* Even if you've turned many machines off, you probably still have a lot of traffic on your network. Having someone watch it and look for unusual communications (do we really send all that ICMP traffic to Bulgaria?) may alert you to problems you haven't spotted in any other way.

Step 6: Designate a war room. One thing that should be apparent about the investigative tasks is that they cannot be performed in isolation. A clue in one area can lead to a breakthrough in another. You need a place to gather the information that you've painstakingly collected and turn it into a picture of what happened. For that, you want a war room that has these characteristics:

- Big enough to seat the entire core team
- Several large easels with multisheet paper pads on them for drawing and notes; colored pens
- Lots of wall space so that you can tape up sheets from the easel
- One or two phone lines, including a speakerphone
- A door that can be locked
- No windows into the hallway
- No whiteboard or chalkboard, or one that you can lock up when it's not in legitimate use

The last point requires some explanation. As we discussed earlier, documentation is everything in an investigation of this type. Because of that, you need to be very careful with the use of an erasable medium such as a whiteboard. Whiteboards have limited space, and there is always a temptation to erase old information to make space for new. It would be a pity if what was erased was valuable and difficult to replace. With the paper pads, you simply tear off a sheet and tape it to the wall or throw it in a corner; if you need it, it is still there. So avoid the use of whiteboards in an investigative situation as much as possible. And save all the sheets from the easels as you finish with them.

Step 7: Schedule regular debriefings. Your people need time to work, and they need peace and quiet to work in. If they are constantly being interrupted for status requests, they'll be less effective. But if you never find out what they're up to, you'll work very slowly and duplicate effort. So schedule a time and place where all members of the team get together and report on what has been found. These reports should be reasonably frequent at first, perhaps once per hour, then less frequent as the situation permits. Prepare and post an agenda so that your people can see in advance when it is their turn and be ready to speak. The last item on the agenda should always be when the next debriefing is to be held. The war room is a very good place for these meetings. Don't linger here, though. Meet, move through the issues very quickly and factually, and then move on, get your people back to work.

Step 8: Schedule regular management updates. You are in the thick of the situation and at the top of the information chain. If you've done your job right, information should begin flowing to you shortly after your people start working and you'll begin to get a picture of how bad things really are. Your management, however, is probably in the dark. They see you exercising control of the situation, which is good. They also see that you've sent half the workforce home for the day, which will seem awfully bad. They see your people ignoring their regular duties and doing esoteric things and seeming to be very agitated. No management team on Earth would be able to sit through all of this without becoming nervous. If they know that a briefing is forthcoming in a little while, they'll generally leave you alone to work until that time. If they don't know, they'll bother you and your team whenever the strain becomes too much to bear.

As early as possible in the investigation, set up a schedule for management briefings. Briefings should be given by you and you alone if possible. Your challenge is to give your management as many facts as you can without indulging in too much speculation or being unduly alarming. The briefings should be short and to the point but still provide time for people who are not security professionals to ask questions that may seem naive or may be uncomfortable to answer. Make it clear from the start that the point of these briefings is not to assign fault but rather to get the organization back into operation as quickly and as safely as possible.

The war room is a very bad place for these meetings. Managers can read the notes taped to the walls as well as you can, and while you want your Forensic Team to indulge in some speculation and brainstorming, you may not want to share those thoughts with your management until you have facts to back them up. So use a different conference room for the management meetings, but employ the same formula: Post an agenda on the wall, stay with the agenda, complete the meeting as crisply as possible, and schedule the next management update in the last agenda item. In this case, it is acceptable and possibly even sensible to use a whiteboard for illustration. Be sure to erase it at the end of each meeting.

The Art of Investigation

Eliminate the impossible. Whatever remains, however improbable, is the truth.

—Sherlock Holmes

A thorough reading of the Sherlock Holmes novels certainly cannot hurt someone who wishes to become skilled in the investigation of computer attacks. Unfortunately, it will not help very much, either. Holmes's ability to rapidly assemble an unbreakable chain of logic from the subtle clues around him is enviable, but it is not something that you or I are likely to be able to duplicate.

The spirit of that thought, however, is very much worth emulating. In any investigation, time is your enemy. You don't know whether the hole the attacker used is still open. You don't know whether or how you can safely resume normal operations. You need to conduct the investigation in a way that will not waste the time you have. Some dead-end searches are inevitable, but you cannot afford too many dead ends.

The catch is that while you are in the middle of such an investigation, you won't have the facts to know for certain which course of action is the correct one. So you must guess—and guess well. The only way you'll know that your guesses were correct is in retrospect. Perhaps you'll find the "smoking gun" that lets you completely nail the case closed, as Mr. Holmes would have done. Or perhaps you'll know that you were successful only because the incident doesn't come up in the conversation at your retirement party. That is why this type of investigation is an "art," not a science.

There are some key principles that will help guide you through the perils and pitfalls of forensic investigations.

> *Occam's Razor: The simplest explanation that fits the facts is often the best.*

The critical key word here is "often." The following saying is taught to medical students when training to diagnose patients.

> *When you see hoofprints, think of horses. But don't forget about zebras.*

Which means that the simplest explanation, while often the best, is sometimes not the right answer. But you should start with the simplest explanation first, and then attempt to disprove it. The difficulty here is that you and your team will be in a very paranoid frame of mind. You've been attacked. Paranoia is at least somewhat justified. This is not bad, but it can lead to wild speculation and "conspiracy theory" thinking if you are not careful.

The best trite saying that applies to forensic investigation is this one.

> *Practice makes perfect.*

In other words, if you wait until you have a serious problem to practice your investigatory skills, you probably won't be very good at investigations. For that reason, you want to practice, practice, practice and work the bugs out of your system so that when trouble strikes, you'll be at least somewhat familiar with what must be done and how to do it, and so will your team—and your management.

A forensic investigation of a network penetration is science in a hurry. You don't have time to waste, so any method that gives you the correct answer is worth considering, but you need to be sure that the answer is the correct one. I recall a case where, after the initial facts were presented, one of the investigators said, "Ha! Wait here!" and left the room. He returned a few minutes later holding a student by the collar and announced that he'd caught the culprit. And indeed the student quickly confessed his guilt. The conclusion turned out to be correct. It wasn't scientific, but it was good enough. Sometimes intuition is all you need; other times intuition can lead you astray.

The hard part of this case was not, as it turned out, finding the perpetrator. It was proving that the perpetrator had confessed to everything he had done. Intuition had found him, but it took a lot of hard work to make sure that we were safe.

- Don't leap to conclusions.
- Don't avoid conclusions.
- Decide, in advance, when to give up. And don't press much beyond that point without good reason.
- Remember that you may never learn the answer.

It is very human to leap to conclusions. People almost cannot help it. The trick in managing a forensic analysis is to train people to justify conclusions, which helps to restrain them a bit when the evidence is light and gives them a direction to proceed when they are sure they are correct.

Another danger in forensic analysis is a reluctance to accept the facts in front of you. Some people call this "analysis paralysis." You can keep searching deeper and deeper, but at some point, you stop learning new things and are just reconfirming the same facts over and over again. In science, this is the right approach. The more facts you have and the more ways those facts are confirmed, the more valuable your conclusions. But science takes time, and time is not your friend in an attack crisis. Your business may be paralyzed until your investigation has been concluded, so you must conclude it with all due haste.

As much as you might like it to be otherwise, your mission in a forensic investigation may not be finding the truth. What you are doing is creating an acceptable level of risk. At some point, you will give the signal to your organization that business can resume as usual. To be ready to give the signal, you must be reasonably confident that doing so will not cause major problems or allow subsequent attacks to succeed using the same method. It is likely that you will never be completely certain that you are safe. So you must decide, in advance, what "reasonably confident" means and then stick with your decision. The best approach is to find an acceptable level of risk, get back on line, and then dig in and learn the truth and confirm that the action you took was the right one.

Many factors will influence you. Consider the pressure you'll face as time goes on. The level of risk that is acceptable to your management will be very low one hour after the incident has occurred. They will want their computers to be clean and safe, and you'll be getting all the support you need. Now think about how that will change after the machines have been off line for one month. By that time, your business will have been seriously affected, your Forensics Team will be exhausted, and your management will be on the verge of a nervous breakdown. The pressure on you will be enormous simply to bring the system back up and live with the results. Unless you're superhuman, this pressure will cause you to question your judgment and relax your standards so that the situation can return to "normal," even though the problem may still exist.

So the best possible results are obtained by setting a level of reasonable confidence in advance, one that is based on technical and security considerations alone, and then working like mad to get there before other issues take precedence. Here are some things you would like to feel confident about knowing:

- When the attacker entered your systems

- Which computers the attacker compromised

- How the attacker gained entry to your systems

- Level of access (limited user, full user, system administrator) the attacker attained on each of the compromised systems

- When each successive level of access was attained

- Modifications the attacker made to your systems

If you can determine these points and justify your answers with observed facts and there are no anomalous facts that cannot be accounted for by your theories, then you can feel reasonably confident that you've accounted for the attack correctly.

Some areas of concern about theories:

- Have you examined enough evidence to make an accurate assessment of the facts?

- Are you sure that the evidence you've examined has not been tampered with?

If you were smart, you've provided for these areas in advance by building into your network a means of accumulating logging information for many different types of events so that activity on your network is reflected accurately in the logs. Having gone to the trouble of logging a great deal of network and computer activity, you have also hopefully taken the trouble to fortify your log repository as strongly as possible so that it was not one of the machines compromised by the attacker. If your logs are thorough and trustworthy, when you combine that information with the information extracted from a compromised machine, you should have a reasonable set of answers to the questions that most concern you.

Three Levels of Confidence

- What do you think?
- What do you know?
- What can you prove?

Devotees of the scientific method will recognize their old friends hypothesis, theory, and law in the three levels of confidence. There is an implicit assumption in the last level that should be made clear, however. "What can you prove?" carries with it an idea of the audience for a proof. "What can you prove to a room full of security experts?" is different from "What can you prove to a room full of FBI agents?" or a court of law. Those are subjects for later. Right now, your job is to make a case to the people on your forensics team. If you cannot convince them and yourself, there is no chance you can convince a legal authority.

The Clean Room

You have before you a contaminated machine. The one thing you know about it is that you cannot trust it to behave as it would if it were clean. You must assume that the code that shuts the machine down, reboots it, connects it to the network, reads or writes backup tapes, lists file directories, shows running processes, and any other normal system function that could be of help to you has been modified to do the bidding of the attacker and cannot be trusted by you.

What you need is a facility that allows you to examine the machine and determine what has happened to it, what has been compromised, and what remains unchanged. The design goals of this facility are simple:

- You don't want to contaminate the evidence.

- You don't want the evidence to contaminate you.

- You want to be able to use tools you can trust to examine files you cannot trust.

This facility, analogous to the clean rooms used in biotechnology, which do not permit infection in or out, will give you a workbench on which you can examine your tainted machine without triggering any booby traps added by the attacker. You are not dealing with a biohazard, so the literal definition of a clean room does not apply. But you want to create a facility that

- is not connected to your organization's network.

- has sufficient equipment and tools to allow your team to work on the problem.

- can allow several people to work concurrently.

- will not interfere with or be disturbed by other activities in your organization.

- cannot be tampered with if the attacker is a member of your organization.

Generally, this facility will need several network hubs and the cables associated with them, several workstations similar to the type that you are examining, extra disk controllers and tape drives, keyboards, monitors, and trusted vendor-distributed software.

The first step is to get the machine into the clean room. This is dangerous enough, though not typically in the physical sense (the machine will probably not explode, for example). But the attacker knew that you would to do this and may have taken steps to prevent your success.

What you would like to do is write a backup tape of this machine and then shut it down and move it to the clean room. However, the backup utility may have been compromised.

Judgment call: Do you write a backup tape on the untrusted machine?

The safest answer is probably "No." But consider the case of an attacker who uses a memory-based file system for storage of his software on your machine. When you turn off the machine, the memory of the machine is wiped, and with it, much of your evidence. So the choice is not an automatic one. If you have many infected machines and you are willing to lose the contents of some machines in order to investigate, then the choice may be easier. In that case, just gingerly investigate one machine, and if there is a booby trap, learn from it and avoid it on others. If you have only one, then you are back to a judgment call. If the machine has been rebooted several times after being infected but before the infection was discovered, then you probably need not write a backup tape, as the evidence will survive a reboot. If the infection is new but the attacker did not gain administrative privilege, then you may be safe in writing a tape, provided that you check to see that the tape backup mechanism is not the tool the attacker is waiting for you to use to compromise root privilege. But if you feel that you can safely make a backup of the machine in the infected state, then you should do so. Some information that will be very useful:

- Full backup of all file systems (including memory-based filesystems)

- List of all processes that are running

- List of all services listening for connections on the network and which ports they are listening on

Of course, the attacker knows this as well, so many attack packages (such as the classic rootkit) go to great pains to modify the programs that list running processes and files so that their tools remain unseen. If you were smart in preparing for an attack (Chapter 12), you hid trusted copies of these programs on all your workstations so that they could be used in just such an emergency. Of course, you can't guarantee that they were undamaged, but, to damage them, the attacker would have had to know specifically where and what they were and would have had to craft an attack specifically against your machines. If this is a script kiddie attack, for example, you might get lucky and find the tools available and undamaged. If not, then you should suspect an inside job.

Having gotten all you can from the running system, your next task is to turn off the computer. To do this safely, you must know the computer you are working with. In general, the best way is to simply pull the plug from the wall outlet, unceremoniously forcing the computer to stop. On more and more computers, the power switch is merely a "suggestion" to the operating system that the machine be turned off or on; attackers may intercept the suggestion and take some action based on it. Pulling the plug gives the computer no warning and bypasses this type of trap. For battery-operated machines such as laptops, you must find a way to remove the battery pack.

Once the machine has been powered down, you can move it to the clean room. The goal of your work in this environment is to remove the primary disk drives from the infected machine and place them on a trusted machine as secondary disk drives. This assumes that the operating system of the trusted machine does not execute code from a secondary drive during the boot and disk recognition sequence. Other operating systems may have different behavior, which you should be cognizant of. If at all possible, the compromised disks should be mounted on the clean room machine as read-only so that nothing can accidentally alter their state. You want to make as much as possible of the trusted software on your clean room machine read-only, as well. If you were smart (see Chapter 12), you prepared a clean room template in advance and can now create new ones quickly and easily (Figure 14-1).

The intention of this setup is to allow you to examine the compromised disks with little fear of triggering a booby trap placed there by the attacker. Your clean system will be neither booting from the contaminated disks nor using any of the utility programs from those disks.

Once you've transferred the contaminated disks to the clean machine, you should make another backup of them to tape. After doing so, have a member of your team compare the backups on another machine to see if the same amount of data is on each one. If so, then you have strong evidence that the attacker did not alter your system backup utilities and confirmation that your decision to risk an initial backup was not a major mistake. You should go the extra mile and make

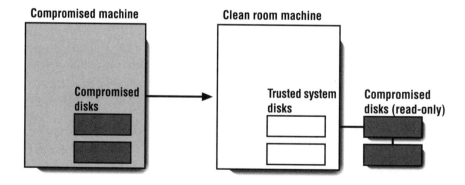

Figure 14-1: Clean room template

sure that all of the backed-up files are identical, however. If they are not the same size, then you have a place to start to look for a compromise: the backup software on the contaminated disks.

Analyzing the Contaminated File System

With the contaminated disks now safely in your clean room and mounted read-only, you can begin to examine them for problems. Exactly how to do this will depend on your choice of approaches to the problem. There are two major schools of thought here: paranoid or simple. A paranoid approach to forensics would be to assume that the attacker has been extremely subtle in his contamination of your system. Nothing can be trusted. Everything down to the format of the file system on disk is suspect. Confidence must be rebuilt from the bottom up. A simple approach assumes that the attacker probably did as little work as possible on your system to avoid detection or simply because of a lack of time or access. In that case, most of the compromised system is likely to work as before, with only a few changes here and there on key files.

> *Judgment call: Should you take a paranoid or a simple approach to the investigation of a compromised machine?*

There's no easy answer. A paranoid approach is the safest one, because you trust nothing and slowly build up a picture of what was done to your machine. But the key word there is "slowly." Unless you have the appropriate tools, and are extremely skilled in using them, a paranoid approach is going to take a long time and will pose a number of roadblocks.

Here are some rules of thumb that may prove helpful:

- If you don't have sophisticated tools or access to people who can use them effectively, favor a simple approach.

- If the attacker was on your system for a very short amount of time, favor a simple approach.

- If the attacker gained privileged access, favor a paranoid approach.

- If you have many systems that have been similarly compromised, favor a simple approach on the first system you investigate.

- If you have only one system that has been compromised, favor a paranoid approach. If that system is vital to your operations and cannot be quickly recovered from backups, strongly favor a paranoid approach.

The approach you select should help you, not bind you. As you dig deeper into the compromised computer, you'll get more information, all of which you should be noting in your log book. If, in light of any new facts, your investigation approach seems flawed, don't hesitate to step back and reassess all your conclusions.

Analysis Tools

Now that you've got your suspect system up on the dissection table and have selected an approach to examining it, examine the tools you have at your disposal. Each operating system has tools and capabilities unique to itself. Others can be found on the Internet, a list that is constantly changing. A very good hobby for a computer security professional is to collect and test forensic tools. Something to remember is that a tool is good because it is useful, not because it is complicated. Another thing to keep in mind is that the author of a forensic tool on the Internet may be using his tool as a part of an attack. Do not use tools from the Internet that you don't get the source code for and cannot compile for yourself. Read through the source code and look for programming that does unexpected things, such as send e-mail or listen on a network port.

> **File System Consistency Checks.** In a way, an attacker is building a ship in a glass bottle. He's working through a very narrow opening and trying to do sophisticated things. He's often in a hurry. All this adds up to the significant possibility that he has made a mistake. By running a consistency checking program (which usually is supplied with the computer's operating system) on a contaminated file system, you may be able to spot a mistake. Files that were open for writing may not have been closed correctly when you pulled the power cord of the contaminated system, and they will stand out during the consistency check. Also, a sophisticated attack involving the file system format may become apparent during this check, as well. Many consistency checking programs can be run with parameters that deny it the ability to write changes to the file system under test. These flags should be used when consistency programs are used for forensic purposes.

> **Modification Dates.** For simple attacks or attacks the attacker did not have time to complete, an examination of the file system for files that are very new can sometime spot modifications made by the attacker. A more sophisticated attacker can set file creation or modification dates, so looking

for the newest files may not be successful. However, the attacker may have used a fixed date long in the past to set his files to. Often, the attacker will use a date identical to that of the files on the vendor OS distribution media. If you were smart (see Chapter 12), you set all of the last-modified times to a known value different from that of the vendor distribution. In that case, examining all the files whose modification dates differ from your known value may prove interesting.

File Permissions. After an attacker has found a complicated and difficult way in, he will often add files to your system to make the next visit much simpler. These files often have additional permissions to allow the attacker to gain access to privileged services quickly and easily. A walk through all the files in each filesystem looking for unusual privileged files can be quite revealing. If you were smart (see Chapters 6 and 12), you eliminated all unnecessary privileged files from your systems and are familiar with the names and characteristics of all that legitimately remain. An attacker may hide a privileged file in an unusual location or replace an existing but infrequently used file with a different one. Some attacks simply give an existing file slightly or significantly more liberal permissions, such as allowing universal read/write access to the user account database. This type of change may be subtle, and it could be very difficult to spot unless you were familiar with the correct values.

Sophisticated Checksums. A common type of attack is known as the Trojan horse attack, or simply a *trojan.* If a program is *trojanned,* it has been replaced with a version that performs many (but not necessarily all) of the original functions it was supposed to perform, and it may perform other functions as well. A command to list running processes might do so, unless those processes had names that were being used by the attacker. Running such a program would show the picture of a system in which all was well, even though processes owned by the attacker were running on the system. A good way to spot programs that have been trojanned is to perform a summary calculation on them, resulting in a unique value that could only have been derived from a particular combination of bits in a file. The catch here is that, because a summary function produces a value that is (typically) smaller than the file itself, it has to abstract a lot of the file information away by means of some algorithm.

Figure 14-2 shows three of the most common types of file summary functions. The first is a 16-bit summary, the second is a 32-bit summary, and the third is a 128-bit summary. It is relatively easy for an attacker to fool the first value (i.e., create a trojanned file that is different from the original but still returns the correct checksum) and considerably harder to fool the sec-

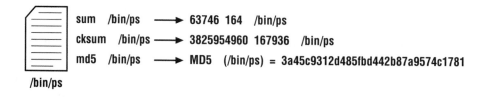

/bin/ps

Figure 14-2: Types of file summary functions

ond; while it is theoretically possible to fool the third, the attacker is unlikely to. Many other summary functions exist and are easily available on the Internet. A good forensics toolkit would have as many as possible. Of course, you need a library of correct checksums for each function, as well, against which to compare the checksum of each program on the contaminated machine. If the contaminated files summarize differently than the correct versions, then you know something has been changed. If the files match on simple checksums but fail on more sophisticated ones, then you have a means to gauge the sophistication of the attacker (or at least the tools the attacker used).

Embedded Strings. Many freely available programs provide a way to examine a binary file (such as an executable program) and look for ASCII strings embedded in the program. If you suspect that a file has been contaminated, you'll want to look a bit further to see if you can determine what it is supposed to do. By examining the strings output for a file closely, you may be able to get a clue to what the program does and who originated it. As attack tools have become more sophisticated, this technique has lost much of its usefulness, because attackers have learned to embed strings in ways that cannot be seen by the strings command, but skillful interpretation of strings output can still pay off from time to time. It is especially useful to develop the habit of looking at a variety of programs (whether you suspect them of being hostile or not) to learn how a normal program appears when examined by strings. Once this skill is learned, it becomes much easier to spot the anomalies in a rogue program.

Decompilation. Binary programs are typically created by feeding source code (the more or less human readable form of the program) to a program called a compiler, creating a computer-readable and -executable version. On some systems it is possible to feed a binary program to a decompiler, which will examine the computer-executable version and translate it back into a form that is more easily interpreted by a human. What you get as a result of decompilation is rarely as readable as the original program was and probably will require deep programming knowledge in the person reading the output for any insight to be gained.

Traceable Execution. Many operating systems provide a means for running a program under observation so that some understanding of its operation can be gained even without access to the source code. Typically, this involves watching a list of system calls flash by as the program executes. The advantage of doing this is that you will see the program attempt to do what it has been designed to do, including making many hidden strings visible. The disadvantages are many, not the least of which is that once you've executed a "tainted" binary on your clean machine, it may no longer be clean and thus no longer trustworthy. This type of forensic analysis should be considered as a last resort and should be done on a machine that can be "sacrificed" if a problem should arise. If it is attempted, one good way to do it is to run the program under a debugger, such as gdb. Many modern debuggers decompile the program as they execute and provide you with a means to "step" through the program, running one portion of the code at a time. If you are careful (and awfully patient), you can stop the program from executing before any damage can be done but still be able to see what damage was intended. Running a contaminated program in this fashion should be done on a machine that has been configured to be as much as possible like the original target machine on which the contaminated program was found. Host name, time of day, IP address, even Ethernet address, if possible, should be the same as the original target. The machine should be connected to an isolated network segment, however, and no contact with the Internet or with your production networks should be allowed.

Sniffers. If you do run contaminated software, you should set up additional clean machines running sniffers to monitor the network traffic generated by the contaminated software. Many sniffer programs are available on the network for all types of operating systems. A sniffer allows you to watch any and all traffic that is placed on a network. You can record many things about the sniffed packets, including their contents, if that is appropriate. In the case of running contaminated software, you should carefully record each piece of traffic and then account for each one so that you can see what anomalies occur. Don't bias your search by looking for specific traffic types, such as TCP streams or UDP packets, or specific sources or destinations. Record everything and sort it out later.

What to Look For

The point of applying all of these tools is to look for items or events that are out of the ordinary. To do this successfully, you'll need to have a good sense of what is ordinary. If you've practiced this type of investigation, your team will already have some sense of it. Another good way to bring unusual things to light is to follow the classic scientific method once again and set up a control experiment. You would do this by duplicating the experiment on a second clean room machine without any contaminated media on it. By running the two side by side, you can see the point at which the contaminated software deviates from the clean software—if it deviates at all.

What you're looking for in all of these experiments are indications of what the attacker has done and what the attacker wants to occur. These indications can take many forms.

New Files. Some files that were created or modified within the period of the attack may have been created by normal processes, others may be a side effect of the attack. Remember that the attacker may have created a file recently but made it appear that the file is quite old.

Unusual Files or Directories. Files that appear to be one thing may actually be another. A Trojan horse program is a good example. It might appear to be a normal system program, except that it would be a different size than the one that came with the system or take a little longer to run than normal or have a different checksum, if examined carefully enough.

Files with Unusual Names. A common attacker technique on Unix systems is to create files that begin with a period (.). A convention in program directory lists in Unix is that a filename beginning with a period is "hidden," meaning that it requires a special option to be listed. Because of this, "dot files," as they are called, are less likely to be noticed. Each directory in a Unix file system contains two standard files, named "." and "..", which refer to the current directory and the parent directory, respectively. A common trick is to create a directory called "...". Because it is a dot file, it will not be seen in the standard listing of a directory. Because it resembles two files that Unix users have been conditioned to ignore, it is often overlooked even in a full directory listing.

Other filenames are less subtle. Many attackers, especially young ones who attempt system penetration for reasons related more to their peer group than for financial gain, use a sort of code system for filenames that is loosely designed to resist brute force string searches. The code mutates regularly, and so do the common words used in it, but following are some examples to give you the basic idea:

HackSpeak	Intended Word
31337	elite (eleet)
3L33t	elite (eleet)
el33t	elite (eleet)
el1t3	elite
warez	software
kewl	cool
k3w1	cool
haq	hack
h4q	hack

As you can see, there are a lot of variations possible on an individual word, both phonetic and representational. The slight advantage that you have as a defender is that these words are designed to be recognized by other attackers as a sort of "tag" similar to gang graffiti. Because of that, they can't be completely free form, so you can collect a list of them, search for them, make some up yourself, and recognize them when you see them. But recognition can be difficult. A good example: The Back Orifice program, which allows an attacker to remotely control a Windows 95 or Windows 98 machine and allows UDP connections on port 31337, which you'll recognize from the hackspeak table. A string search or filename search would never find this, but it is there all the same.

Files with Normal Names in (Slightly) Unusual Places. Earlier, we discussed the habit of doing forensic-style analysis on a regular basis to keep in practice for emergencies and to develop a good feel for what is normal so that what is not normal stands out. In general, this is a good idea. Sometimes, however, this familiarity can be used against you, as in the case of the "..." directory. For example, it is a common Unix convention to place software packages in a directory by themselves. In this directory is a collection of other directories, which usually follow a standard naming convention: bin for binary programs, lib for loadable libraries and static data files, etc for administrative programs and sometimes configurations files, man for manual pages, and so forth.

If you were to see a file called /usr/local/perl5/lib/info, would it mean anything to you, or would it seem like a perfectly normal file in the Perl 5 package? The correct answer is that you don't know until you look at it. This type of misdirection is a classic way of hiding information or files. You might be tipped off if the file were executable, for example, and if it were executable with root privilege, that would be a big red flag. But it might be a simple text file that contains the output of a password collector hidden elsewhere and thus not call attention to itself in any special way.

Normal Files in Unusual Places (Such as Under /dev). This is another aspect of misdirection. The /dev directory (/devices under some versions of Unix) contains special files that trigger action for device drivers when accessed correctly. The filenames are often quite obscure, and one more obscure filename can be easily lost. Usually, files hidden here are normal files (as opposed to "special" device files), because an attacker would not normally be able to create new devices on the fly without rebooting the system.

This is also one of the places where attackers look for clues to how to break into the system as well. One classic trick is to look for a normal file with a name similar to that of a backup device. A common mistake for novice systems administrators is to attempt to back up a disk volume to a tape device while running as root. If the tape device used is not an actual device on the system, Unix will cheerfully create a file under the /dev directory with this name and proceed to back up the volume to that file. The naive sysadmin comes back later, sees that the backup has finished, ejects the (blank) tape, and files it. If an attacker gains access to the system, even though key system files might be unreadable to him, the backup file may be, and he can read and analyze it at leisure.

Unusual Processes. This test must be performed on the contaminated system; it cannot be done on the clean room system without contaminating it. Are there any processes that are running on the contaminated system that do not belong there? Or are there processes that belong there but are running in an unusual fashion? To get this information requires that you have a trusted means of listing running processes, which may mean that you've hidden such a set of programs on your machines before they were infected (see Chapter 12) or loaded them later or verified that the existing programs were unmodified.

An unusual process may have an odd name (which is unlikely) or it may have a perfectly normal name. One way to tell if a process is supposed to be there is to examine the parent of that process. If the parent of a system process is unusual (it was started from a login shell rather than the system boot process, for example), then it is suspect. Operating systems provide tools for examining running processes that can sometimes be illuminating. These tools vary from implementation to implementation and OS to OS.

Unauthorized Network Listeners. This test must also be performed on a contaminated system, but it can often be done from the outside rather than depending on untrustworthy tools. Programs such as `strobe`, `netcat`, `nmap`, `tcpscan`, and `udpscan` are widely available that allow you to probe a suspect machine and see which ports it is willing to accept connections on. If you were smart (see Chapter 6), you reduced the number of listeners on each machine to the bare minimum necessary for the machine's normal operation, so any unusual listeners should stand out.

Network listeners such as this usually indicate that the attacker has left a backdoor into the system for some type of access later. By carefully monitoring your network, watching for attempts to access these ports, you can sometimes gather clues as to the identity of the attacker or at least move in that direction.

Chapter
15

Log Analysis

IN THIS CHAPTER:

- Integrity Checks
- Log Analysis
- The Hunt
- Developing Theories
- Legalities

In a security crisis, the most important questions you can ask about your logs are

- Are they safe?
- Are they complete?

These questions should be the critical parameters for the design of your logging system. As we discussed in Chapter 9, the design of your logging system is crucial to the security of your entire enterprise, because it is in the logs that you will find out what an attacker has attempted or accomplished. If the logs cannot be kept safe, then the attacker is free to present whatever view of your world he would like you to see.

The best way to move in this direction is to design a logging system that is extraordinarily difficult for an attacker to reach. Earlier, we discussed a logging system that scaled well to many different hosts, yet was very difficult to compromise (Figure 15-1). This logging system was designed to reside in physical isolation from all other systems on the network, in both the network and the physical senses; it is inaccessible except by a very small number of authorized people. Network hubs, power supplies, and the machines themselves should all be in a locked and sealed area, with strong access control and access logging.

The only means of information transfer between the monitored network and the logging system is a small number of network connections (shown in the figure

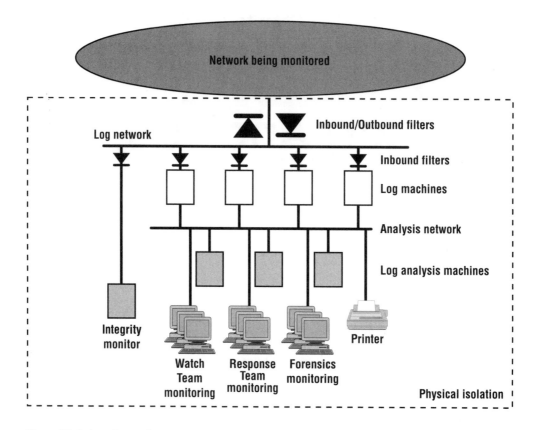

Figure 15-1: Logging system

as a single connection). This network connection is guarded by a filtering system. The filtering system is designed to let logging messages in but allow no other inbound connections, and to allow no outbound connections whatsoever. This type of filtering would typically be implemented with a router so that the filtering would not induce significant latency and so that additional access control could be added in an emergency.

The inbound logging traffic enters the logging system by means of a log network. This network is of sufficient bandwidth to cope with an extremely high volume of log activity. Log traffic is sent to several machines, which are split by function. For example, one machine might handle router activity, another core server activity, another workstation activity. A large number of different machines can be accommodated here.

The inbound network connection of each logging machine has been modified so that it will accept only log traffic and can generate no traffic onto the log network. This modification could be done in software at the kernel level of each machine, or it could be done by hardware modification to the network connection by clipping the TRANSMIT wire of the network interface and thus allowing no outbound transmissions on that network interface. The best answer is, of course, making both modifications.

In addition to the logging machines, another machine resides on this network. This machine is the integrity monitor. It is the job of the integrity monitor to sniff the traffic on the log network and to analyze the traffic to see if other protocols are present. If that is ever the case, then the integrity of the log network has been compromised, and it is the responsibility of this machine to sound an alarm. In addition, this machine may be used to monitor log traffic and look for other signs of interest, such as a machine that is generating too much or too little logging traffic.

Behind the logging machines is the analysis network. This network is physically separate from all other networks in the organization. Its purpose is to allow access from the log analysis machines to the data stored on the logging machines. Access can occur through whatever mechanism is convenient that does not place unnecessary load on the log machines. A good example would be the NFS (Network File System) protocol, though in fact, any number of systems could be used.

Each log analysis system is designed to look for a particular issue or set of issues. Many different analysis machines can be placed on the network, and they can be functionally arranged or merely arranged for proper load balancing. Indeed, there is some advantage to making these machines of a homogenous nature so that any machine can handle any set of tasks; by doing so, you improve the robustness of your monitoring system and also your ability to add capacity to it.

The log analysis systems are set up completely separate from the rest of your network, but you will want to have three sets of analysis monitoring stations set up to access the results of the analysis, one set for the watch team, one set for the Response Team, and one set for the Forensics Team.

The purpose of all of this isolation is so that you can have an unbreachable core to your system that will always be available to tell you what went wrong and provide you with vital clues for fixing it. This system can be of other uses than just security, in that logging of all types can be sent here and handled safely and reliably. A good way to think about this would be as the equivalent of the "black box" flight recorder on aircraft. The reason airplanes carry black boxes (which, incidentally, are always painted international rescue orange, not black) is so that after a major catastrophe, the lives lost will not have been lost entirely in vain. The information in the black box can (sometimes) tell the crash investigators what went wrong. Other planes can then be modified so that the same problem does not occur again. Good black boxes are one of the reasons commercial aviation is commonplace, reliable, and safe. A good network "black box" can help you through a variety of catastrophic situations as well, if it is set up and maintained properly.

Integrity Checks

You can ensure that your logs have not been tampered with in a number of ways. The key problem with all of them is making sure that the integrity checks themselves have not been tampered with. You can ensure that your integrity checking mechanisms are safe in the following ways:

- Keep them physically secure.

- Make them difficult to reach from the network.

- Have many different types of checking mechanisms, and sound an alarm if a discrepancy appears between them.

- Limit the number of people who can examine or modify all of them.

The last point is very interesting. As you drastically reduce the ways in which people can access and possibly modify your logging and log assurance systems, the greatest threat to them will come from your own people. This is not to say that a secured logging system induces your people to become more hostile to it. Consider a "clean room" at an integrated circuit manufacturing facility. This is a room that has been swept of all large particles of dust and debris, because such particles can seriously interfere with successful chip fabrication. Open windows allow particles in from the outside, so these rooms have sealed windows. Doorways also can contaminate the room, so the doors to the rooms are unfigured like an airlock on a spacecraft. Tools and instruments brought in from the outside are a problem, so each one is specially cleaned before it is allowed to enter the room. The workers' clothing and shoes carry microscopic debris, so they wear special "bunny suits" and are swept clean by jets of air before entering the room. The air of the room itself is meticulously filtered. After all of these precautions, the room is pretty clean. But chip factories have special teams to deal with room contaminations, because sometimes problems still occur. After years of operations, most of the simple physical problems, such as plastic tool handles that shed particles after serious wear and outgassing ceiling tiles, are well understood and can be dealt with. What the contamination teams discover in almost all cases is that unexpected contamination is caused by the one unpredictable element in the room: the people.

People skip decontamination procedures when they are not supposed to. People chew gum where gum is not allowed. People have unpleasant and embarrassing skin conditions that they do not report. And sometimes, people deliberately bring in material to contaminate the room for malicious reasons, such as revenge or, once in a while, sabotage.

Most clean room workers cause very few problems and have the highest regard for their jobs and the contamination protocol. But all it takes is one bad or careless worker to cause a problem.

Your logging systems are in much the same situation. You work diligently to eliminate ways in which an outside agency could contaminate or modify those machines. You provide cross-checking systems to ensure that the logs remain secure. But the more people you trust with access to the systems, the more likely you are to have a problem by either accidental or deliberate cause.

Of course, you must give access to some people, such as the watch, response, and forensics teams. But you don't have to give full access to all those people all the time. You can apply a number of limitations:

Extremely Limited Physical Access to the Machines. Lock the machines away where they cannot be touched, rewired, or interfered with. Of course, you'll need to make provisions for them to be backed up reliably and regularly.

Independent Monitoring Systems. Have, as shown in Figure 15-1, an independent verification system with extremely limited access so that many groups could observe the display indicating the integrity of the logs at a particular moment, but very few would be allowed access to the system itself, and only with logged and verified access. There might be other verification systems in place on the other logging machines, but their results must be correlated with this system to be trusted.

Layered Access to the Machines. Design into the logging systems a progressive access mechanism so that different groups have different layers of access. For example, the Watch Team might have read-only access to a specified user interface, while the Response Team and Forensics Team have deeper but perhaps still read-only access to the raw data; only a very limited group, such as the group responsible for maintaining the monitoring software, have read-write access to the systems, and only two people (yourself and a backup, perhaps) have read-write access to the independent integrity verification systems.

Login to Analysis Systems Restricted to Response Team Manager. An alternative to traditional account access might be that the Response Team Manager on duty is the only one who can log Response Team and Forensics Team members into the log analysis systems. By doing this and verifying that they are logged out at the end of a session, only the RTM has access, but all the other team members can use the system.

Two-Man Rule. A slightly better alternative is one in which *both* the Response Team Manager and a team member are required to log into a system in a two-factor authentication mechanism, such as each person knowing half a password, or better still, a dynamic authentication token, such as a SecurID card, in which the RTM knows the PIN (the static code that is the prefix for the dynamic part) and the team member is issued the token. In any of these ways (assuming that neither party is allowed to "eavesdrop" on another's typing), two people are required to allow login to a core logging system.

You may wish to think of other alternatives for keeping your systems physically secure and limiting access to key, trusted personnel appropriate to your organization, but however you choose to do so, the best way to ensure the integrity of your logs is to permit no opportunity for the integrity to be compromised. Nevertheless, you will want some active methods for log verification, as well. A number of mechanisms can work quite well:

Entry Counts. This is a simple method that lends itself to implementation on an independent system. A sniffer listens for log entries, counts them, and displays the log counts at particular times of day. The logging systems themselves maintain their own counts in a similar fashion and display them at the same times as the independent systems. If the numbers disagree, there is a problem.

Monotonically Increasing Counts. In addition to simple counting, another check is to verify that the count of log entries is always increasing or staying the same, never decreasing (known in mathematics as a *monotonically increasing number*). If you take a count of log entries now, and then wait some period of time (a second, a minute, an hour) and check again, the new count will always be greater than or equal to the first count. If the count is ever smaller, there is a problem. Of course, this method works best when the time period is very short compared to the number of log entries that could come in.

Periodic Sampling. A simple yet effective check is to periodically sample a file. A program on the logging system would periodically read through a log file and collect, for example, every 463d line. The number of these entries should also increase monotonically. The first N lines in the array of sampled lines (where N is the number of lines in the previous sample) should match exactly. If they don't, there is a problem. Also, if there are M lines in the new sample, and M minus N is a very large number (larger than 10, for example), then the interval between samples is too long, which should result in a warning to the logging software support staff.

Duplicate Logs. By having multiple machines store each log file, you can perform the same checks on each independently. By comparing the results and looking for discrepancies, you can notice any differences between the two. Duplicate logs checked in this fashion require an attacker to compromise each system simultaneously (or at least within the same window between checks) to avoid detection. If the checks occur sufficiently often and the overall security of the machines is satisfactory, compromising the systems should be very difficult. Besides providing redundant checks, duplicate logs increase the overall robustness of the logging system and make it easier to survive and recover from a catastrophic hardware failure.

Note that in all of these mechanisms, you'll need to account for the concept of *log rotation*. You cannot allow your logs to grow without bounds, simply because doing so will make it increasingly difficult to process the logs each day. For logs with a great deal of daily traffic, in a short while their size will become unmanageable, even for the most powerful systems. You need a way to periodically have the logging system move old logs to a place where they can be archived, while continuing to accumulate new logs. Depending on the log volume, you may choose to rotate your logs hourly, daily, weekly, or when they reach a certain size. For security purposes, it is typical to select a reasonable time period, such as daily rotation and apply it to all logs. This simplifies the writing of tools to analyze the logs and makes it easier to locate a particular log file when looking for historical data on a particular event.

Note also that many of these methods, when executed across several machines, require the machines to be in precise time synchronization. With many machines, such as Unix platforms, this is quite easy, using the network time protocol (NTP). Remember, however, that one type of attack on your system might be to corrupt the NTP synchronization between the logging machines and the rest of your network. Fortunately, there are many inexpensive time sources now available that depend on the Global Positioning System (GPS) signals from orbiting satellites for time synchronization. GPS systems are basically hyperaccurate clocks broadcasting time signals from many satellites at the same time. A GPS receiver locates itself on the surface of the Earth by measuring fractional discrepancies from several satellites at the same time and using those discrepancies to compute the distance from the satellites and by extension the position of the receiver. A GPS time source is simply a receiver that never moves that can translate the GPS time signal into NTP updates.

By having an isolated GPS time source for your logging system, you render it independent of time sources on the rest of the network. By comparing network time with logging system time, you can provide a valuable cross-check for accidental or possibly malicious discrepancies between the two systems.

Another check that should be made against logs is to look for missing entities. The integrity checks described up to this point are against log entries that were made. A simple defeating strategy would be simply blocking any log messages from a target machine to the logging system. To counteract this possibility, the logging system should come to expect messages from machines that log regularly and warn if such messages fail to arrive.

The opposite side of this problem is one of log saturation. An attacker might cause various machines to generate hundreds or thousands of logging messages per minute in an attempt to overwhelm the logging system and perhaps slip by the integrity checks. A good logging system should notice this and warn about the flood of messages. A very good logging system would have quick ways to divert excess messages away from the core logging systems, perhaps storing them safely on a backup server, so that the standard checks are not affected and the core logging systems can continue to operate as normally as possible.

Log Analysis

Once you've satisfied yourself that your log files are uncontaminated, your next task is to begin to analyze log files for evidence related to the attack. This part of your job is in line with the teachings of Sir Arthur Conan Doyle and his alter ego, Sherlock Holmes. What you will be doing is searching your records for clues that will allow you to piece together what happened, and from there, to choose your response. As we said in Chapter 14:

Eliminate the impossible. Whatever remains, however improbable, is the truth.

—Sherlock Holmes.

If you have adequate logs of enough of the events on your network and your logging systems are uncontaminated, your work should not be extremely difficult. If, however, you lack information for key areas, now is when you will regret it.

Following are the key priorities in a search through your logs.

1. *Look for traffic.* Suppose that machine A has been compromised. Your immediate task would be to look for traffic from any machine or network that was directed toward machine A. Alternatively, suppose that you suspected machine X of being the source of the attack. In that case, you would collect logs relating to traffic from machine X to any machine on your network.

2. *Look for anomalies in the traffic.* Of the traffic you've collected, what appears normal and what appears odd? If the target is a file server and you see logged file requests from machines on your network, you will not suspect those at first. If, however, one request comes from Bulgaria, then that is a good place to start. Collect the anomalies and begin the process of explaining them.

3. *Look for linkages in the traffic.* Suppose that machine A has been compromised, and you see an unusual entry in its log whose source was machine X. You would want to begin looking at all traffic from machine X to any machine on your network. You also want to find any of your machines that have been touched by machine X and examine them for contamination. If a machine has been contaminated, then you also want to examine the logs of any traffic it has been generating for anomalies, as well.

4. *Look for patterns in the traffic.* Suppose you see that machine A, which has received an SMTP connection from machine X, suddenly starts sending ICMP packets to machine Y, but before the SMTP connection there was no traffic of any kind from A to Y. You now have a possible vector for the contamination.

5. *Look for broken or unusual patterns in the traffic.* You've collected vast amounts of logging information on all of your machines under normal operations. You should be able to look at that information and have a sense of what the normal operations of a particular machine are. For example, if a file server for the engineering department suddenly starts answering file requests from the sales department, it has departed from its normal pattern. It may be a legitimate departure, but you have to know to ask the question before you will have the answer.

6. *Create hypotheses.* Now that you've accumulated a big pile of data and seen some unusual things in the data, the time has arrived to speculate. One of the biggest problems that incident investigators (even experienced ones) have is that they begin to speculate too soon and get lost in the problem. Unfortunately, another major problem of investigators is that they take too much time and demand too much confirmation to form an opinion. Better to take a middle position: Accumulate a reasonable amount of data, find a reasonable amount of anomalies, and then begin to speculate about the problem.

7. *Attempt to support your hypotheses with the data.* Once you've made the leap and created some hypotheses about what happened, look for data to support it. Be conservative: Don't try to put a square peg in a round hole. If a datum fits the hypothesis, it will probably fit nicely and not need to be forced. If you find yourself forcing the fit by requiring amazing coincidences or superhuman attackers to make your hypothesis work, then put the

hypothesis on the back burner. You may not be wrong, but you want to look in more obvious places first. If you can make a reasonable case, then a hypothesis supported by data is now a theory.

8. *Attempt to disprove your hypotheses with the data.* Be ruthless here. Try to shoot holes in your pet theory with the facts at hand. See if any other facts in your logs can make your theory invalid. You are not trying for conclusive, scientific proof, but you are trying to avoid wasting time. Once you have a theory that is supported by and not obviously contradicted by the available facts, then move forward with it.

The Hunt

Log analysis is a flavorless name for it, but what you are doing is looking for the bent twig, the crushed insect, the faint disturbance in the dust that points you in the direction of the attacker and his misdeeds. It is a serious business, but it can be enjoyed, as well. Of course, your job is not to be sporting and give your quarry a head start and a fair fight. Your job is to play rough and win quickly, so the best hunts are the ones you win before they've really begun because the quarry's gone home early.

For cases where you are testing each other, the hunt is best shared with your team. You are not a pilot until you fly alone, but you learned to fly by watching others and by emulating (or in some cases avoiding) their examples. You learn to fly alone because someday you might have to. Let your people "solo" during exercises, and if they have to fly alone for real late one night when no one else is available, they'll be ready to do so. Celebrate such victories. But here, where it's not a game, where every second counts, where someone has crept into your network and intends to do you harm, take every bit of help you can get and end the hunt quickly.

Developing Theories

In Chapter 14, we discussed the use of a "war room." This is the ideal place for developing theories and testing them out. Collect your data, gather your team together, and start to think. There are some tricks to doing this successfully, though.

Put everything on paper. Draw pictures, graphs, diagrams. Make lists. Rewrite things. But don't make the mistake of using an erasable whiteboard or a computer to do this. First, nothing is more frustrating than wanting to refer to a list or diagram that you've erased to make room on the whiteboard.

Second, paper is evidence; whiteboard dust is not, and bits on a computer may not be. Use up lots of paper, put the time and date at the top of each piece, and tack them up on the walls.

Don't have a computer in the war room. If you have things to discuss with the group, print them out at the source and bring the printouts to the war room. You'll notice that the diagram of the logging system in Figure 15-1 shows a dedicated printer. Well, it's for exactly this purpose. Print out log excerpts and bring them to the war room for discussion and analysis. If possible, have your machine time and date each page.

The other reason for avoiding a computer is so that you and your team will use your brains rather than using the computer as a crutch. Explaining your ideas to a group of people brings them into focus and refines them. Think of how many times you've experienced the all-too-common phenomenon of having a great idea that sounds dumb as soon as you've put it into words. Or the flip side: As you're talking out a problem, the solution appears in your mind. These are powerful tools for burning away the irrelevancies and focusing on the problem. Use them.

Brainstorm, but do it realistically. This will take practice, as all good brainstorming does. In a classic brainstorm, anything goes. Anybody can propose any idea, no matter how silly, and it gets considered. All well and good when time is not a problem, but you're working against the clock. What you need to do is to develop a rhythm with your team so that reasonable ideas are generated quickly and silly ones suppressed, and yet you don't overlook anything major. The way you develop rhythm is to practice, practice, practice. That allows your team to learn each other's ways of thinking and learn how to communicate. A team of sharp people who know their tools and can communicate with each other effectively can outthink an attacker any day of the week.

Don't suppress anything that seems reasonable, no matter how far fetched. Despite your need to move quickly, intuition can sometimes spark an idea that seems crazy at first but turns out to be all too plausible once you look into it. And such an idea can spark in the mind of anybody. So train your team to think clearly, and put the results of their thinking on paper if their logic *or* their gut tells them to consider it.

Do suppress initial criticism. Nothing short-circuits a brainstorm like early or vehement criticism. No one likes to be criticized, and it is only with the greatest self-discipline that most people can handle serious criticism at all. Your first goal with any theory is to find facts that support it. That is everyone's job for the first part of any brainstorm. In fact, it can be a good idea to go around the room and ask everybody to point out a fact that supports each particular theory. If the idea is a bad one, the responses—or lack of them—will make that fact stand out just as quickly as criticism will, without the bruise to the self-confidence of the theorist or the negative impact on the brainstorming process.

Make sure that your theories stand up to the facts. The second part of the theorization process gives naysayers a chance to vent their criticisms. But criticisms should be based on *observed fact,* not opinion. A comment of "That's the stupidest idea I've ever heard" should be shut down cold, while "That's impossible because of log entry 27" is exactly what you're looking for. Not opinions, not the "weight of authority," just facts.

Rate the theories according to experience. Once you've got some good theories, that are supported by the known facts but cannot be contradicted by them, have everybody vote on their "gut feelings," and rate the theories in order of priority. Intuition can be wrong, but it can also be right. By factoring it in at the right moment you can let the trained intuition of your team add weight to a good theory or lessen the credence of a bad one.

Go and find out. Now that you've got some theories on the table that seem reasonable, figure out what information you need to go and find out, and assign teams to do so.

This type of meeting can be very quick and enormously productive if a team has experience with the technique.

Legalities

The reason all those pages were time and date stamped is so that they can act as evidence, if you intend to pursue legal action in such a case. Being able to reproduce how you arrived at a conclusion, with documentation and meeting notes, is extremely valuable evidence.

The decision to pursue prosecution is one that you should make as early as possible in the course of the incident. Your ability to pursue prosecution is something that you, your management, and your legal staff should have discussed well in advance of any incident. Presumably you clarified what then would be needed from your team in order to prosecute and then try to supply it.

One thing that should come up in this conversation is the concept of a *standard of evidence,* in which the quality of evidence is specified. Your legal staff should be able to tell you what is required to realistically prosecute, and you can judge if and how you can provide such evidence. This may not be possible for all incidents, but the better the body of evidence you can provide, the more likely you are to be seen favorably by the judge and jury.

Another concept is the *chain of evidence,* in which evidence you collect is properly accounted for at all points throughout the life of the case. If, for example, the murder weapon cannot be accounted for during the six months between the arrest and the trial, it may not be considered a valid piece of evidence, because during that time another gun could have been substituted or identifying marks changed. You want to develop a good chain of evidence procedure if you are going to prosecute. You want to arrange with your legal staff for evidence to be sealed and stored in a way that is acceptable to them and the courts. You also want to arrange for copies of evidence to work from while the originals are locked away. And you want a safe means of storing the evidence from a 1 A.M. penetration attempt until the start of normal business hours in the morning when you turn the evidence over to the legal staff.

The evidence we're talking about here is, of course, all the paper hanging on the walls of your war room, the log books written by each member of your team, meeting notes for each meeting, and the log book for your Watch Team.

Chapter

16

Damage Control

IN THIS CHAPTER:

- Priorities
- Advance Preparation
- Post-Mortem Analysis

You've had the problem, and you've eliminated contamination. But your network is still down. To use a naval analogy, the torpedo has damaged your ship, you've sunk the submarine that shot the torpedo at you, but you still have to fix the hole that's letting water into your hull.

Network security problems can be grouped into two rough categories. *Passive problems* are activated by action; they don't get worse if you do nothing. In the case of the trojanned application, for example, nothing happens if you don't run the application. *Active problems* get worse even if you do nothing. A good example was the Internet worm of several years back. Once it got onto a system, it ran as a separate process and began looking for other machines to infect. With a passive problem, you might have time to sit down and think about how to correct it; an active problem requires immediate corrective measures.

The best way to control damage to your systems is to deploy excellent defenses so that the problem of damage control never arises. But that is little comfort if you find yourself with a rampant problem that snuck by your defenses. In this chapter, we discuss some things you can do to handle the situation and some steps you can take in advance to make yourself ready for action in circumstances where there's no substitute for taking direct and decisive action.

Priorities

As with any crisis situation, knowing what to do in a crunch is half the battle.

Advance planning and practice will save you.

> *Try not to have to make it up as you go along.*

Following are some general priorities for damage control.

1. *Gain control of the situation.* Any work you do on damage control is wasted if the source of the problem has not been dealt with. If an attacker can reinfect your machines at will, then working to scrub them is much less important than preventing the reinfection. For serious problems, it's best to work in parallel with another person or group. One team works to block the source of the problem, and the other works to contain it. If your problem has become this bad, you've got quite a bit of work ahead of you before you can trust your network again, but you should do everything in your power to limit the damage as much as you can.

2. *Stop any active problems.* The goal here is to give yourself time to think. If an active problem is forcing your hand, then take care of it as soon as possible. There are two major dangers here: underreaction and overreaction. If you are hesitant about solving an active problem, it's going to get much worse very quickly. You need to be decisive. A very good way to be decisive is to make liberal use of power switches. Turn off the equipment that has been infected, and make sure that it cannot be turned on again without your consent. If, as you're reading these words, you feel that there's no way you'd have the authority to do that, then your first task in preparing for security problems should be to get that authority now, before you need it, because sometimes there's no other choice. But you need to be careful not to go too far. Adrenaline excitement can make you crazy, and if you've seen too many movies, you might think about taking a fire axe to your computer room cabling or something equally difficult to recover from. Turn things off and make them stay off, but remember that you're going to have to repair anything you disable.

3. *Map out the total area of damage.* This is the tough part, because you've got to figure out which machines are damaged without triggering problems. (See the discussion in Chapter 14 about forensic analysis and clean room machines.) Remember also that once you've turned an infected machine off, you don't want to turn it back on except under controlled circumstances. You also want to be very conservative here. If a machine might have been damaged, then you have to treat it as you would a damaged machine, on the theory that it's much better to rebuild an undamaged machine than it is to forget to rebuild a damaged one.

4. *Prioritize the damaged systems in order of criticality.* Your goal is to get your network back into operation. That means that you want to fix the machines most germane to that task first. But leave a little room for experimentation. You want to bring your servers back up quickly, but you don't want to practice disinfecting techniques on critical machines. So plan to fix a few easily replaceable machines first and learn the fine points of what must be done; then work on the critical machines.

5. *Develop a plan to restore the systems in order of priority.* You know what must be done, so develop a plan for the work.

6. *Execute your plan.* Put your team to work. Make sure you encourage lots of regular updates and communication in this process so that you can be sure that things are going as they should.

Some other issues that you want to keep in mind:

- Mark all damaged systems "Do not touch. Do not power up." Confiscate their power cords, and put tape across their power switches.

- Create an information clearinghouse so that people can find out where on the priority list their favorite server is without bothering the workers.

- Create an escalation policy so that misprioritized systems can be repaired sooner if the proper approval is given.

- Schedule management updates and generate brief daily reports, listing accomplishments so that there is a sense of progress.

Advance Preparation

The key to any kind of effective damage control is advance preparation. Thinking through a number of crisis situations can tell you a lot about the kinds of things you'll need to survive a crisis. You'll almost certainly miss something important when a crisis happens, but the practice you get by thinking through crises in advance will help you improvise where you need to.

Advance preparation can help immensely in the following areas.

- *System reconstruction.* This is an easy one to practice if you have the available hardware. You want the ability to be able to rebuild any system (including any custom software) from blank hardware. This means that your backups really have to work, and you'll need a way of reinstalling the system software to match that of the trashed computer. Nothing is a good substitute for practice in this endeavor.

- *Diagnostics*. How do you know that the system you've just rebuilt is functionally the same as the one you are trying to resurrect? You need a collection of acceptance tests for your computer systems. You'll need very stringent ones for critical systems, less stringent ones for more general computers.

- *Prioritization*. If you know in advance which systems are critical and which can wait for reconstruction, then you'll save a lot of time. By thinking through the priorities for repair at a general level and deciding the order in which various types of systems must come back on-line in order to restore your business, you'll eliminate a lot of heated discussions during a crisis.

- *Forensic tools*. In Chapter 14 we discussed a number of forensic tools and techniques that can be used to help rebuild damaged systems and to determine the extent of contamination. The last thing you want is to have to invent tools like this in a crisis. Build them, test them, and keep them up to date, and you can apply them to network damage to restore service as quickly as possible. This applies especially to clean room machines.

- *Practice*. Tools are great, but if you haven't used them or haven't tested your ability to rebuild key servers in a while, then you're not ready for a serious problem.

Post-Mortem Analysis

Finally, after all the shouting is over and things are stable again, don't forget to conduct a post-mortem review of everything you did to cope with the crisis.

- Evaluate the effectiveness of your advance preparations.

- Determine what other types of advance prep work would have benefitted you the most during this crisis.

- Analyze the effectiveness of your procedures.

In most crisis situations, there is someone who digs into the situation and becomes the hero of the hour. Everybody works hard, but one person stands out as having taken charge of the situation or as being right there with help, advice, or legwork when it was needed. A good way to end your post-mortem meeting is to take a poll of your team and see if a hero emerges by consensus. If one does, find some way to recognize this person and show your appreciation that he or she was able to rise to the occasion and help bring the crisis to a rapid conclusion.

After the applause dies down, ask the final post-mortem question: "How would we have handled this situation if our hero had been on vacation?" If you don't know the answer, then you've still got work to do.

Of course, you're in the security business, which means you've *always* got more work to do.

Appendix

A

Glossary

active system

System that requires human participation in order to function correctly. See **passive system.**

anonymizing

Process of taking a collection of data and stripping from it any evidence of its origin or ownership, while still retaining the essential structure of the data.

attacker

Someone who is attacking your computer network. This term is used to avoid the confusion caused by other terms (see **hacker**).

auditing

Examination by an independent party of one or more devices to determine how well they are protected against a variety of attacks.

background check

Investigation of a potential employee, contractor, or business associate designed to help in determining if the subject is actually who they say they are and whether the subject is an acceptable risk for a particular position or relationship.

compromised machine

Machine that has been altered by an attacker so that some of its functions are now under the control of the attacker; a machine that cannot be trusted.

contaminated

Another term for **compromised.**

daemon

Process that performs some service or function independently of a user login session. For example, the program used to listen for log entries using the syslog function is called the syslog daemon.

Dark Side

Idiomatic term for people who use their computer security skills in unethical, immoral, illegal, or inadvisable ways.

denial of service

Type of attack in which the goal is not to steal something but to prevent others from using a service. You can prevent many types of DoS attacks and attenuate the effect of others, but an attacker can always find some way to deny service.

failover

Process by which a nonfunction server is detected and traffic for that server is redirected to a backup that is still operational.

filter

In the security context, a system for examining events in an ongoing stream of events and choosing a way to handle each event based on some characteristic of the event. Incoming packets may be filtered based on their source address, their destination address, the service they are connecting to, the time of day, the mood of the network administrator, or many other characteristics. Filtering in this case involves taking some action, such as discarding the packet, sending the packet to a different destination, or editing the contents of the packet.

forensics

In the context of this book, the process of determining how an attack was made and the amount of damage caused by the attack, and to gather the information necessary to determine how much work is necessary to repair the damage.

fortification

Process by which a device is made more secure by reconfiguration and modification. Also known as *hardening*.

FUD

Fear, uncertainty, and doubt. A technique, often used in sales, for making a customer afraid *not* to purchase a particular product or service.

gzip, gunzip

Unix program used for compression (or decompression) of files.

hacker

Word used by many to mean a talented but unorthodox computer programmer and by many others to mean those who attack computer systems and networks. See **attacker.**

host

Common Internet term for a computer with a network connection that is connected to the Internet.

ISP

Internet service provider—an organization that connects a person or business to the Internet.

latency

Delay between the transmission and reception of information. Imagine two machines, A and B, that are exactly synchronized to the correct time of day and the same time zone. If A sends a message to B and records the exact time of the transmission and B records the exact time of its reception of the transmission, the difference between the two times is the latency of that particular channel through the network.

Laugh Test

Simple test for whether you've gone far enough with a particular approach to a security problem. If you present your solution to a trained and experienced security professional, will the solution be laughed at? If so, then chances are good that you haven't applied enough thought, money, personnel, or skill to the problem. Compare **Wow Test.**

legacy components

Parts of your network that were designed, configured, or installed before your current security policies took effect. These devices are probably not going to be in security compliance and may be difficult to bring into compliance.

logging

Means by which a network system reports that a particular event has occurred or that a particular condition is now in effect.

log rotation

Process by which the logs captured by a running process are removed to prevent excessive file sizes and stored to aid in location of archival data for a specific date and time.

mechanism

Programmer's slang for a process that requires little or no human input to perform its function. A means for accomplishing a goal.

network hops

Number of routers connecting any two nodes of the Internet. If host A is on network X, which routes to network Y, which routes to network Z, and host B is on network Z, then A is three hops from Z. The more hops there are between two nodes, the greater the latency of network transmissions between the nodes.

nondisclosure agreement

Legal agreement between two parties used to inhibit discussion of sensitive issues with people or organizations not party to the agreement.

NTP

Network Time Protocol, an Internet mechanism for ensuring that a group of machines can remain in reasonable synchronization with each other. NTP, when properly implemented, can generally keep machines within a second or better of synchronization, which is adequate for most purposes.

passive system

System that operates correctly and adequately when unattended by human beings.

patch

Self-contained modification to a device or software. Patches are generally issued by software vendors to fix flaws in their shipped products. The ability to assess patching levels and to locate and apply patches is an essential part of system fortification.

permissive design

Design philosophy in which everything is allowed except things that are specifically forbidden. Compare **restrictive designs.**

ping

Mechanism, typically implemented via the TCP/IP ICMP protocol, to determine if a machine is operating and is reachable via the network. Machine A pings machine B, and if B receives the request, it acknowledges the request. If A receives the acknowledgment, then A knows that B is "alive." Pings are often used by attackers to scan a network (known as a *ping sweep*) to see which machines on the network are available for further investigation and attack. A ping reply confirms *not* that a machine is operating correctly, only that it is operating well enough to respond to the ping request. Since ping requests are handled at a very low level in the operating system kernel, a machine may respond to a ping but yet be completely unable to carry out its primary functions. However, a machine that does not respond to pings is either unreachable or dead.

replay attack

Particular form of attack in which a portion of a network transmission is recorded and then "played back" at a later time. Usually, this type of attack is associated with poorly designed cryptography. Example: An authentication mechanism transmits a credential for a user over the network. If the credential is encrypted in the same way each time, then an attacker may be able to record the encrypted string and incorporate it into a transmission of his own. Without knowing the password, he could gain access to the system. A properly designed encryption scheme would vary the encrypted form of any credential so that no two instances of it were the same, and a replay of a previous form would be guaranteed not to succeed.

restrictive design
> Design philosophy in which everything is forbidden except for things that are specifically permitted. Compare **permissive design.**

signature
> Essential characteristics of an item that can be applied by a computer to many similar items to determine if the item is of a specific type. A packet filtering device may be configured to look for a particular signature (packets originating from a specific network or going to a specific service, for example) to determine whether or not to filter a particular packet.

sniffer
> Device used for passively monitoring a network for traffic. A sniffer listens to all traffic on a given network segment and watches for patterns of activity that might signal an attack or a dangerous condition. There are many types of sniffer software available on the Internet. An attacker may attempt to plant sniffers on your network, typically to listen for unencrypted login traffic so that user names and passwords can be recorded and used by the attacker.

social engineering
> Gaining access to or information about a target by human-to-human interaction. Sometimes referred to in other contexts as "street theater," an attacker engages a member of the target organization in such a way as to present that person with a plausible excuse for violating a security principle. This type of exercise is often done in a series of small steps, each building upon the last, until a goal is achieved.

strong authentication
> Means for identifying some entity, such as a person who is adequately difficult to defeat. A fixed password is not considered particularly strong authentication, because it can be recorded or eavesdropped or written down and thus work for anyone who knows it. A smart card, which changes its response to each challenge, is much stronger.

tar
> Unix program used to collect a directory tree of files into a single archive file or to expand an archive file into a directory tree.

template
> Prototype configuration for a specific device that can be easily replicated when one of the devices is to be installed. The goal of designing a good template is to do all the configuration and testing work once and then clone copy after copy of the properly configured device for actual use.

thinking pathologically

Way of considering a situation or technology from the viewpoint of how it might fail or be abused. Also known as *thinking evil thoughts.*

trojanned

From the phrase "Trojan horse," which implies an object that appears to be one thing but carries within it a secret that can be used as part of an attack. A program that has been trojanned has been modified so that it behaves normally under some circumstances but behaves incorrectly under other circumstances that benefit the attacker. An example is a program to list files in a directory that would not list any file that began with "warez."

unblanding

System administrator's term for taking a generic, fresh-from-the-box machine configuration and turning it into a configuration tailored for a specific environment.

Wow Test

Simple test to see whether you've gone too far with a particular approach to a security problem. If you present your solution to a trained and experienced security professional, will the person say "Wow!" If so, then chances are good that you have applied way too much thought, money, personnel, or skill to the problem. Compare **Laugh Test.**

Index

Addison-Wesley Professional

How to Register Your Book

Register this Book

Visit: **http://www.aw.com/cseng/register**
Enter the ISBN*
Then you will receive:

- Notices and reminders about upcoming author appearances, tradeshows, and online chats with special guests
- Advanced notice of forthcoming editions of your book
- Book recommendations
- Notification about special contests and promotions throughout the year

*The ISBN can be found on the copyright page of the book

Visit our Web site

http://www.aw.com/cseng

When you think you've read enough, there's always more content for you at Addison-Wesley's web site. Our web site contains a directory of complete product information including:

- Chapters
- Exclusive author interviews
- Links to authors' pages
- Tables of contents
- Source code

You can also discover what tradeshows and conferences Addison-Wesley will be attending, read what others are saying about our titles, and find out where and when you can meet our authors and have them sign your book.

Contact Us via Email

cepubprof@awl.com
Ask general questions about our books.
Sign up for our electronic mailing lists.
Submit corrections for our web site.

cepubeditors@awl.com
Submit a book proposal.
Send errata for a book.

cepubpublicity@awl.com
Request a review copy for a member of the media interested in reviewing new titles.

registration@awl.com
Request information about book registration.

We encourage you to patronize the many fine retailers who stock Addison-Wesley titles. Visit our online directory to find stores near you.

Addison-Wesley Professional
One Jacob Way, Reading, Massachusetts 01867 USA
TEL 781-944-3700 • FAX 781-942-3076